The Global Economic Crisis
through an
Indian Looking Glass

Thank you for choosing a SAGE product! If you have any comment, observation or feedback, I would like to personally hear from you. Please write to me at contactceo@sagepub.in

—Vivek Mehra, Managing Director and CEO,
SAGE Publications India Pvt. Ltd, New Delhi

Bulk Sales

SAGE India offers special discounts for purchase of books in bulk. We also make available special imprints and excerpts from our books on demand.

For orders and enquiries, write to us at

Marketing Department
SAGE Publications India Pvt. Ltd
B1/I-1, Mohan Cooperative Industrial Area
Mathura Road, Post Bag 7
New Delhi 110044, India
E-mail us at marketing@sagepub.in

Get to know more about SAGE, be invited to SAGE events, get on our mailing list. Write today to marketing@sagepub.in

This book is also available as an e-book.

The Global Economic Crisis through an Indian Looking Glass

Adarsh Kishore
Michael Debabrata Patra
Partha Ray

SSAGE www.sagepublications.com
Los Angeles • London • New Delhi • Singapore • Washington DC

First published in 2011 by

SAGE Publications India Pvt Ltd
B 1/I-1, Mohan Cooperative Industrial Area
Mathura Road, New Delhi 110 044, India
www.sagepub.in

SAGE Publications Inc
2455 Teller Road
Thousand Oaks, California 91320, USA

SAGE Publications Ltd
1 Oliver's Yard, 55 City Road
London EC1Y 1SP, United Kingdom

SAGE Publications Asia-Pacific Pte Ltd
33 Pekin Street
#02-01 Far East Square
Singapore 048763

Published by Vivek Mehra for SAGE Publications India Pvt Ltd, typeset in 10/12.5 pt Aldine401 BT by Star Compugraphics Private Limited, Delhi and printed at Chaman Enterprises, New Delhi.

Library of Congress Cataloging-in-Publication Data

Kishore, Adarsh, 1946–
    The global economic crisis through an indian looking glass/Adarsh Kishore, Michael Debabrata Patra, Partha Ray.
        p. cm.

    Includes bibliographical references and index.

    1. Global Financial Crisis, 2008–2009. 2. Financial crises—India. 3. India—Economic conditions—21st century. 4. India—Economic policy—21st century. I. Patra, Michael Debabrata. II. Ray, Partha. III. Title.

HB37172008.k57   330.954'0532—dc23   2011   2011021984

ISBN: 978-81-321-0651-7 (HB)

The SAGE Team: Elina Majumdar, Aniruddha De, Amrita Saha, and Rekha Sahani

To our children

Arush,
Abhijeet,
Ronjini,
and
Debaditya

who
will inherit
the post-crisis world.

Contents

List of Tables

List of Figures

List of Charts

List of Boxes

डॉ. सी. रगंराजन
Dr. C. RANGARAJAN

जय हिन्द

अध्यक्ष
प्रधानमंत्री की आर्थिक सलाहकार परिषद्
विज्ञान भवन सौध ई हाल
मौलाना आज़ाद रोड
नई दिल्ली—110 011
CHAIRMAN
Economic Advisory Council to the Prime Minister
Vigyan Bhavan Annexe, 'E' Hall
Maulana Azad Road
New Delhi-110 011

January 17, 2011

Foreword

The recent global crisis was truly global, dwarfing all other crises that have occurred in post-World War II history. It was a spectacular reflection of the flip side of globalization. While the seeds of the crisis were sown in the US subprime mortgage market, the crisis spread rapidly to other advanced economies, to emerging market economies, and finally to the low-income countries. It is no exaggeration that it has come to be known as the "great recession," an obvious allusion to the "Great Depression" of the 1930s. Given its stretch, it is not without reason that the global crisis has attracted attention of policy makers, academia, journalists, and people of all callings and vocations.

What caused the crisis? What are its dimensions? What has the world done to come out of it? What could we have done differently to avoid the crisis? How do we see the future? Like anyone else, I have myself spent some time reflecting on these questions. What stand out glaringly in the recent crisis are two kinds of regulatory failure in developed countries: (*a*) not all segments of the financial system were adequately regulated or supervised; and (*b*) there was imperfect understanding on the part of regulators on the nature and implications of the various complex derivative products. The shock waves produced by the financial crisis will have their own effect on the structure of capitalism. Acceptable capitalism would require more regulation. Runaway financial innovations

दूरभाष 011-23022311, 23022313 फैक्स 011-23022318 ई-मेल chrtfc@nic.in, c.rangarajan@nic.in
Telephone : 011-23022311, 23022313 Fax : 011-23022318 e-mail : chrtfc@nic.in, c.rangarajan@nic.in

that are dysfunctional do more harm than good. Also, global imbalances had been building up in the years prior to the outbreak of the crisis, and prescient warnings were being conveyed by supranational bodies such as the International Monetary Fund (IMF) and the Bank for International Settlements (BIS). Yet the role of these macro imbalances continues to be widely debated and is still unsettled. These imbalances have made the task of recovery more difficult. The G-20 has emerged as the new forum of discussions on how best to fashion the global recovery and set the agenda for the future. I am glad to see that the present book has deftly handled all these issues.

The book synthesizes four major aspects of the crisis, viz., its genesis; its impact on the world, in general, and on India, in particular; the response; and the aftermath. It traces the origins of the crisis to the post-dotcom crash years of high growth during which accommodative macroeconomic policies allowed global imbalances and financial excesses to grow unfettered in an environment of asset bubbles and complicit financial regulation. The book has surveyed the impact of the crisis on the global economy at large and across geographical boundaries in various dimensions. In dealing with the unprecedented policy responses, the book describes the national and subsequent coordinated policy actions through entities like the G-20, the IMF, and other international financial institutions and the UN. Finally, the book draws out the ongoing debates spurred by the crisis, the lessons, and challenges that lie ahead. All through, the narrative and commentary is supported by incisive analysis and the latest available information.

The fact that the authors have had a firsthand understanding and a ringside view of Indian policy setting (in different capacities), and at the same time, the living experience of the international efforts to deal with the crisis is reflected in their competent and insightful treatment of a most topical theme that continues to draw both heat and light, and animated engagement in the public space. Their effort is distinctive in that it provides an Indian perspective to the subject and fills an important gap in the swelling literature on the global crisis. I compliment the authors on their contribution and strongly commend the book to readers from all walks of life.

(C. Rangarajan)

Preface

The current global crisis, which is widely regarded as paralleled only by the Great Depression of the 1930s, has fascinated policymakers, academia, and the general public alike. While arguably, the intensity of interest and perhaps also that of the impact of the crisis differs, there is possibly unanimity in asking one question: has the world changed fundamentally? Will life be the same again? In response to this crisis, as perhaps never before, there has been an outpouring of reactions—sound bytes; op-eds; analysts' quick fixes and eye-catchers; academic papers, official reports—assessments, evaluations, even judgments on every aspect in all shades. Much more shall come before this crisis is fully understood and behind us. This book joins this ever-expanding catharsis with a different angle of vision—it attempts to peer into the crisis through an Indian looking glass. The chance privilege of a ringside position—from within India and also from a global perch—of the crisis, as it mutated into the perfect storm, brings with it humility. This book, therefore, is not exclusive; neither is it exhaustive. It lays no claim to originality. Apart from tracing the genesis of the crisis and its impact on the world economy with special reference to India, we also try to cover the global response and the aftermath.

As we put pen to paper, there is the overpowering sense that the book is premature and the nativity expedited. There is still so much happening all around. But finality often comes from a long hindsight and we are acutely conscious of the eminent political leader of the 20th century, who when asked about the impact of the French Revolution (of the 18th century), remarked, "It is too early to comment!" Thus, we chose to write about things as they happen and are still very live; in the process of being and becoming, as it were. Admittedly, close proximity to events in historical time could have the potential disadvantage of inability to discern the sublime from the mundane. This book could arguably suffer from this shortcoming. To make up, every effort has been made to provide information on developments till mid-2010 so as to empower the reader to be discerning.

Our choice to write is driven by three reasons. First, we thought that such a synthesis will be of value for its span of coverage. Second, the absence of a prior—whether relating to causes, impact, or measures—relating to the crisis, could add value to the discourse. Third, providing an Indian dimension to the global crisis would be of interest to the readers. All through, we were driven by a conscious desire not to be diagnostic but to be tentative and inquisitive even at the cost of being descriptive, much like the account of the seven blind men and the elephant!

Finally, a transparency warning is in order. This book was written when the authors were working in the IMF as representatives of the Government of India. While the institutional affiliations or the work place of the authors could have influenced the line of research, its coverage, tone, or emphasis, the views expressed are exclusively of the authors and not to be attributed to the IMF, Government of India, or the Reserve Bank of India.

We are indebted to Dr C. Rangarajan for graciously consenting to write a foreword to the book, and to Prof. Arvind Panagariya and Prof. V.S. Vyas for their kind endorsements.

In the aftermath of the Asian crisis of 1997–98, Asians typically began their speeches with an apology, while non-Asians began with a joke. In the wake of this crisis, we wonder if it is the other way around! With the benefit of hindsight, we choose the non-Asian tradition. There is a joke that "the easiest way to make a small fortune is to start off with a large one." This book attempts the big picture with the hope that fortune favors the brave. In the context of the current crisis, the height of "optimism" has been described as a "banker who irons five shirts on a Sunday!" We sincerely hope that our readers will be kinder as we offer them this book and lots to think about.

1

Introduction

At the time of writing, the world at large is watching for signs of strengthening of what has come to be termed as "green shoots," however wan, indicating that the grip of the severe recession on the global economy is beginning to loosen and thaw. Still, the severe financial conflagration that began it all looms as large as it did at its outbreak in mid-September 2008 and the evaporation of confidence as chilling. The traction sought to be achieved by wide-ranging and unorthodox policy actions is in the process of fully materializing—while some calm has returned to financial markets, the downturn in economic activity is still worrisome and broad in its ambit. There seems to be general agreement that the global economy could continue to deteriorate for some time unless policymakers act in coordination to restore and sustain financial stability and economic activity, and that exiting from the policy interventions could be premature at this point for most countries.

The Backdrop

In August 2007, when the US subprime crisis started unraveling, the global economy had begun to slow. Advanced economies felt the slackening first and by mid-2008 started slipping into what then appeared as mild recessions. Emerging and developing economies were incipiently turning but continued to grow at fairly robust rates, leading many to herald so-called decoupling, as if a new epoch in the history of the global economy was taking root. Underneath, global imbalances grew larger, misalignments became more pronounced, and the financial abscesses continued to fester. To be fair, by then, authorities were worrying about market liquidity and bad assets with some concerns about the solvency and funding of large financial institutions. Suddenly in September 2008 there was an explosion—nightmare took over. As if preordained, incidents began to happen with metronomic and frightening severity—the rescue of the largest US insurance company, intervention in a range of systemic institutions in the United States and Europe, and a gripping sense of panic as fears of counterparty risk suffused the international financial community. Banks faced huge losses and a number of the most established financial names went into oblivion. Markets froze up, credit stopped, and liquidity evaporated. Volatility surged to all-time highs as a disorderly deleveraging cascaded across the global financial system. The world was jolted in to recognizing the existence of bizarre securitization and the "shadow banking system." Global trade collapsed and capital flows retracted at a rapid pace from the entire developing world. For emerging and developing economies, which earlier had appeared to have been spared due to their supposedly miniscule exposure to the US subprime market, the crisis flared with a ferocity not known before. International financial markets closed up on them as their own equity and exchange markets dropped like stones. For those with relatively large dependence on external sectors, whether through current account deficits or just external financing or both, the bottom seemed to have fallen out with no end to the cataclysm in sight. Soon the crisis spread from financial markets, exports, and capital inflows to credit, jobs, corporates, and consumers.

Current Situation

At this juncture, while a complete global meltdown appears to have been halted, the global economy is still besieged, financial systems even more so. Business and consumer confidence has been hit hard by the heightened uncertainty about the success of rescue efforts and, therefore, about the prospects of the resumption of future growth. The specter of stagflation stalks developed and developing countries alike and the tale of human immiserization continues to unfold. Economic weakness and accentuated financial strains appear to be caught in the rictus of a macabre tango. The global downturn deepened in the first half of 2009, especially in the advanced economies, while the intensity of the contraction in the developing countries has been no less albeit varied in terms of the impact on trade, commodity prices, and financial sectors. In India as in China, the downturn has been somewhat muted in view of relatively lower reliance on international trade in relation to economic size and more resilient domestic demand. The second half of 2009 has seen these economies rebound faster out of the crisis than the fragile recovery that has started in some other parts of the world.

According to the update of the *World Economic Outlook* made in January 2010 by the IMF, the global economy is expected to have contracted by 0.8 percent in 2009 in purchasing power parity terms, representing a 380-basis point downturn from the growth of 3.0 percent in 2008. Advanced economies would have shrunk by 3.2 percent [ranging between (–) 2.5 percent in the US, (–) 3.9 percent in the Euro Area, and (–) 5.3 percent in Japan] while in emerging and developing economies, growth is expected to have slumped to 2.1 percent from 6.1 percent a year ago. In terms of market exchange rates, the decline in world output was of the order of (–) 2.1 percent. The volume of world trade in goods and services is projected to have declined by a precipitous 12.3 percent. With non-oil commodity prices expected to have fallen by 18.9 percent, advanced countries are likely to have recorded close to zero inflation while in developing countries, it is expected to have eased to 5.2 percent from 9.2 percent in 2008. Even with current levels of policy intensity—policy rates at or close to zero, sustained quantitative easing, fiscal stimulus of 1.8 percent of Gross Domestic Product (GDP) in G-20 countries in 2009 and 1.3 percent of GDP in 2010—the end of the trough is not seen until early 2010 and could get pushed out further if the policy responses fail to gain grip. The prospects for developing countries would worsen if external financing constraints tighten further, trade and financial protectionism escalates, and stress in domestic financial systems heightens and spreads. A global growth of 3.9 percent has been projected for 2010, with output increasing by 2.1 percent in advanced economies. Growth was expected to pick up to 6.0 percent in developing economies on the back of a recovery of world trade growth to 5.8 percent, with non-fuel commodity prices rising by a similar magnitude.

As far as financial stability is concerned the October 2009 issue of the IMF's *Global Financial Stability Report* noted that there has been some improvement since mid-2009. Nevertheless, the risks of reversal remain with indicators of financial stress continuing at elevated levels. Global write-downs on account of loans and securities is estimated to be of the order of US\$2.8 trillion, out of which more than US\$1 trillion was incurred by US banks; the UK and Euro Area banks too suffered substantial losses at around US\$600 billion and US\$800 billion, respectively. Concerns are increasingly being voiced as to whether banks are robust enough to absorb these losses.

This crisis, unlike others, did not catch us by surprise; its scale and intensity did, but not its advent. Consequently, there has been a proliferation of writing and media bytes on it from people of every walk of life. A great deal has issued purely in the form of narrative, situating the crisis in history and geography. A lot of attention has been drawn by the complex nature of the phenomenon, the interactions and co-movements, the institutions and instruments, and no less by the manner in which authorities in almost every country responded in their determination to ensure that the Great Depression of the 1930s was not revisited. Unlike in other crises, there has been a distinct effort on the part of nations to act in concert through various fora and show solidarity to do what it takes to rescue the world from this apocalypse. This too has drawn an animated interest. A parallel stream has focused on the human suffering that has ensued—and this aspect is still unraveling beyond the visible loss of wealth, property, jobs, livelihood, and welfare—and the warning bells on the need to ward off a human holocaust are ringing loud and clear. Lessons are being gathered and ways to prevent recurrence are being intensely debated. But, by far the greatest concentration of thinking is going in to understand what is going on. Each strand has drawn its own following, its constituency in a sense, to an extent that each is a body of expanding knowledge in its own right.

Scope of the Book

This book is an attempt to bring these diverse but interconnected elements together. In this collation, the primary consideration is to avoid both the pejorative and the complicated, both of which are indeed distinct characteristics of this crisis. The aim of this endeavor is to, as factually and objectively as possible, set out for the layperson, the student, the academic, and the policymaker what we think happened and so swiftly. By doing so, the book attempts to contribute by informing and empowering this wider swathe of readership so that the collective consciousness retains a desire not to let such a crisis happen again. The book is also "different" in that it seeks to look at the crisis from an Indian perspective; however, it is by no means India-specific—it has a generalized flavor that makes it equally applicable to the "periphery" of nations, as distinct from the "core," that got ensnared in the crisis that was not of their doing.

The rest of the book is organized into six chapters, each with a specific focus and theme but integrated into a unified canvas.

Chapter 2 traces the origins of the crisis. While in a strict chronological sense, the roots of the crisis can be located in the Great Moderation of the last decade that ushered in a golden age for the world in terms of exuberant growth with remarkable price stability, the focus of this chapter is on the immediate pre-crisis years that witnessed a large buildup in macro imbalances at the turn of the century and the accommodative policy environment that transferred the dotcom bubble frictionlessly to the housing sector. The US housing sector is discussed in some detail to provide a perspective on the incubation of the crisis.

Chapter 3 undertakes a dissection of the possible causes of the crisis. In view of the evolutionary state of the crisis itself, the identification of causes is unavoidably in various shades of gray. The chapter is exploratory rather than definitive in its descriptive survey of the key actors, nature of risk management in the afflicted financial institutions, the underlying models that drove the risk management strategies, and the type and structure of financial products they dealt in to sidestep regulatory requirements in the relentless search for returns. A natural complement is an evaluation in this chapter of the regulatory structure and the role of national entities such as central banks in their positions as lenders of last resort as well as of multilateral institutions in crisis management.

Chapter 4 sets out the quantifiable dimensions of the toll that the crisis has taken. The brunt of the impact has been on the financial sector and, in this context, the chapter provides the latest updates of the volume of actual and potential losses on financial assets in the major affected economies, and the size of capitalization, injected and required, in the troubled financial institutions. Turning to macroeconomic costs of the crisis, the chapter addresses the latest available projections of the downturn in the global economy and its duration, disaggregated between advanced and developing economy blocks as well as by region with a focus on Asia, the inflation scenario, and external outlook in terms of projections of current accounts and capital flows. Risks to the outlook are outlined with a view to presenting the policy challenges that lie ahead.

Chapter 5 is centered on the impact of the crisis on the Indian economy. Here, the approach is a combination of narration and quantification. The objective is to capture the specific aspects of the onset of the crisis along with the policy responses with particular emphasis on the sequencing thereof. Interwoven into this description is an effort to measure the size of the policy effort and the impact on market conditions and on key macroeconomic variables. The chapter also attempts to reflect on the main challenges that may confront the conduct of macroeconomic policies in India as crisis resolution takes place.

Chapter 6 deals with the policy responses taken in the major affected areas—the US and Europe—and the multilateral initiatives for coordinated action. An important part of this chapter is the G-20 processes and the agenda for global policy endeavor that is emerging from its summit declarations. Other initiatives, mainly in the form of distinguished opinion and key reports, are also discussed. The central role played by the IMF in galvanizing the evolution of ideas into actions is another aspect of this chapter. The chapter also delves into the global financial architecture and specifically into the role of the IMF and international financial institutions in this regard, identifying the gaps in the architecture and the speed and resolve with which the IMF, particularly, has moved to bridge the gaps to the extent feasible. While the channeling of resources to the affected areas through adaptation and change is the main theme, other initiatives in the form of improvement in surveillance and regulatory coordination are also addressed in this chapter.

Chapter 7 attempts to draw some lessons from the crisis with a view to improving our understanding of how and why the crisis occurred, and to minimize the probability of its recurrence or at least to mitigate the aftereffects, should it occur again. The exercise is sensitive to the fact that the situation is still fluid and evolving, and that a consensus on several of the issues involved is far from being struck. Notwithstanding the fuzziness, the goal is to gather the lessons as they are thrown up rather than by hindsight. The main focus of this chapter is on macroeconomic policies, financial regulation, and the global architecture. Summarizing the experience of this looking glass examination of the current crisis, this chapter also addresses the important questions that have been raised, many unresolved and several that are likely to remain so. Against this background, it peers into the future and the likely shape of the global economy after the crisis has passed.

2

Origin of the Crisis

Introduction

The current crisis is widely compared with the Great Depression of the 1930s, as stated earlier, presumably in an effort to draw some parallel to the shock and awe it has created (Eichengreen and O'Rourke 2009; Reinhart and Rogoff 2009). Close similarity has been found in terms of the contraction of global industrial output and world trade, while the decline in stock markets is found to be larger in the current crisis. The stronger response of monetary and fiscal policies this time around has been cited as a saving grace, providing a glimmer of hope that the three-year-long downturn that characterized the Great Depression may be avoided. Yet, in terms of the suddenness with which this crisis overtook the world, the size of the financial black hole at its epicenter and the sheer breadth of its impact, it is perhaps without precedent. The Asian crisis of the late 1990s was regarded as spectacular—this crisis dwarfs it, even eclipses it. Today, after the initial blame games have quickly died away, a stunned and hushed silence reigns and the question that commonly faces the world has been succinctly posed in the April 2009 *World Economic Outlook* of the IMF: "*How did things get so bad so fast?*"

This chapter explores the environment in which the seeds of the crisis were sown and the elements that enabled it to take root and fester unabated until it metamorphosed into its colossal form. The approach is eclectic as the situation is still nebulous, that the crisis is still not fully understood, and that efforts to assign causes and draw lessons are still initial and tentative. In a basic fashion, this chapter launches the journey into the heart of the crisis and back. This chapter thus provides the wherewithal for delving into the proximate causes of the crisis, which is the subject of Chapter 3. Here, three distinguishing features of the milieu in which the crisis occurred are chosen for a focused scrutiny: (a) the macroeconomic environment and the buildup of global imbalances, (b) asset price inflation and the bubble in the US mortgage market, and (c) the legal architecture for home ownership that enabled the interaction of these factors. The lethal combination of these factors is succinctly captured in a statement of the Chairman of the US Federal Reserve Board (Fed), Ben Bernanke:

> It was sparked by the end of the U.S. housing boom, which revealed the weaknesses and excesses that had occurred in subprime mortgage lending. However, as subsequent events have demonstrated, the problem was much broader than subprime lending. Large inflows of capital into the United States and other countries stimulated a reaching for yield, an underpricing of risk, excessive leverage, and the development of complex and opaque financial instruments that seemed to work well during the credit boom but have been shown to be fragile under stress. The unwinding of these developments, including a sharp deleveraging and a headlong retreat from credit risk, led to highly strained conditions in financial markets and a tightening of credit that has hamstrung economic growth. (Bernanke 2008)

The Macroeconomic Setting: Calm before the Storm

The story goes back to the preceding seven years of high global growth, perhaps the highest since the 1980s if not in recorded history (Table 2.1). The global economy was not overheating because this growth was associated with rising productivity and, moreover, inflation was low and stable in most countries, barring sporadic and short-lived flares here and there. With the increasing prosperity of the world economy, global consumption and saving rose, though not in a well-distributed manner, and kept long-term interest rates low. Short-term interest rates were also low as monetary policy, lulled by the absence of inflation risks, accommodated the growth boom and sought to create conditions to extend it as much as possible. Other factors were also at work in keeping interest rates benign. There grew in those years an increasing popularity of inflation-targeting with some central banks setting monetary policy exclusively for price stability. With inflation remaining muted, whether by good design or plain good luck, central banks earned a credibility bonus and this worked to anchoring inflation expectations all around.

TABLE 2.1
Global Growth, Trade, and Inflation

(percent)

Country Group	Variable	1981– 1990	1991– 2000	2001– 2009
(1)	*(2)*	*(3)*	*(4)*	*(5)*
1. World	GDP Growth	3.2	3.1	3.4
	Inflation	16.2	16.7	3.9
	Trade Volume	6.5	7.2	4.0
2. Advanced Economies	GDP Growth	3.2	2.8	1.5
	Inflation	5.9	2.8	2.0
3. G7 Economies	GDP Growth	3.1	2.5	1.2
	Inflation	4.7	2.4	1.8
4. Emerging and Developing Economies	GDP Growth	3.4	3.6	5.9
	Inflation	38.4	50.4	6.6
	Private capital flows, net (US$ billion)	10.2	123.3	163.3

Source IMF, *World Economic Outlook* database, April 2009, Washington D.C.

At the epicenter, i.e., in the US, a conducive macroeconomic environment—a decade-long housing boom, fueled by easy monetary policy—was setting the stage for the savage turmoil that was to follow. A regime of low interest rates—introduced in response to the post-9/11 recession and the collapse of the new economy (or dotcom) bubble injected an enormous amount of liquidity into the global monetary system. This reduced short-term interest rates to their lowest levels in 50 years (Table 2.2).

As pointed out in an influential view, this proved subsequently to be the starting point of the conflagration:

Relatively low interest rates worldwide for much of the 2000s drove investors to seek higher yields, and relative stability in financial markets, reflecting the low cost of funds and solid economic growth, led to significant under-pricing of risk. Lending standards were weakened and leverage increased. The rise in leverage sharpened the exposure to liquidity risk for financial institutions as they depended increasingly on wholesale markets for funding and these funds became increasingly short term. New, complex financial products obfuscated risks and

TABLE 2.2
US Interest Rates

(percent)

Year	Discount Rate	Federal Funds Rate	Treasury Bill Rate	Lending Rate (Prime Rate)	Mortgage Rate
(1)	(2)	(3)	(4)	(5)	(6)
2000	5.00	5.45	5.33	8.50	8.21
2001	5.52	5.98	5.27	9.05	7.03
2002	1.25	1.73	1.66	4.75	7.00
2003	2.25	1.24	1.17	4.25	5.92
2004	2.00	1.00	0.89	4.00	5.74
2005	3.25	2.29	2.32	5.25	5.71
2006	5.26	4.29	4.20	7.26	6.15
2007	6.25	5.25	4.96	8.25	6.22
2008	4.48	3.94	2.86	6.98	5.76
2009	0.86	0.16	0.04	3.61	5.33

Source   CEIC database, available at http://www.ceicdata.com

contributed to serious mis-pricing. Risk controls failed and good old-fashioned fraud also created significant losses. All of this combined to precipitate unprecedented turmoil in global financial markets beginning in mid-2007. (Dunaway 2009)

Global Macro-imbalances

As alluded to in the foregoing, high growth brought in its train the so-called global imbalances, i.e., widening current account deficits in the United States and large current account surpluses in Asia and in oil exporting countries. The counterpart was large net capital flows from Asian and oil surplus countries to the United States—the strange phenomenon of capital flowing uphill, i.e., from developing to developed countries. The roots of these imbalances were twofold: high saving in Asia and oil exporting countries and low saving/high consumption in the United States; and a strong global preference for investment in US assets in view of the perception of low risk and high liquidity. These imbalances did ignite fears, the main one being that they could not go on forever, they would have to unwind, and, when that would happen, there would be large swings in the major currencies, particularly the US dollar. In the sunlit phase of high global growth, however, these fears remained underestimated, mostly subliminal, and the imbalances continued to grow.

External current account deficits or surpluses in some major economic areas—notably the United States, oil exporting countries, and Asia—reached record-high levels by 2002–06, and expectations which gained ground that they would stay large or increase for some time were borne out by actual outturns (Table 2.3). Several forces were at work—an acceleration in the pace of growth of international trade in goods, services, and financial assets relative to the rate of growth in domestic trade; the global integration of emerging market economies; greater competition; reduced exchange rate pass-through which, while related to globalization, also reflect other factors, including more credible monetary policy frameworks. Many observers, including the IMF, expressed concern that corrections to sustainable levels would likely require large exchange rate adjustments, especially against the US dollar, with possibly disruptive effects on global financial markets and economic activity. In contrast, other observers appeared less concerned, arguing that a benign resolution of global imbalances was likely with today's deep economic and financial integration (Blanchard 2009). The globalized world of trade and finance, characterized by the rapid expansion of two-way capital flows and the corresponding increases in gross external asset and liability positions, contributed to an environment in which large current account surpluses or deficits were sustained. Correspondingly, there were wealth transfers from countries with appreciating currencies to countries with depreciating currencies which brought benefits in terms of portfolio diversification but had the potential to turn into a liability if macroeconomic policies were not consistent with a credible medium-term policy framework aimed at external and internal balances. Investor preferences would quickly change and the fallout from disruptive financial market turbulence would likely be elevated, as the ensuing events showed with devastating impact.

In the era of the classical gold standard prior to 1914, globalization included large net capital flows and current account deficits and surpluses and large reversals. There are, however, important differences. Under the gold standard, the emerging markets of the time ran current account deficits while the major European economies had surpluses. In the current era, core industrial countries run either persistent deficits or surpluses, with domestic saving–investment imbalances redistributed primarily among industrial countries rather than from the core to the periphery as in the earlier era. Furthermore, gross external positions are generally larger today. Moreover, the global economy is now on a managed floating exchange rate regime, and external adjustment depends no

TABLE 2.3
Current Account Balance in Select Countries

(as % of GDP)

Country	2000	2005	2006	2007	2008
(1)	*(2)*	*(3)*	*(4)*	*(5)*	*(6)*
Select Asian Countries					
China	1.7	7.2	9.5	11.0	10.0
Thailand	7.6	–4.3	1.1	5.7	–0.1
Taiwan	2.8	4.9	7.2	8.6	6.4
Korea	2.3	1.8	0.6	0.6	–0.7
Singapore	11.6	22.7	25.4	23.5	14.8
Malaysia	9.0	15.0	16.7	15.4	17.4
Philippines	–2.9	2.0	4.5	4.9	2.5
Hong Kong	4.1	11.4	12.1	12.3	14.2
Select Oil-Producing Countries					
Saudi Arabia	7.6	28.7	27.9	25.1	28.9
United Arab Emirates	17.3	18.0	22.6	16.1	15.8
Oman	15.5	15.2	12.1	5.9	6.1
Qatar	23.2	33.2	28.3	30.9	35.3
Bahrain	10.6	11.0	13.8	15.8	10.6
Iran	13.0	8.8	9.2	11.9	5.2
Libya	29.8	38.4	45.8	33.8	39.2
Russia	18.0	11.0	9.5	5.9	6.1
Select Advanced Economies					
Greece	–7.8	–7.5	–11.1	–14.1	–14.4
France	1.6	–0.6	–0.6	–1.0	–1.6
Spain	–4.0	–7.4	–8.9	–10.1	–9.6
Ireland	–0.4	–3.5	–3.6	–5.4	–4.5
Iceland	–10.2	–16.1	–25.3	–15.4	–34.7
Italy	–0.5	–1.7	–2.6	–2.4	–3.2
United Kingdom	–2.6	–2.6	–3.4	–2.9	–1.7
United States	–4.3	–5.9	–6.0	–5.3	–4.7
Memo Items					
Advanced Economies	*–1.1*	*–1.1*	*–1.3*	*–1.0*	*–1.1*
Euro Area	*–0.6*	*0.4*	*0.3*	*0.2*	*–0.7*
Major Advanced					
Economies (G7)	*–1.6*	*–1.8*	*–2.0*	*–1.4*	*–1.4*
Newly Industrialized					
Asian Economies	*3.5*	*5.3*	*5.5*	*5.7*	*4.4*

Source   IMF, *World Economic Outlook* database, April 2009, Washington D.C.

longer on gold flows but on changes in exchange rates and international reserves, along with relative price movements, short-term capital flows, and valuation effects. The probability of cataclysmic effects of adjustments became, accordingly, all the greater.

In the advanced economies, the counterpart of current account deficits were wider fiscal deficits, overturning, in a sense, the dominant paradigm of the day (Table 2.4). In the US particularly, the fiscal position deteriorated over the past several years. While the external current account deficit broke new records with every passing year, it was financed primarily by sales of government agency and corporate paper, including to a number of Asian central banks. Fiscal policy became even more stimulative with the passage of further tax cuts and higher defense expenditures. While this provided short-term support to the economy, it came at the cost of a substantial deterioration in the medium-term fiscal position. Fiscal policy was activated to provide support to demand, but at the cost of a serious deterioration in long-run sustainability

TABLE 2.4
General Government Balance in Select Advanced Countries

(as % of GDP)

Country/Country Groups	2000	2005	2006	2007	2008
(1)	(2)	(3)	(4)	(5)	(6)
Canada	2.9	1.5	1.3	1.4	0.4
France	–1.5	–3.0	–2.4	–2.7	–3.4
Iceland	1.7	4.9	6.3	5.4	–1.2
Ireland	4.7	1.5	2.9	0.2	–6.4
Italy	–0.8	–4.3	–3.3	–1.5	–2.7
Japan	–7.6	–5.0	–4.0	–2.5	–5.6
United Kingdom	1.3	–3.3	–2.6	–2.6	–5.4
United States	1.6	–3.3	–2.2	–2.9	–6.1
Memo Items					
Advanced Economies	0.0	–2.4	–1.5	–1.2	–3.5
Euro Area	0.1	–2.5	–1.3	–0.7	–1.8
Major Advanced Economies (G7)	–0.2	–3.4	–2.4	–2.3	–4.7
Newly Industrialized Asian Economies	–0.2	1.5	1.9	3.4	0.8
European Union	–0.1	–2.5	–1.5	–0.9	–2.3

Source IMF, *World Economic Outlook* database, April 2009, Washington D.C.

and eventually the macroeconomic outlook. In the larger European countries, medium-term fiscal consolidation soon became a priority. Given the limited scope for discretionary action by the early 2000s, it was felt that automatic stabilizers should be allowed to operate fully around the consolidation path, even if that results in "temporary" breaches of the 3 percent of GDP deficit limit. In Japan, given the very high public deficit and debt, modest structural fiscal consolidation appeared appropriate. For several of these countries, the pressing need for a credible medium-term framework to restore balance began to be expressed by the IMF as early as 2003 in its *World Economic Outlook*. In emerging markets, the policy priorities varied widely across regions. In Latin America, the pace of fiscal consolidation and structural reform was sustained. In Asia, the scope for policy maneuver was regarded as greater, though many emerging and developing countries continued a broad-based effort to improve medium-term public debt sustainability—encompassing tax reforms, improved expenditure control, institutional strengthening, and structural reforms.

In the United States as in other advanced economies, measures to boost national saving assumed considerable urgency. With public debt projected to remain high into the medium-term, it was feared that no fiscal cushion would be available to deal with the coming pressures from the retirement of the baby boomers. All these economies face significant fiscal pressures from aging populations. Public spending on old-age pensions is expected to rise by about 4–5 percent of GDP over the next 50 years. Without offsetting increases in saving rates from current levels, which were widely perceived as low in relation to medium-term requirements (Table 2.5), these increases would put unbearable strains on public finances and debt burdens.

How did the global imbalances emerge and swell? Since the post-Bretton Woods international monetary and financial system, three features have worked to delay adjustment in global imbalances. First, a country issuing a reserve currency can finance current account deficits for an extended period relatively costlessly. Second, a country managing its exchange rate can resist upward pressure on the value of its currency and delay adjustment in its balance of payments for an extended period. Third, there could be incentives to delay adjustment in terms of gains in net exports or capital flows (Dunaway 2009). It is in this context that the then US Treasury Secretary Henry M. Paulson pointed out aptly:

TABLE 2.5
Gross National Saving in Select Countries

(as % of GDP)

Country	2000	2005	2006	2007	2008
(1)	*(2)*	*(3)*	*(4)*	*(5)*	*(6)*
France	21.5	19.7	20.5	21.0	20.8
Germany	20.1	22.0	23.8	25.8	25.7
Italy	20.2	19.0	19.0	19.4	18.0
Japan	28.0	27.2	27.7	28.9	26.7
United Kingdom	15.0	14.7	14.2	15.3	15.1
United States	18.0	14.8	15.5	14.2	11.9
Memo Items					
China	*36.8*	*51.0*	*54.1*	*57.6*	*58.9*
India	*23.8*	*34.3*	*35.8*	*37.6*	*37.4*

Source IMF, *World Economic Outlook* database, April 2009, Washington D.C.

If we only address particular regulatory issues—as critical as they are—without addressing the global imbalances that fueled recent excesses, we will have missed an opportunity to dramatically improve the foundation for global markets and economic vitality going forward. The pressure from global imbalances will simply build up again until it finds another outlet.[1]

The Growing Asset Price Bubble

The robust optimism generated by high global growth, the massive slosh of capital flows, and low interest rates produced a heady cocktail. Asset prices across all classes of instruments, ranging from stocks to housing prices to commodity prices, surged as investors around the world were driven by a relentless search for returns, including those of relatively lower credit quality. This occurred not just in the US but across the Atlantic in Europe as well as in a broad range of developed and developing countries (Table 2.6). The benign environment spurred an underestimation of risks and soon led to the creation and purchase of ever-riskier assets. The quest for yield spread across financial entities, corporates and individuals, and carry trade—selling a certain currency with a relatively low interest rate and using the funds to purchase a different currency yielding a higher interest rate without hedging against the risk of adverse currency movements—became a household term.

TABLE 2.6
**Equity Market Indices in Select Countries
and Country Groups**

(percentage change)

(1)	2004	2005	2006	2007	2008
	(2)	(3)	(4)	(5)	(6)
World	12.8	7.6	18.0	7.1	–42.1
Emerging Markets	22.4	30.3	29.2	36.5	–54.5
Latin America	34.8	44.9	39.3	46.9	–52.8
Europe, Middle East, and Africa	35.8	34.9	21.3	25.8	–56.7
Asia	12.2	23.5	29.8	38.3	–54.1
China	–0.8	15.9	78.1	63.1	–51.9
India	16.5	35.4	49.0	71.2	–65.1
France	16.3	7.8	31.7	10.9	–44.9
Germany	14.4	7.7	33.0	32.5	–47.2
Italy	28.6	–1.3	28.1	2.7	–52.1
Japan	14.7	24.1	5.1	–5.4	–30.5
United Kingdom	15.5	3.7	26.2	4.7	–50.6
United States	8.8	3.8	13.2	4.1	–38.6

Source *Global Financial Stability Report*, IMF, April 2009, Washington D.C.

The obsession of monetary policy with commodity price stability also stoked the asset bubble—monetary policy was until recently regarded as too blunt an instrument to counteract asset price booms.

Households and House Prices

In the US, the benign macroeconomic conditions sparked off a housing boom funded through an increase in mortgages originated by banks and non-banks. A large portion of these mortgages was securitized. In addition, evidence shows that a decrease in lending standards played a significant role. Credit to households rose rapidly after 2000, driven largely by growth in mortgages. Interest rates below historical averages and financial innovation contributed to rising household indebtedness, and despite low interest rates, debt service relative to disposable income increased sharply. Leveraging in the form of high loan-to-value (LTV) mortgages left households vulnerable to declines in house prices, tightening credit conditions, and a slowdown in economic activity or even moderate declines in house prices would have been enough to push many borrowers into negative equity.

Similar to previous episodes (Finland, 1991; Japan, 1992; Norway, 1987; Spain, 1977; and Sweden, 1991), house prices rose sharply in the years preceding the crisis. Prices peaked six quarters prior to the beginning of the banking crisis, after rising by more than 30 percent in the previous five years.

Financial innovation and the sheer complexity of the system referred to earlier, however, led to the underestimation of systemic risk. The widespread perception was that risk had been sufficiently passed on to those investors who could more safely hold it because of their longer-term and less-leveraged liability structure. The "surprise" was that banks' exposures to the housing sector through their structured investment vehicles (SIVs), conduits, and trading books were much larger than anticipated. Consequently, the housing downturn became a threat for financial and macroeconomic stability.

Some of these patterns are also found in varying degrees in other countries. In the run-up to the crisis, credit aggregates grew extremely fast in the UK, Spain, Iceland, and several Eastern European countries. As in the US, these credit expansions fueled real estate booms. House prices rose rapidly in most of Eastern and Western European countries, including the UK and Iceland. As in the US, these housing booms were generally supported by sharply increased household leverage. Increased international financial integration helped these patterns along. For Eastern Europe and some other emerging markets, a clear relationship can be documented between credit growth and capital inflows. In many of these countries, risks were exacerbated by widespread unhedged foreign currency borrowing by households.

The Housing Market in the US

Subprime Mortgage Market

The US residential mortgage market was US$10 trillion in 2006, representing one-quarter of the total debt market in the US. Within the US residential mortgage market, the subprime segment was relatively small at US$1.5 trillion (Figure 2.1).

FIGURE 2.1
Structure of US Residential Mortgage Market

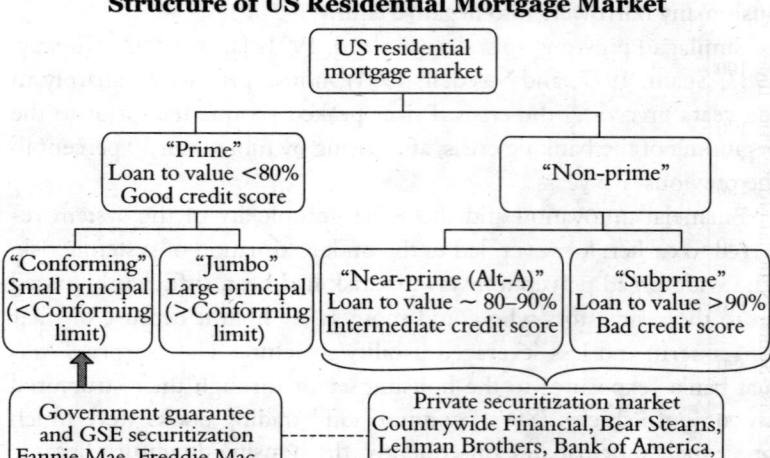

Source Rant (2008).

With the increase in house prices, the subprime mortgage market experienced an exponential growth (Chart 2.1). Subprime mortgages accounted for over 20 percent of all mortgage originations in 2006, up from 6 percent in 2002; the Alt-A mortgage (see Box 2.1 for definition) market alone grew from US$85 billion in 2003 to US$400 billion in 2006 (Agarwal and Ho 2007).

The 2001 *Interagency Expanded Guidance for Subprime Lending Programs* defines the subprime borrower as one who generally displays a range of credit risk characteristics, including one or more of the following:

- Two or more 30-day delinquencies in the last 12 months, or one or more 60-day delinquencies in the last 24 months;
- Judgment, foreclosure, repossession, or charge-off in the prior 24 months;
- Bankruptcy in the last five years;
- Relatively high default probability as evidenced by, e.g., a credit bureau risk score of 660 or below (depending on the product/collateral), or other bureau or proprietary scores with an equivalent default probability likelihood; and/or
- Debt service-to-income ratio of 50 percent or greater; or otherwise limited ability to cover family living expenses after deducting total debt service requirements from monthly income.

CHART 2.1
House Prices and Mortgage Originations

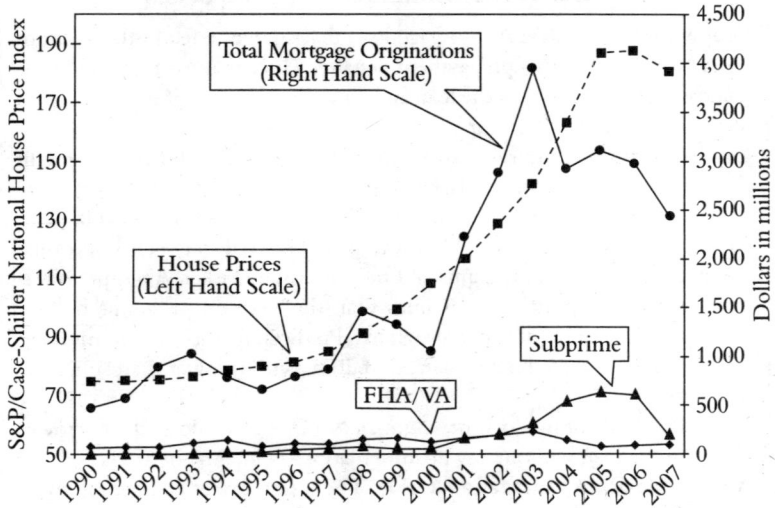

Source   Agarwal and Ho (2007).
Note   FHA: Federal Housing Authority; VA: Veterans Administration.

Thus, people who cannot qualify for conventional competitive mortgages often turn to subprime mortgage products. These products carry relatively higher interest rates and fees in order to compensate for the riskier applicants. Subprime lending practices, in turn, gave rise to specific terminologies (Box 2.1).

The difference in the quality of borrowers between the jumbo and subprime mortgage lenders is quite marked—while the delinquency rate for the prime conventional loans ranged between 2 and 4 percent, for subprime conventional loans it was 10 percent at its minimum (Chart 2.2).

Trends in US Housing Prices

The housing market bubble was exacerbated by a jump in US house prices which registered a unidirectional increase from the early 1990s till mid-2006 (Chart 2.3). During 1997–2006, *real* home prices increased by 85 percent. By early 2007, however, house prices started moving southwards—initial signs of the imminent bursting of the bubble.

BOX 2.1
Select Terms from the Subprime Crisis

Prepayment penalty: A mortgage loan that charges a fee in the event of an early payoff carries a prepayment penalty. The penalty can be as high as 3 percent of the balance of the loan and typically is charged if the loan is paid off within the first three years.

Credit scores: A comprehensive statistical model rates a borrower's credit risk. The lower the score, the riskier the applicant. In order to qualify for the best mortgage programs, a credit score should not be lower than 700.

Alt-A: Short for alternative-A, these programs fall between traditional competitive mortgage programs and the subprime market. Alt-A programs have looser underwriting guidelines than the A-credit programs but are not as loose as many subprime programs. Predictably, these programs carry rates and fees that are higher than A-credit paper but lower than subprime programs.

No Doc: Short for no documentation, a No Doc loan allows the borrower to obtain the loan without any documentation on income or assets.

Adjustable-Rate Mortgage (ARM): The interest rates charged on these mortgages are tied to an interest rate index. If the interest rate index rises, the mortgage interest rate and the monthly payment go up. If the interest rate index falls, the mortgage interest rate and monthly payment go down.

Amortization: This term refers to the gradual paying down of a loan. For example, traditional mortgage terms require that each payment include, in addition to interest, part of the loan principal, continually lessening the amount you owed and extinguishing the debt within a set period of time.

Interest-only Mortgage: The borrower is required only to make interest payments for a specified number of years. When this initial period expires, the loan changes so that the monthly payment includes principal and interest. At this point, the mortgage begins to fully amortize and monthly payments could increase significantly. The monthly principal payment could be greater than the conventional fixed-rate mortgage payment because there are fewer years to pay down the principal.

Loan-to-value Ratio (LTV): The ratio compares the value of the loan with the fair market value of the home. The lender uses it to determine if its potential losses (in the event that you do not pay) may be recouped by selling the house.

Negative Amortization: This can occur when one chooses to make the minimum payments based on an offered "teaser" rate. The minimum monthly payment often does not cover the interest owed each month for a certain period of time. The interest that is not covered by these monthly

(Box 2.1 continued)

(Box 2.1 continued)

payments becomes part of the principal. As a result, the balance of the loan increases and could eventually exceed what was intended to be borrowed in the first place.

Nontraditional Mortgages: These products are more complex than traditional fixed-rate or adjustable-rate mortgages. They present greater risk of negative amortization and payment shock. Typically referred to as *alternative* or *exotic*, these products take many different forms. They include interest-only mortgages and payment-option ARMs.

Option-ARM: This product typically offers the borrower three different monthly payment options: (*a*) payments of principal and interest, (*b*) interest-only payments, or (*c*) minimum monthly payments ("teaser" payment options that are less than interest-only payments).

Teaser Rates: These are low rates that lenders offer to make mortgage products more attractive. When the "teaser rate" period expires, the lender raises the interest rate for the remainder of the loan period. This new rate may be fixed or may change periodically, depending upon the terms of your loan.

Sources   *Washington Times*, June 8, 2007; *A Guide to Mortgage Products—A Glossary of Lending Terms*, Federal Reserve Bank of Boston, 2007, available at http://www.bos.frb.org

CHART 2.2
Mortgage Delinquency Rates

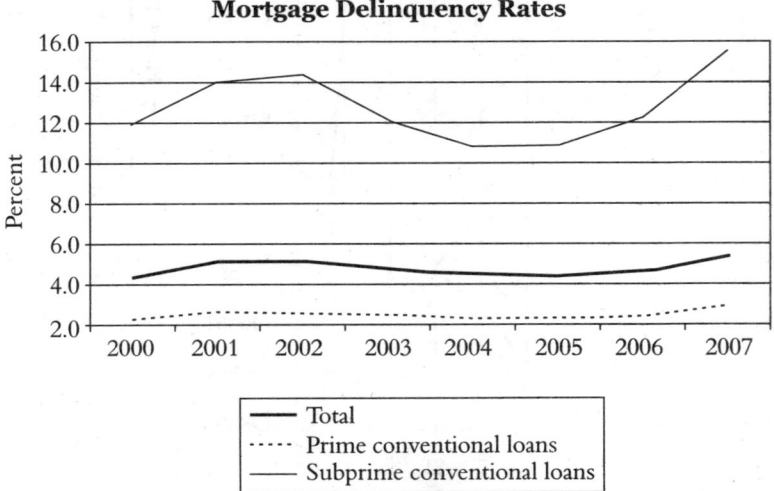

- —— Total
- ----- Prime conventional loans
- —— Subprime conventional loans

Source Mortgage Bankers Association of America.

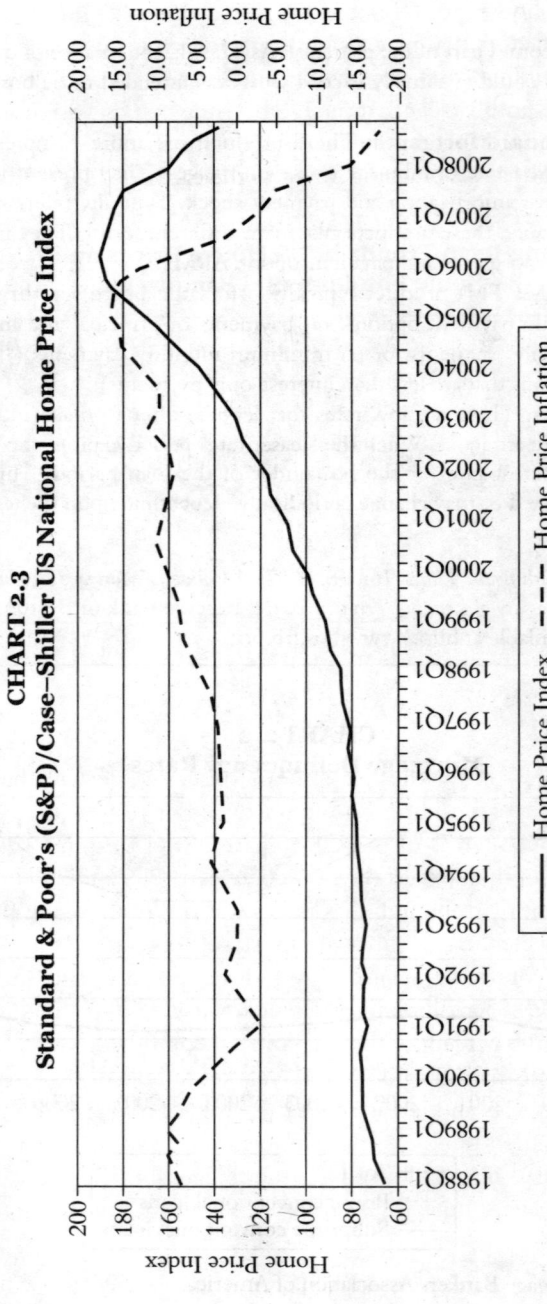

CHART 2.3

Standard & Poor's (S&P)/Case–Shiller US National Home Price Index

— Home Price Index   - - - Home Price Inflation

Source http://www2.standardandpoors.com/portal/site/sp/en/us (accessed in May 2009).

Trends in home prices in the US stood out in contrast to some fundamental factors that play a significant role in influencing housing demands—building costs, population, and interest rates (Chart 2.4). In retrospect, it is amply clear that the US housing market was driven by a bubble. "Home prices certainly did not seem justifiable … it looked like the rocket might come crashing down to the earth" (Shiller 2008).

CHART 2.4
**Long-term Trends in US House Prices and
Some Fundamental Factors**

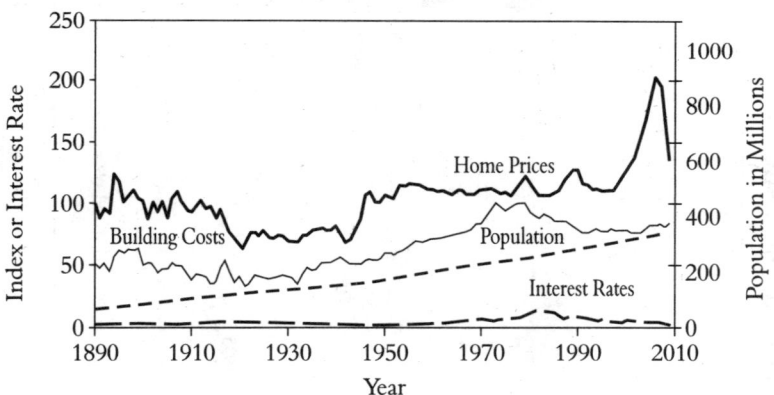

Source Shiller (2007).

A possible reason for the rise in home prices could have been the increase in cost of building houses in terms of prices-to-cost ratio in 79 metropolitan areas of the US (Chart 2.5). The trend was fairly unidirectional in the upward direction between 1995 and 2006.

The accelerating trend in house prices was not restricted to the US. It was also reflected in a number of industrialized countries in Europe. The total value of residential property in developed countries increased by more than US$30 trillion over 2004 to over US$70 trillion in 2005, an increase of 100 percent of those countries' combined GDP. Thus, it was much larger than the global stock market bubble of the late 1990s (in which there was an increase over five years of 80 percent of GDP) or the stock market bubble of the US in the late 1920s (increase of 50 percent of GDP). Thus, it looked like the "biggest bubble in history" in 2005 (*The Economist*, June 16, 2005). In this context, it was observed:

> While home price booms have been known for centuries, the recent boom is unique in its pervasiveness. Dramatic home price booms since

CHART 2.5
US House Price-to-cost Ratio

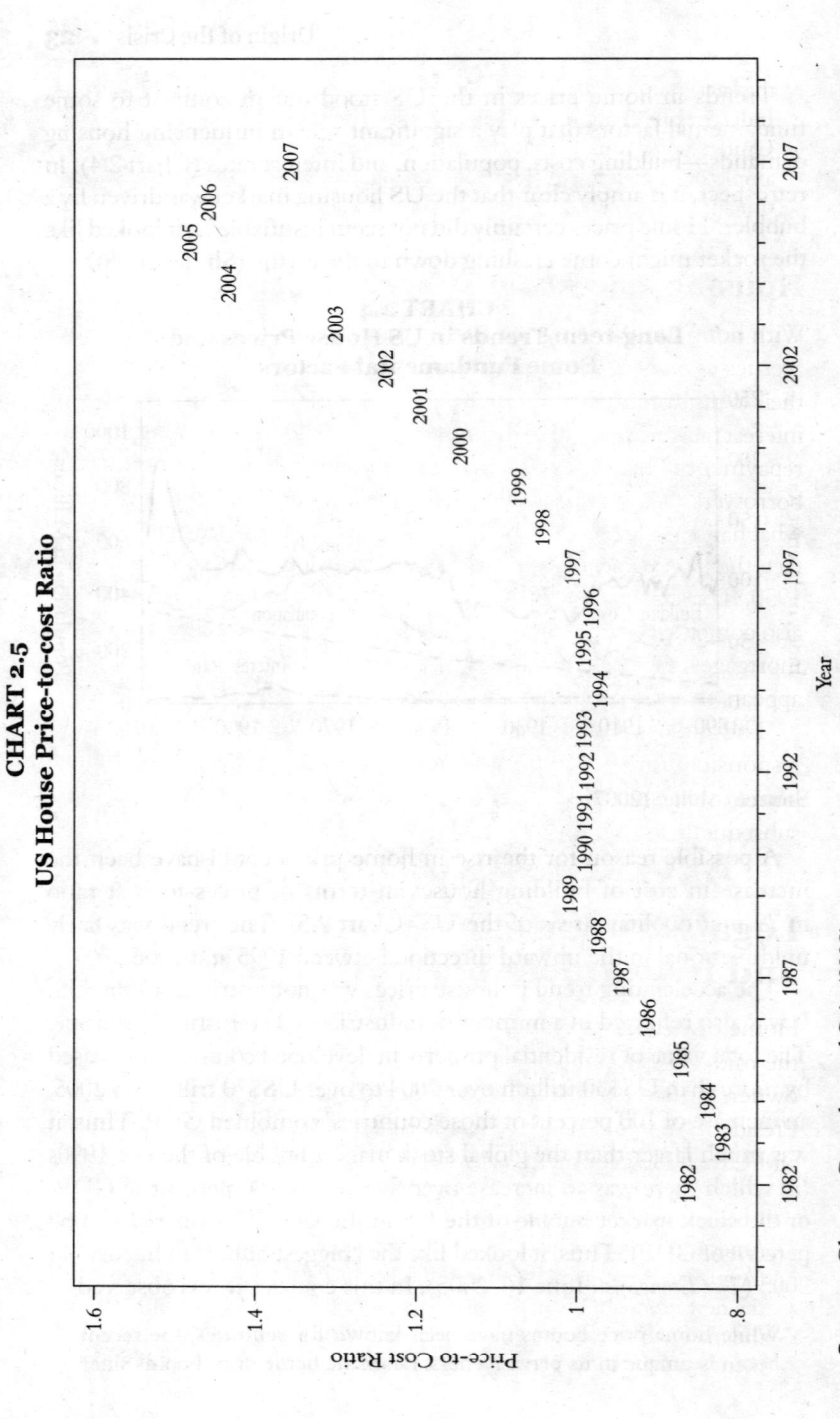

Source Glaeser, Gyourko, and Saiz (2008).

the late 1990s have been in evidence in Australia, Canada, China, France, India, Ireland, Italy, Korea, Russia, Spain, the United Kingdom, and the United States, among other countries. There appears to be no prior example of such dramatic booms occurring in so many places at the same time. (Shiller 2007)

Housing Prices and Subprime Crisis

With house prices rising and low interest rates, additional home equity accrues to owners due to price appreciation and borrowers could repay their loans by refinancing. On the contrary, if house prices are falling and interest rates are high, then the home equity could be zero or negative and repayment of loans by refinancing may not be possible. Consequently, borrowers face increased debt servicing difficulties. This is precisely what happened in early 2007. The 1997–2006 house price bubble was, in fact, the largest speculative surge of real housing prices in the US since 1950. The collapse of this house price bubble in late 2006/early 2007 also coincided with a surge in loan defaults in the market for residential mortgages, especially in the case of the recent loans. With hindsight it appears that the subprime crisis was waiting to happen.

The collapse of house price was by no means the only factor responsible for the subprime crisis. The legal structure encouraging home ownership in the US also played some role, as depicted in the subsequent section.

Legal Structure for Home Ownership and Investment Banking

Home ownership is a crucial ingredient of the American dream. Since the mid-1970s, there were a number of laws which encouraged home ownership at any cost. This is reflected in the remarks of the then President George W. Bush (while speaking at the Department of Housing and Urban Development, Washington, DC on June 18, 2002):

I believe when somebody owns their own home, they're realizing the American Dream. They can say it's my home, it's nobody else's home. (Applause.) And we saw that yesterday in Atlanta, when we went to the new homes of the new homeowners. And I saw with pride firsthand, the man say, welcome to my home. He didn't say, welcome to government's home; he didn't say, welcome to my neighbor's home; he said, welcome to my home. I own the home, and you're welcome to come in the home, and I appreciate it. (Applause.) He was a proud man. He was proud that he owns the property. And I was proud for him. And I want that pride to extend all throughout our country.[2]

In retrospect, there are reasons to believe that US lawmakers pushed the dream too far. In fact, it has argued that the housing crisis was the direct result of 30 years of government policy that forced banks to make bad loans to uncreditworthy borrowers. Such policies are now regarded as outcomes of "crackpot egalitarianism" (DiLorenzo 2008).

To go back in history, the origin of this public policy in favor of "affordable" housing lies in the 1938 decision by President Roosevelt to found Fannie Mae (Federal National Mortgage Association) to add to housing liquidity by purchasing and insuring home mortgages. In 1968, Fannie Mae was privatized and any public guarantee for its debts was purely implicit. In 1970, Freddie Mac (Federal Home Mortgage Corporation) was set up to extend the work of Fannie Mae and to offer mortgage backed securities as a way of collateralizing home mortgages and spreading the risks. The root of easy housing policy can, in fact, be traced to legislations like the *Home Mortgage Disclosure Act* (*HMDA*), *1975* and the *Community Reinvestment Act* (*CRA*), *1977*.

Home Mortgage Disclosure Act (HMDA), 1975

The *HMDA* of 1975 was one in a series of federal antipoverty laws enacted by the United States Congress in the 1960s and 1970s.[3] Congress believed that some financial institutions had contributed to the decline of some geographical areas by their failure to provide adequate home financing to qualified applicants on reasonable terms and conditions. Thus, one purpose of *HMDA* was to provide the public with information that would help show whether financial institutions were serving the housing credit needs of the neighborhoods and communities in which they were located. A second purpose was to aid public officials in targeting public investments from the private sector to areas where they were needed. Finally, subsequent amendments required the collection and disclosure of data about applicant and borrower characteristics. As the name implies, *HMDA* is a disclosure law that relies upon public scrutiny for its effectiveness. It does not prohibit any specific activity of lenders, and it does not establish a quota system of mortgage loans to be made in any Metropolitan Statistical Area (MSA) or other geographic area as defined by the Office of Management and Budget.

Community Reinvestment Act (CRA), 1977

The CRA was intended to encourage depository institutions to help meet the credit needs of the communities in which they operated, including low- and moderate-income neighborhoods, consistent with safe and sound operations. It was enacted by the Congress in 1977. The regulation was substantially revised in May 1995, and was most recently amended in August 2005. In basic terms, the CRA requires banks to lend in the low-income neighborhoods where they take deposits.

As the financial crisis unfolded, the notion that the CRA is at its root gained currency. It had been argued that the CRA tended to encourage banks to help meet the credit needs of lower-income borrowers and borrowers in lower-income neighborhoods. Critics of the CRA contend that the law pushed banking institutions to undertake high-risk mortgage lending. While, admittedly, CRA led to some sort of financial inclusion in the US, how far was it responsible for the subprime crisis? Two distinct opinions have emerged.

At the one end of the spectrum is the view that the CRA, made even more stringent during the Clinton administration, trapped banks in a Catch-22 situation, so that, "...if they comply, they know they will have to suffer from more loan defaults. If they don't comply, they face financial penalties ... which can cost a large corporation like Bank of America billions of dollars" (DiLorenzo 2008).

A contrary opinion has been expressed by Fed Governor Krozner (2008):

> I believe the CRA is an important model for designing incentives that motivate private-sector involvement to help meet community needs. The CRA has, in fact, been helpful in alleviating the financial isolation of many areas of concentrated poverty.... Contrary to the assertions of critics, the evidence does not support the view that the CRA contributed in any substantial way to the crisis in the subprime mortgage market.

Did the CRA cause the mortgage market meltdown? The question has been probed empirically (Bhutta and Canner 2009). Two basic conclusions emerged. First, only a small portion of subprime mortgage originations is related to the CRA. Second, CRA-related loans appear to perform comparably to other types of subprime loans. Taken together, the available evidence does not seem to support the contention that the *CRA* contributed in any substantive way to the current mortgage crisis. The jury is still out; only time will tell.

Depository Institutions Deregulation and Monetary Control Act (DIDMCA), 1980

The *DIDMCA* of 1980 preempts state usury ceilings during a time of record high interest rates. When interest rates increased in the late 1970s and state usury ceilings did not rise with them, lenders were unwilling to originate loans. Thus, low usury ceilings prevented lenders from making profitable loans during times of high interest. *DIDMCA*'s preemption allowed lenders to charge a high interest rate despite the state's cap. Two years after, the *Alternative Mortgage Transaction Parity Act* (*AMTPA*) was signed into law. The *AMTPA* preempted state statutes that regulated alternative mortgage transactions, such as those with balloon payments, variable rates, and negative amortization. Similar to *DIDMCA*, volatile market conditions, rising interest rates, and lenders' difficulty in making fixed interest prompted the *AMTPA*'s passage.

By the late 1990s, the effects of deregulation started to unravel. With increasing availability of alternative mortgage products, first-time buyers with low credit scores were able to purchase homes. The deregulation aimed at opening the housing market to low-income, low-credit-score borrowers had actually paved the way for the risky and expensive loan products that created today's foreclosure crisis. Because of *DIDMCA* and *AMTPA*, the subprime mortgage lender emerged. By 2006, subprime lenders held 20 percent of the mortgage market.

Repeal of the Glass–Steagall Act of 1933

The *Glass–Steagall Act* of 1933, officially known as the *Banking Act* of 1933, mandated the separation of banks according to the types of business they conducted. Investment banks, whose securities-related activities resulted in relatively large risks, were to be separate from commercial banks whose depositors needed greater protection. The establishment of such an Act has many good arguments. First, conflict of interest characterizes the granting of credit lending and the use of credit investing by the same entity. Second, depository institutions possess enormous financial power by virtue of their control of other people's money; their influence must be limited to ensure soundness and fair competition in the market for funds. Third, securities activities can be risky and can threaten the integrity of deposits. Since the government insures deposits, it could be required to pay large sums if securities losses led to bank failures. Finally, managers of depository institutions may not be conditioned to operate prudently in more speculative securities businesses.

Despite these compelling reasons, the *Glass–Steagall Act* was repealed during 1999–2001, and the *Gramm–Leach–Bliley (GLB) Act*, that allowed commercial and investment banks to consolidate, came into existence.[4] In some sense, the booming of the investment banking business can be traced to the repeal of the *Glass–Steagall Act* and while it may have been directly responsible for the crisis, its role in the investment banking cannot be ruled out. In fact, many observers believe that the *GLB Act* allowed various financial firms to focus too much on meeting the expectations of Wall Street analysts and the high rewards inherent in investment banking and to avoid recognition of the risks necessary to achieve them (Verschoor 2009). In fact, the "Volcker Rule" proposed in January 2010, debarring a commercial bank to own, invest in, or sponsor a hedge fund/private equity fund/proprietary trading organization attempts to bring back the spirit of the *Glass–Steagall Act*.

Where does the discussion on these legislations lead us? As far as the crisis is concerned, it is difficult to establish a one-to-one correspondence between these laws and the adverse developments in the US home finance market and investment banking. However, some elements of these laws did provide a fillip to homeownership and created the spurt in investment banking business. Thus, an indirect influence of these laws on the US mortgage market crisis cannot be ruled out.

Conclusion

As this chapter has shown, the current crisis was brewed in the cauldron of economic prosperity and well-being, sophistication of financial innovation and the deepening of finance—ingredients that were widely believed to be factors antithetical to the possibility of its occurrence. It highlighted the strong co-movement of financial and macroeconomic stress across economies. Links binding economies together in a globalized world—the interdependence of macroeconomic activity, international trade, and financial ties in the form of bank lending and investment flows—have helped to spread prosperity in good times. In bad times, however, they have provided the conduits for contagion. In a longer-term perspective therefore, financial integration may be an essential part of a prospering world economy, but growing financial linkages inevitably increase the transmission of stress, especially in the absence of circuit breakers.

One fact has emerged in stark relief—periods of financial stress in the US are usually global and pervasive in their impact. Even strong macroeconomic fundamentals or prudent policies in other economies cannot prevent their transmission. Since its earliest days, the United States has suffered periodic financial crises. The first dates to 1792. In the 19th century, bank panics occurred regularly. Then came the great stock market crash of 1929 and the failure of two-fifths of the nation's banks in the Great Depression. Almost all of these perturbations had global implications.

Every financial crisis originates in a failure of "vision." It is not that, before the crisis, no one foresees problems, "excesses," and losses. There are usually warnings. But what are routinely overlooked are the fatal interconnections that transform problems into panic. People panic because the future goes dark. They do not know what to expect, so they expect the worst. Herd behavior quickly sets in whereby being pessimistic often becomes synonymous with keeping pace with the Joneses. Markets cascade uncontrollably downward. It is argued that the current crisis did not occur merely because "subprime" mortgages experienced unexpectedly large losses or even because many of these loans were "securitized" in complex bonds. It occurred because doubts and lack of confidence snowballed into generalized panic. Hardly anyone expected the panic; once it happened, large but bearable losses became a crisis. So then, what triggered the loss of confidence and brought on the panic? It is to this subject that the next chapter turns.

Notes

1. "Remarks by Secretary Henry M. Paulson, Jr, on the Financial Rescue Package and Economic Update," *US Treasury Press Release*, November 12, 2008.
2. Speech delivered by US President George W. Bush, June 18, 2002, available at http://www.hud.gov/news/speeches/presremarks.cfm

3. The US Congress passed the first of these statutes in 1968, when it enacted Title VIII of the *Civil Rights Act* prohibiting discrimination in housing finance. In the 1970s, as urban centers continued to decline, Congress passed three more statutes designed to address the twin ills of discrimination and disinvestment. One of these statutes was the *HMDA*; the other two were the *Equal Credit Opportunity Act* of 1974 and the *CRA* of 1977.

4. For example, in 1998, Citibank merged with Travelers Group, an insurance company, and formed the conglomerate Citigroup, a corporation combining banking and insurance underwriting services under brands including Smith-Barney, Shearson, Primerica and Travelers Insurance Corporation. This combination would have violated the *Glass–Steagall Act*.

3

Proximate Causes
of the Crisis

Introduction

As set out in the previous chapter, the backdrop to the crisis of 2008–2009 was provided by global economic imbalances, an accommodative macro environment, the subprime crisis in the US housing market and the populism and deregulation imparted by the legal structure. Against this setting, we now explore the proximate causes and actors that turned the subprime crisis into a global financial conflagration.[1] This distinction is merely for expository convenience and in some sense the division between the two sets of factors (and hence the line of demarcation between Chapters 2 and 3) is somewhat fuzzy. As the US was at the epicenter, it may be noted at the outset that the discussion in the chapter is essentially about the US situation. This US-centric focus should not, however, be interpreted as absence of these factors elsewhere in the world.

While the final word on the diagnosis of the proximate causes of the global crisis is yet to be pronounced, at the risk of broad generalization, we focus our attention on three major factors: (*a*) structured financial products, (*b*) lack of effective regulation and supervision, and (*c*) institutions that seem to have played an important role in transmission and propagation of the crisis such as investment banks, government sponsored institutions in the US, and the rating agencies. Other factors like accounting norms and the perverse incentive structure in the financial sector are also dealt with.

In the face of the prevailing uncertainty, it is useful, as in the preceding chapter, to begin with an influential view:

...although the subprime debacle triggered the crisis, the developments in the U.S. mortgage market were only one aspect of a much larger and more encompassing credit boom whose impact transcended the mortgage market to affect many other forms of credit. Aspects of this broader credit boom included widespread declines in underwriting standards, breakdowns in lending oversight by investors and rating agencies, increased reliance on complex and opaque credit instruments that proved fragile under stress, and unusually low compensation for risk-taking. (Bernanke 2009)

Admittedly, there are arguments and counterarguments about the extent of responsibility that can be assigned to any particular factor that was playing out a role in the genesis of the crisis. Annex I gives a sense of this ongoing debate in a nutshell.

Credit Boom

We have already seen in Chapter 2 that the period preceding the crisis, viz., 2000–06, was marked by easy monetary policy when interest rates reached an all-time low. It was also evident in hindsight that this could have been the response to the dotcom bubble, with policy efforts shifting it to the housing market rather than pricking it. Be that as it may, the data confirm that there was a massive credit growth during the period 2002–05 in the US and the Euro Area (Chart 3.1).

In some sense, the financial crisis marked the end of a major global credit cycle that significantly benefited the growth of the housing sector and mortgage markets in most advanced Organization for Economic Cooperation and Development (OECD) economies and in a large number of emerging economies as well. Yet, to be fair, for several years, central bankers, bank regulators, and economists monitoring global financial markets had worried about the widespread underpricing of risk in the credit boom and more importantly, the surge in indebtedness that is the mirror image of the credit expansion. A financial crisis was seen as an accident waiting to happen somewhere in the global financial system. Opaque hedge funds were often mentioned. As noted in the previous chapter, this was accompanied by very low Federal Funds Rates during the period from 2003 to 2006—these rates were even negative in real terms in 2002 and 2003 (Taylor 2007). This lethal combination found reflection in an extraordinary increase in credit and household debt (Wolf 2009). Along with a spurt in total US public and private debt,

CHART 3.1
Private Credit Growth: US and the Euro Area
(12-month percent change)

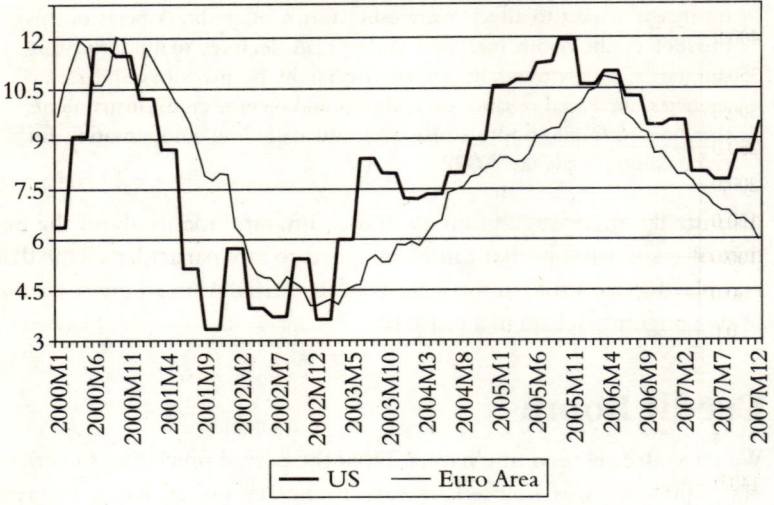

Source IMF, *World Economic Outlook* database, Washington D.C.

and within private sector debt, debt of the financial sector (as a percent of GDP) tended to surpass the debt of the households and nonfinancial business sector since the mid-1990s (Chart 3.2).

Interestingly, previous global bank lending booms in the early-1970s and mid-to-late 1980s were hump-shaped phenomena lasting between two and five years. The credit boom which started in the mid-1990s and ended only recently was different. It lasted twice as long, the increase in the bank lending to GDP ratio was more marked, and it was concentrated in the household sector in its later stages to an unusual extent. It also seems to have been focused on the advanced economies and was US-led, with the boom in the US starting in the mid-1990s compared with start dates of 2001–02 for most other economies.[2] The impact of a given change in credit standards might be expected to be largest for the United States, where household financial problems are arguably most severe. A rapid increase in household debt since 2002 made it possible for households to maintain consumption and residential investment at higher levels than would have been feasible based on their income alone.

As mentioned earlier, this increase in debt was enabled largely by strongly rising house prices, which reduced collateral constraints for

CHART 3.2
US Debt: Evolution

TOTAL US PUBLIC AND PRIVATE DEBT
(as percent of GDP)

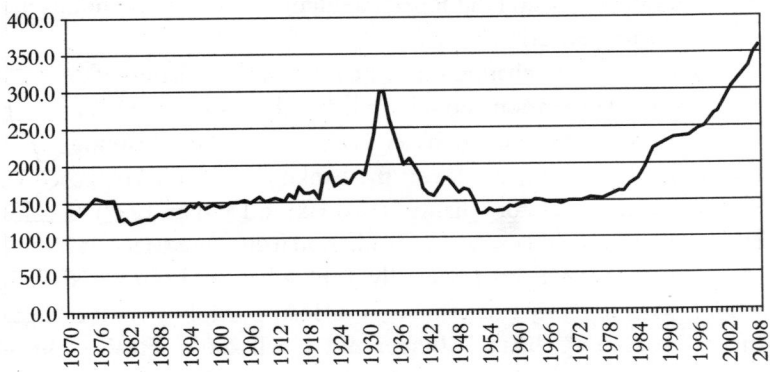

PRIVATE SECTOR DEBT
(relative to GDP)

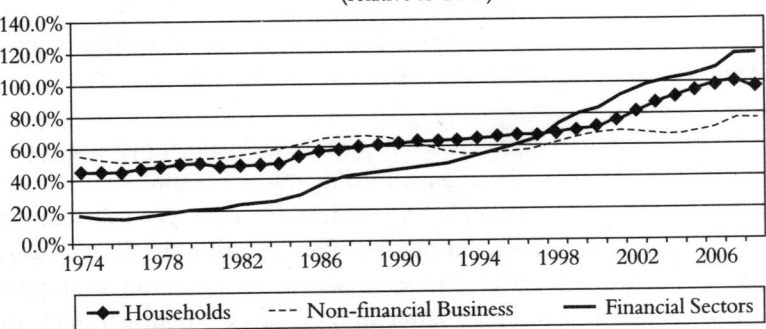

◆ Households   --- Non-financial Business   — Financial Sectors

Source Wolf (2009).

households that would otherwise have been unable to borrow as much, or at all. Households in the US were also able to use proceeds from home sales, cash-out refinancing, and home equity loans to extract their rising home equity: some private estimates suggest that home equity extraction financed on average about 3 percent of personal consumption (including repayment of non-mortgage debts) from 2001 to 2005. One source of vulnerability became the combination of low saving and high household debt. While the ratio of US household saving to disposable income started declining from about 7.5 percent in 1992, it fell particularly sharply during the early 2000s to almost zero by 2005. A significant rise in debt service payments during this period, to over 14 percent of disposable income by 2007, made households more exposed to income and interest rate shocks. Household spending was destined to weaken in response to high debt and debt service burdens, falling employment, and the general tightening of credit conditions that occurred when the crisis broke.

There are various channels in which such accumulation of debt and massive credit expansion could have led to the crisis. First, an increase in value of collateralizable goods tends to release credit constraints, fuels further wealth effects, and leaves the banking system overexposed via the "financial accelerator" channel (Kiyotaki and Moore 1997). Second, in periods of fast credit expansion, banks find it difficult to recruit enough experienced loan officers (especially if there has not been a crisis for a while). This leads to a deterioration of loan portfolios via the "institutional memory" channel (Berger and Udell 2004). Finally, during expansions, adverse selection is less severe and banks find it optimal to trade quality for market share, increasing crisis probability through an "informational capital and adverse selection" channel (Dell'Ariccia and Marquez 2006). In effect, a credit boom is often associated with fall in lending standards, which really sows the seeds of the next crisis. This crisis is no exception.

The connection between financial crises and bank liquidity creation has also drawn wide attention within the "credit boom" strand in the recent literature. For example, an examination of the aggregate liquidity creation of banks before, during, and after five major financial crises in the US from 1984:Q1 to 2008:Q1 uncovered several interesting patterns, such as a significant buildup or drop-off of "abnormal" liquidity creation before each crisis, where "abnormal" is defined relative to a time trend and seasonal factors (Berger and Bouwman 2008). Banking and market-related crises differ in that banking crises are preceded by abnormal positive liquidity creation, while market-related crises were generally preceded by abnormal negative liquidity creation. Bank liquidity creation has both decreased and increased during crises, likely both exacerbating and ameliorating the effects of crises.[3] Off-balance-sheet guarantees such as loan commitments moved more than on-balance-sheet assets such as mortgages and business lending during banking crises. In the context of this crisis, there was a massive liquidity expansion till the third quarter of 2007 (Chart 3.3).

CHART 3.3
Liquidity Creation and the Subprime Crisis

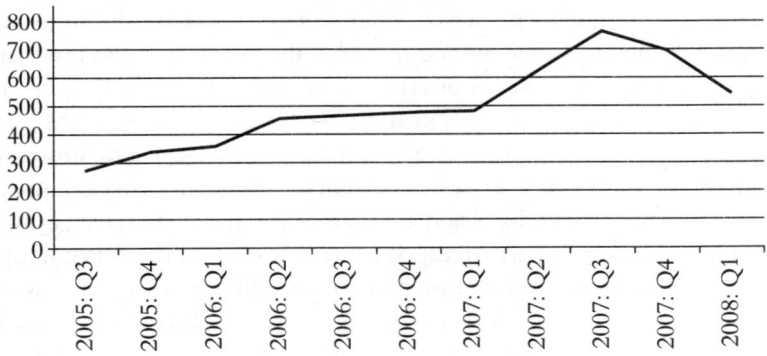

Source Berger and Bouwman (2008).

Securitization and Structured Products

In the olden days, when one needed to borrow money to buy a house, one used to go to a bank. The bank used to give the borrower the money and the borrowers promised to repay the bank with interest over a certain length of time. Gone are those days. Today, it is quite uncommon in the advanced countries for the bank that originally made the loan to be the institution that actually receives the interest payments. Instead, those payments are likely to have gone into a pool from which structured products and derivatives like mortgage-backed securities (MBSs) were created by the US government sponsored enterprises (GSEs) or, particularly in the last few years, arranged by large private institutions.

Nature of Derivatives and Structured Products

What are derivatives? In a generic sense, derivatives are financial securities whose prices are dependent upon or derived from one or more underlying assets. The derivative itself is merely a contract between two or more parties and its value is determined by fluctuations in the underlying asset. The most common underlying assets include stocks, bonds, commodities, currencies, interest rates, and stock market indexes. Most derivatives are characterized by high leverage.[4]

Composition-wise, derivatives includes the following major financial products: (*a*) interest rate contracts (as defined as the notional value of interest rate swap, futures, forward, and option contracts); (*b*) foreign exchange rate contracts; (*c*) commodity contracts; and (*d*) equity contracts (defined similarly to interest rate contracts). Futures and forward contracts are contracts in which the buyer agrees to purchase and the seller agrees to sell, at a specified future date, a specific quantity of underlying assets at a specified price or yield. These contracts exist for a variety of underlying assets, including traditional agricultural or physical commodities as well as currencies and interest rates. Futures contracts are standardized and are traded on organized exchanges that set limits on counterparty credit exposure. Forward contracts do not have standardized terms and are traded over the counter (OTC). Options are contracts in which the buyer acquires the right to buy from or to sell to another party some specified amount of underlying assets at a stated price (strike price) during a period or on a specified future date, in return for compensation (such as a fee or premium). The seller is obligated to purchase or sell the underlying assets at the discretion of the buyer of the contract. Swaps are obligations between two parties to exchange a series of cash flows at periodic intervals (settlement dates) for a specified period. The cash flows of a swap are either fixed or determined for each settlement date by multiplying the quantity of the underlying instrument (notional principal) by specified reference rates or prices. Except for currency swaps, the notional principal is used to calculate each payment but is not exchanged.

Over the years, derivatives have turned out to be important vehicles of risk mitigation and the derivatives business has shown tremendous growth; illustratively, the amounts outstanding in the credit default swap (CDS) market had almost doubled just within a year in 2007—from US$28.6 trillion to nearly US$58 trillion (Table 3.1).[5]

What are structured products? Structured finance encompasses all advanced private and public financial arrangements that serve to efficiently refinance and hedge any profitable economic activity beyond the scope of conventional forms of on-balance-sheet securities (debt, bonds, equity) in the effort to lower cost of capital and to mitigate agency costs of market impediments on liquidity (Jobst 2006). Thus, in some sense, the process of securitization is the key to the process of formation of structured financial assets. Securitization refers to the process of conversion of assets (usually forms of debt) into securities which can be traded more freely and cheaply than the underlying assets and generates better returns than if the assets were used as collateral for a loan.

TABLE 3.1
Over-the-counter (OTC) Derivatives

(amounts outstanding in billions of US$)

Type of Derivatives	2000	2005	2006	2007	2008
(1)	(2)	(3)	(4)	(5)	(6)
1. Notional Amounts Outstanding	**95,199**	**299,261**	**418,131**	**595,341**	**591,963**
1.1. Foreign exchange contracts	15,666	31,360	40,271	56,238	49,753
1.2. Interest rate contracts	64,668	211,970	291,581	393,138	418,678
1.3. Equity-linked contracts	1,891	5,793	7,488	8,469	6,494
1.4. Commodity contracts	662	5,434	7,115	8,455	4,427
1.5. Credit default swaps	0	13,908	28,650	57,894	41,868
1.6. Unallocated	12,313	30,794	43,026	71,146	70,742
2. Gross Market Values	**3,183**	**9,800**	**9,791**	**15,813**	**33,889**
2.1. Foreign exchange contracts	849	997	1,266	1,807	3,917
2.2. Interest rate contracts	1,426	5,397	4,826	7,177	18,420
2.3. Equity-linked contracts	289	582	853	1,142	1,113
2.4. Commodity contracts	133	871	667	1,899	955
2.5. Credit default swaps	0	243	470	2,002	5,652
2.6. Unallocated	485	1,710	1,709	1,788	3,831
Memorandum Item					
Gross Credit Exposure	*1,080*	*1,900*	*2,036*	*3,256*	*5,004*

Source *Quarterly Review*, March 2009, Bank for International Settlements.

One example is the MBS which pools illiquid individual mortgages into a single tradable asset.

The basic idea of securitization or structured products is that bundles, or pools of income-producing financial assets, usually loan-like obligations such as mortgages, corporate loans, auto loans, or credit card receivables, but potentially also revenue sources such as royalty streams are sold to an entity (a special purpose vehicle [SPV]) that issues claims on the pool income to investors. Once the claims have been sold, the underlying asset is said to have been securitized. Securitization transactions are designed in a way such that the investors have no recourse to the party that sold the claims to the investment vehicle, and creditors of the selling party typically have no ability to pursue the assets sold to the investment vehicle. Structured products have flourished in the US mortgage market and various types of products have emerged in recent years (Box 3.1).

Structured finance offers the issuers enormous flexibility in terms of maturity structure, security design, and asset types, allowing them to provide enhanced return at a customized degree of diversification commensurate to an individual investor's appetite for risk. Hence, structured finance contributes to a more complete capital market by offering any risk–return trade-off along the efficient frontier of optimal diversification at lower transaction cost. However, the increasing complexity of the structured finance market and the ever-growing range of products being made available to investors invariably create challenges in terms of efficient assembly, management, and dissemination of information.

Credit derivatives are financial instruments that isolate and transfer credit risk. As a common working principle, such derivatives involve the sale of contingent credit protection for pre-defined credit events of lending transactions. Credit derivatives sever the link between loan origination and associated credit risk, but leave the original borrower–creditor relationship intact. One may distinguish between credit derivatives in the narrower and in a wider sense. The latter classification includes pure credit derivatives such as CDSs, total return swaps, and credit spread options as well as hybrid products and securitization products with credit derivative elements such as CDOs of bonds and loans. Some unfunded/partially funded structured finance transactions such as credit-linked notes (CLNs) and synthetic CDOs (SCDOs) are credit-derivative-based securitization transactions that provide refinancing through cash flow restructuring and tranche-specific credit

Box 3.1
The Alphabet Soup of Structured Financial Products

ABS (Asset-backed Security): An ABS is a security collateralized by assets such as bonds, credit card repayments, loan repayments, or real estate. For example, an **ABCP (Asset-backed Commercial Paper)** refers to a short-term investment vehicle with a maturity that is typically between 90 and 180 days and is typically issued by a bank. The notes are backed by physical assets such as trade receivables, and are generally used for short-term financing needs.

CDO (Collateralized Debt Obligation): A structured/pooled security backed by a pool of bonds, loans, and other assets. Thus, it is a generic name for collateralized bond obligations, collateralized loan obligations (CLO), and collateralized mortgage obligations (CMO).

SCDO (Synthetic Collateralized Debt Obligation): An SCDO uses credit derivatives to transfer credit risk in a portfolio. This is in contrast to a traditional CDO, which is typically structured as securitization with ownership of the assets transferred to a separate SPV.

CLO (Collateralized Loan Obligation): A structured bond backed by the loan repayments from a portfolio of pooled personal or commercial loans, excluding mortgages. The structure allows a bank to remove loans from its balance sheet so as to reduce its required capital reserves (normally imposed on the loan amount), while retaining contact with the borrowers and fees for servicing the loans.

CMO (Collateralized Mortgage Obligation): A type of ABS backed by mortgage payments. Typically, such securities provide a higher return than normal fixed-rate securities but purchasers suffer prepayment risk if mortgage holders redeem their mortgages.

SPV (Special Purpose Vehicle): An SPV is a legal entity created by a firm (known as the sponsor or originator) by transferring assets to the SPV to carry out some specific purpose or circumscribed activity or a series of such transactions.

CDS (Credit Default Swap): A CDS is an insurance-like contract that is sold as protection against default on loans. More technically, CDO is a bilateral financial contract in which one counterparty (e.g., buyer) pays a periodic fee in return for a contingent payment by the other counterparty (e.g., seller) upon the occurrence of a credit.

MS (Mortgage Swap): An asset swap attached to fixed-rate mortgage payments. MSs allow investors to enjoy the flows from a portfolio of mortgages without taking a mortgage asset onto their balance sheet. The principal reduces if and when the outstanding mortgage principal reduces (which can occur if the mortgage holder pays off the mortgage or defaults).

(Box 3.1 continued)

(*Box 3.1 continued*)

MBS (Mortgage Backed Securities): MBSs are debt obligations that represent claims to the cash flows from pools of mortgage loans, such as residential property. Mortgage loans are purchased from banks or mortgage companies and then assembled into pools by a governmental, quasi-governmental, or private entity. Most MBSs in the US are issued by the Government National Mortgage Association (Ginnie Mae), a US government agency, or Fannie Mae and Freddie Mac, both US GSEs.

Sources Incisive Media Investments (2005); Invetopedia, available at http://www.investopedia.com; Securities and Exchange Commission (2008).

risk transfer (CRT). These hybrid products, which are considered credit derivatives in a wider sense, usually condition the repayment of securitized debt on a defined credit event in a bilateral hedge (in the case of CLNs), the premium income generated from credit protection sold on reference assets (in the case of SCDOs), or the returns from investing and/or writing credit protection on securitization transactions as constituent assets of a diversified pool of CDOs and/or ABSs (Figure 3.1).

Subprime lending was financed by the securitization process, involving brokers and lenders packaging subprime loan debt into MBS, which were rated and bought by investors seeking high-risk, high-payout investments. Besides, subprime securitization involved the spreading of the risk that subprime loans created for the lender. Once originated, the lender could pass the risk of default to investors on Wall Street. The mortgage note was held by a servicer who assumed the responsibility of demanding payments from the borrower and distributing them to the investors. In many cases, these MBS were held by foreign investors. Thus, subprime lending and securitization became popular on Wall Street. Hedge funds and risky investors not only provided funding for loans by investing, but demanded more subprime loan packages (Figure 3.2).

Trends in Mortgage-based Structured Products

As a result of the popularity of the MBS, its share in total mortgage debt began soaring—from around 10 percent in the early 1980s it rose to 40 percent in early 1990s, touching 55 percent in early 2000 (Chart 3.4).

FIGURE 3.1
Types of Structured Products

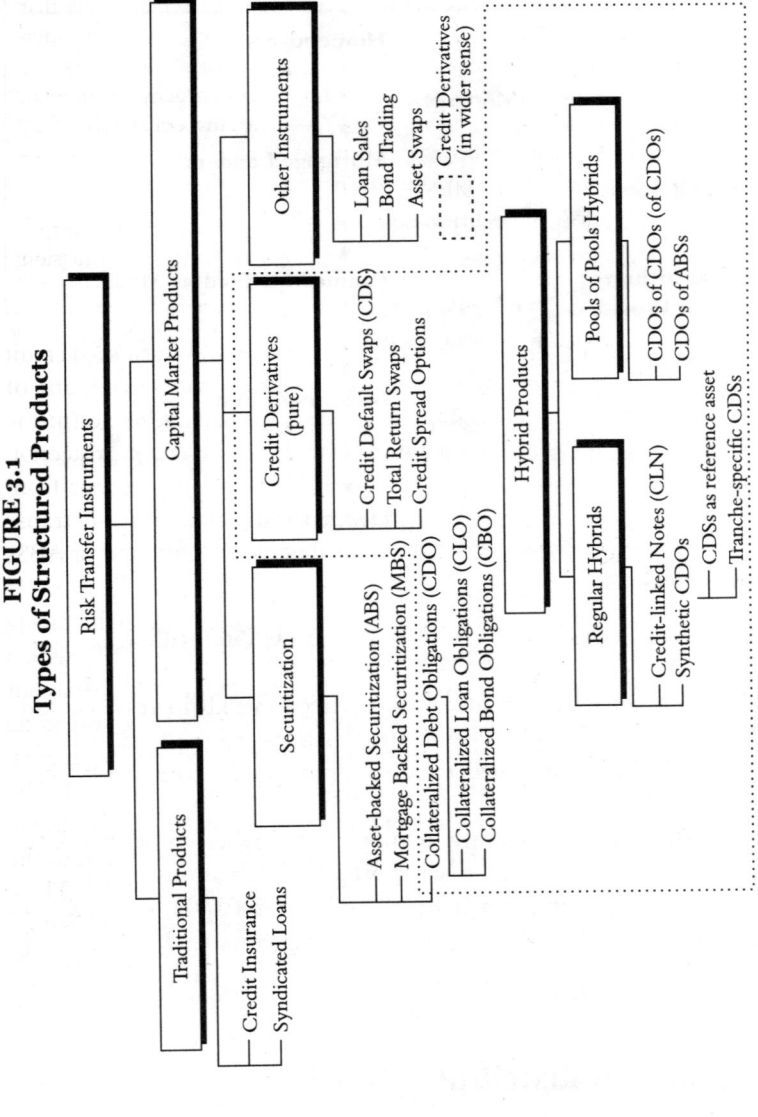

Source Jobst (2006).

FIGURE 3.2
A Simplified Mortgage Funding Process

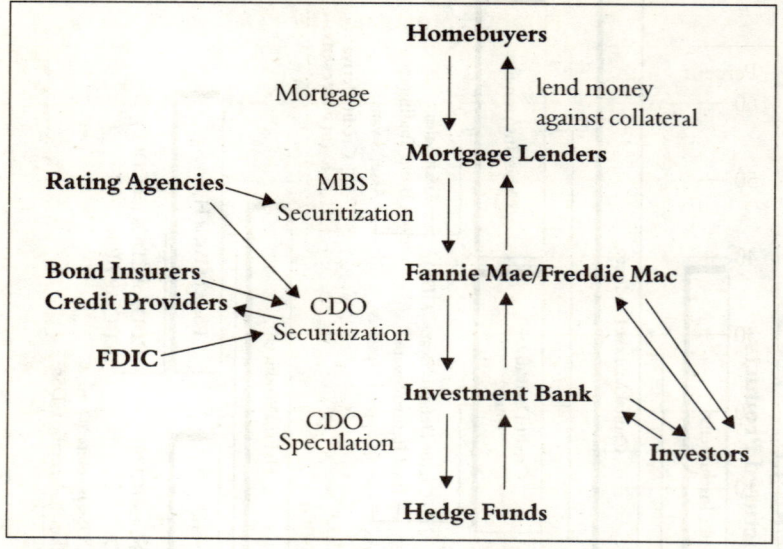

Source Authors.

The outstanding value of CDOs crossed US$60 trillion by 2007 (Chart 3.5).

US mortgage-related securities experienced a steady increase—from around US$500 billion in 1996 to a peak surpassing the US$3 trillion mark in 2003 and continued to remain over US$2 trillion till 2007 (Chart 3.6).

Interestingly, mortgage originations were highly correlated with house prices. As the latter rose, mortgage originations followed a northbound trajectory. Furthermore, during 2003–06, there was a quantum jump in the subprime mortgage originations, a lead indicator of the imminent crisis. The spread of securitization was not limited to the US alone (Table 3.2).[6]

Originate-to-distribute Model

A crucial element of the process of securitization is the "originate-to-distribute" model whereby originators/arrangers did not hold these assets on their balance sheets, provided they could repackage the assets in securitized form, and ratings agencies rated them at appropriate

CHART 3.4
Share of Mortgage-backed Securities in
Total US Mortgage Debt (%)

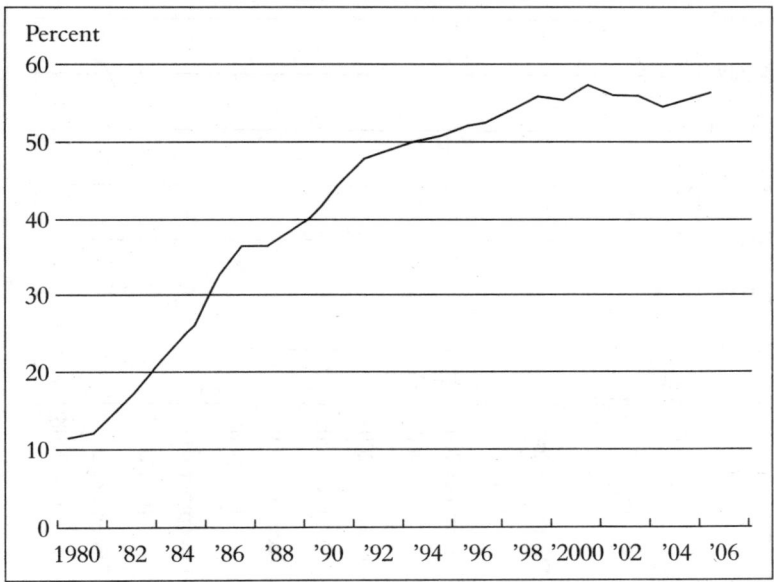

Source Rosen (2007).

"attachment points" at which investors would purchase. Rating agencies drew additional fees to advise arrangers how to meet attachment points. If securitized products were rated below these points, they could be combined with other low rated ABSs to form CDOs. Thus, each agent becomes completely oblivious to the risks involved in the structured product (Figure 3.3).

Relationship between the Structured Products and the Crisis

Complex structured products appear to have been a major causal actor in the crisis. Existing risk management techniques were inadequate to capture the risks associated with these structured products, rating agencies failed to account for the risks in rating these instruments, and supervisors did not adequately identify the risks associated with these instruments. What was lucrative to a few market operators failed to generate sufficient understanding among all concerned.

CHART 3.5
Credit Default Swaps (CDS) in the US
(outstanding amount, in billions of dollars)

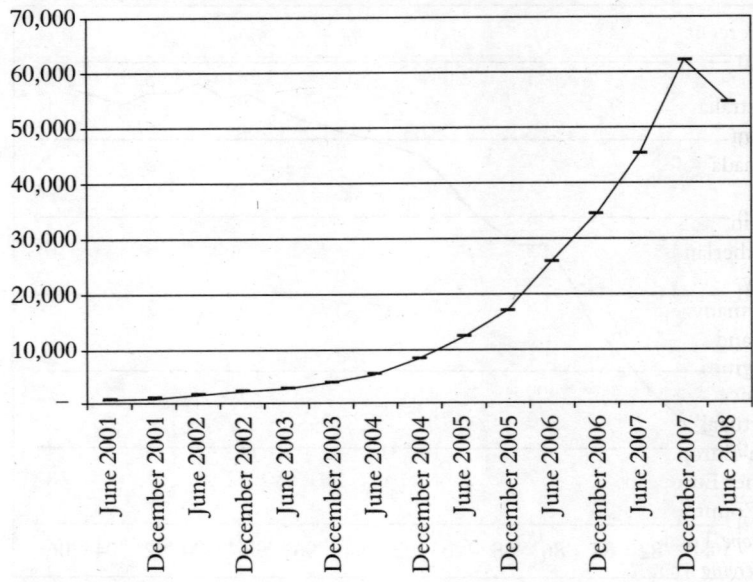

Source Zingales (2008).

CHART 3.6
Mortgage-related Security Issuance
in the US (US$ billion)

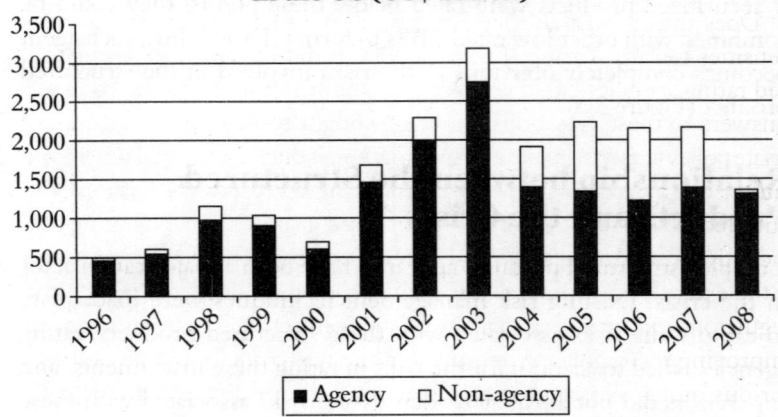

■ Agency   □ Non-agency

Source Securities Industry and Financial Markets Association (SIFMA), US,
available at www.sifma.org.

TABLE 3.2
Securitization Issuance by Originating Country/Region

(US$ billion)

	2003	2004	2005	2006	2007	2008
US	3,671	2,649	3,139	3,241	2,952	1,521
Australia	71	76	77	91	68	16
Japan	33	51	81	83	76	58
Canada	17	18	25	29	45	79
UK	86	130	157	242	237	400
Spain	44	41	50	55	84	119
Netherlands	24	23	49	36	56	107
Italy	38	43	41	38	36	121
Germany	8	10	19	47	26	74
Ireland	4	3	1	13	14	60
Belgium	3	3	1	3	6	51
France	9	10	9	10	5	21
Portugal	12	10	10	7	15	22
Pan-Europe	13	19	63	143	132	41
Other European Countries	7	12	8	11	12	32
Europe Total	*248*	*303*	*407*	*604*	*622*	*1,047*
Emerging Market Economies	*48*	*46*	*55*	*64*	*53*	*55*
World Total	**4,087**	**3,142**	**3,782**	**4,112**	**3,817**	**2,777**

Source International Financial Services, London, available at http://www.ifsl.org.uk

Does this mean that these structured products have inherent propensities towards financial instability? Or, did the financial regulators and rating agencies fail to comprehend the structure of these products? Answers to these questions are being sought to determine the appropriate policy response. Going forward, if the products are after all inherently faulty, one needs to seriously consider newer products without the bundled characteristics of the structured products or changing the incentive structure of a typical investment banker. On the contrary, if the extent of comprehension of the products is limited amongst the regulators and rating agencies then the solution has to be in terms of improving the regulatory regime and the rating methodology. Like in various other fields including in life itself, the reality may perhaps lie somewhere in between.

What is the relationship between the structured products and the crisis? There could be five frictions associated with the structured

FIGURE 3.3
Originate-to-hold and Originate-to-distribute Models
Originate-to-hold Model

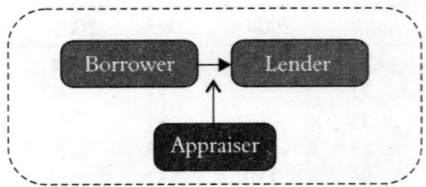

Originate-to-distribute Model

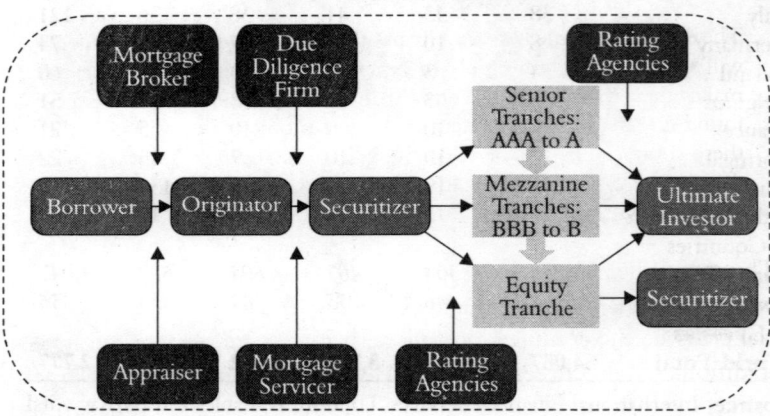

Source Kolb (2010).

products that played a major role in the subprime crisis (Ashcraft and Schuermann 2008):

- Many products offered to subprime borrowers are very complex and subject to misunderstanding and/or misrepresentation.
- Existing investment mandates do not adequately distinguish between structured and corporate ratings—asset managers had an incentive to reach for yield by purchasing structured debt issues with the same credit rating but higher coupons as corporate debt issues.
- Without due diligence of the asset manager, the arranger's incentives to conduct own due diligence are reduced; moreover, as the market for credit derivatives developed, the arranger was able to limit funded exposure to securitizations of risky loans.

- Together, the above factors worsened the friction between the originator and arranger, opening the door for predatory borrowing and lending.
- Credit ratings were assigned to subprime MBS with significant error—even though the rating agencies publicly disclosed their rating criteria for subprime investment, investors lacked the ability to evaluate the efficacy of these models.

In sum, structured products paved the way for predatory lending, and involved severe moral hazard and principal agent problems. It is perhaps from this standpoint that Warren Buffet commented:

> The derivatives genie is now well out of the bottle, and these instruments will almost certainly multiply in variety and number until some event makes their toxicity clear. Central banks and governments have so far found no effective way to control, or even monitor, the risks posed by these contracts. In my view, derivatives are financial weapons of mass destruction, carrying dangers that, while now latent, are potentially lethal. (Buffet 2002)

Thus, over the past three decades, the sea change in the way that credit is extended in America created problems. At the heart of the financial crisis lie the complex, opaque derivative securities created not by traditional Main Street banks but by Wall Street-based investment bankers and financial companies. Wall Street created, originated, and sold an alphabet soup of derivative securities, and it was such synthetic instruments—not traditional mortgage loans, small-business loans or other standard lending originated by banks—that unleashed a flood of credit, created a vast excess of housing, weakened the capital structure of the banking industry and undermined popular confidence in banks (Wilmers 2009). In previous generations, home buyers obtained mortgages and other loans from local or Main Street, banks, which typically held those loans until they were fully repaid—and therefore had an interest in making loans that borrowers could afford. But then Wall Street started slicing, dicing, and packaging mortgages into bundles that served as the basis for bonds sold in the securities markets. Traditional bank deposits were no longer the primary funding source for credit. Instead, loans were being financed by the capital markets and packaged and sold by Wall Street. Mortgages were originated by one firm, packaged by another, sold by a third, and serviced by yet another, but none of them worried about whether the mortgages would be repaid, because they did not hold the loans on their books!

Lack of Effective Financial Regulation

Lack of effective financial regulation has been regarded as a primary responsible factor in this financial crisis. The fact that advanced countries, in general, and the US, in particular, remained relatively unscathed in the earlier financial turmoils like the East Asian crisis or the Long-term Capital Management (LTCM) crisis perhaps made the regulators in these countries somewhat complacent. Besides, there was a large shadow banking system comprising entities like investment banks, hedge funds, or financial conglomerates like the American International Group (AIG) that could largely bypass regulatory oversight. There was, in fact, a perceived philosophy that self-regulation works best in the financial markets. In some sense, this is reflected in the then Fed Chairman Alan Greenspan's notion of "light touch regulation." It is interesting to note that in distilling the initial lessons of the crisis, the IMF emphasized the role of financial regulation, which was not equipped to detect the risk concentrations and flawed incentives, as one of the key factors underlying the crisis. It is in this context that this chapter raises two specific questions. First, in what way was regulation responsible? Second, in the light of proposed action plans of various governments as well as international institutions, how do we see the future of financial regulation?

Rationale for financial regulation

Why do we need regulation in a market economy? After all, traditional economic theory held that a freely competitive economy can ensure maximization of welfare. Yet, the reality is often marked by various distortions. Thus, there could be three main purposes driving any economic regulation: (*a*) constraining monopoly power and prevention of market distortion, (*b*) protecting consumer interests, and (*c*) mitigating externalities associated with market failure (Brunnermeier et al. 2009). While both (*a*) and (*b*) are important, it became clear by the early 1970s that the presence of externalities is by far the key reason for financial regulation. After all, the market for any commodity, say oranges, is markedly different from the market for financial products, say, bank credit. Since the fundamental basis for the financial market is in some sense "faith," a breakdown of a financial firm could be far most costly than revealed in its balance sheet. Illustratively, when a company fails, the bankruptcy value of its inventories can, to a limited extent, fetch value for its shareholders. Banks, on the other hand, are highly leveraged—the whole basis of credit creation is the implicit assumption that all depositors are not going to come at the same time. If all the depositors come to the bank all at the same time, there is a "run" on the bank which is far more systemic than the failure of a commodity/ service producing company.

At this stage, it is useful to review the structure of the US financial industry so as to probe into the causes of regulatory failure.

Structure of the US financial regulation

The US has one of the most complex financial systems in the world. If one adopts a functional taxonomy, then broadly speaking, the US financial services sector provides four major types of financial services: (*a*) payment and liquidity products (e.g., banks), (*b*) credit products (e.g., banks, insurers, and securities firms), (*c*) investment products (e.g., investment banks), and (*d*) products that transfer financial risk (e.g., insurance products, futures products) (US Department of Treasury 2008a). Even within deposit accepting institutions (what in popular parlance are termed as banks), there are a number of entities that overlap in business activities and industry structure: (*a*) commercial banks, (*b*) bank holding companies (BHC) and financial holding companies, (*c*) thrifts (historically "Savings and Loans" or S&Ls are depository institutions focused on providing mortgage lending to residential customers), (*d*) credit unions, and (*e*) industrial loan companies (financial institutions that can be owned by commercial firms). The US financial system is also large and multifaceted, with characteristics distinguishing it from systems in other major countries. Four such characteristics could have led to vulnerabilities in the current crisis: (*a*) the relative size and importance of capital markets, (*b*) the relative size and importance (till recently) of standalone investments banks, (*c*) the regional and local nature of much of the deposit banking system, (*d*) the nature of the regulation of the insurance sector, (*e*) the size of the federal government's direct and sponsored involvement in market-based credit intermediation, and (*f*) the complexity of the structure of US regulation and supervision (Group of Thirty 2009).

Over the years, the US economy has witnessed a steady decline in importance of the depository institutions—this has been counterbalanced by an increasing importance of government sponsored institutions and issues of ABSs (Table 3.3). This, in some sense, is reflective of the building up of the shadow banking sector, which, under a less involved regulatory oversight, tends to create the incentives for rash financial innovation described in the previous section.

The regulatory structure of the US depository institution is fragmented in nature. Furthermore, banking in the US is regulated at both the federal and state level and depending on a banking organization's charter, type, and organizational structure, it may be subject to numerous federal and state banking regulators. At the federal level, five agencies simultaneously divide and share regulatory and examination authority: (a) the Office of the Comptroller of the Currency (OCC), (b) the Fed (Board of Governors of the Federal Reserve System), (c) the Federal Deposit Insurance Corporation (FDIC), (d) the Office of Thrift Supervision (OTS), and (e) the National Credit Union Administration (NCUA). Compared to other advanced countries, the US also has one of the most highly regulated banking structures focusing on privacy, disclosure, fraud prevention, anti-money laundering, antiterrorism, anti-usury lending, and promoting lending to lower-income segments. Often regulations facing each type of institution are governed by separate laws which have evolved over the years (Box 3.2).

Interestingly, consequent to each crisis till the early 1930s, the US economy had created a separate regulator (Table 3.4).

Given the financial regulatory structure in the US, a number of institutions were involved in the regulation and supervision of US financial system (Table 3.5). The coordination between them has not been cohesive all the time. This was another factor that was responsible for weak regulation and delayed detection of the subprime crisis.

Regulatory failure appears to have also played a role in transmission of the crisis. The US subprime crisis got transmitted to other US financial institutions and other countries via the credit risk transfer (CRT) market. Specifically, there were four weaknesses in the CRT market that catalyzed the propagation of the financial crisis: (a) active involvement of unregulated entities in the market, (b) divergent regulatory treatment of CRT transactions across different financial institutions, (c) insufficient supervisory data on CRT transactions, and (d) insufficient capital requirement for CRT transactions (Espenilla 2009). Illustratively, in the CDS

TABLE 3.3
Composition of the US Financial Sector

(share of financial sector assets in percent)

Institutions	1980	1990	2000	2005	2006	2007	2008
(1)	(4)	(5)	(6)	(7)	(8)	(9)	(10)
1. Monetary Authority	3.6	2.4	2.5	2.4	2.3	2.0	2.5
2. Depository Institutions	57.9	41.4	31.3	31.0	30.5	30.2	29.5
(a) Commercial Banking	36.1	27.9	24.2	23.8	24.1	24.1	24.3
(b) Savings Institutions	20.2	11.8	5.2	5.3	4.6	4.3	3.4
(c) Credit Unions	1.5	1.7	1.8	1.9	1.9	1.8	1.8
3. Insurance Companies	14.3	14.9	11.8	11.6	10.8	10.2	9.6
4. Pension Funds	8.4	8.8	6.7	4.8	5.0	5.0	5.0
5. Mutual Funds	1.7	7.4	11.7	10.1	10.5	11.3	12.8
6. GSEs and Other Agencies	8.4	14.0	20.7	19.9	19.3	20.0	20.5
7. ABS Issuers	0.0	2.5	6.8	10.7	12.2	12.1	10.3
8. Finance Companies	5.5	5.7	5.3	5.7	5.4	5.0	4.5
9. Brokers and Dealers	0.2	1.1	1.1	1.6	1.7	2.2	1.8
10. Others	0.2	1.9	2.2	2.2	2.2	1.9	3.5
11. Total	**100.0**	**100.0**	**100.0**	**100.0**	**100.0**	**100.0**	**100.0**

Source Compiled from the Flow of Funds Accounts, March 2009, US Federal Reserve, available at www.federalreserve.gov

---

BOX 3.2
Evolution of Laws Governing the Regulation
of US Financial Sector

The *National Bank Act of 1863*: A dual banking system (referring to the parallel state and federal banking systems that co-exist in the US) came into existence when the US Congress, seeking to finance its Civil War debt and ensure financial stability, passed the National Bank Act of 1863. This law created a federal bank charter and established the OCC as the office in charge of chartering and overseeing the newly created national banks.

The *Federal Reserve Act of 1913*: In the post-Civil War period, the US banking system suffered from periods of severe illiquidity, runs on deposits, and panics, the worst of which hit the US economy in 1907. In response, the US Congress passed the Federal Reserve Act of 1913 that created the Federal Reserve System.

Legislations following the Great Depression: After the stock market crash of 1929 and the subsequent Great Depression, massive bank failures prompted the US Congress to enact a series of legislations.

- The key statute, focused on the commercial banks, was the *Banking Act of 1933*. Four sections of that statute, known as the *Glass–Steagall Act*, mandated the strict separation of commercial and investment banking.
- The *Federal Home Loan Bank Act of 1932* (*FHLB Act*) created the FHLB System of 12 cooperatively owned regional banks that borrowed funds on behalf of state-chartered members and were overseen by the **Federal Home Loan Bank Board** (**FHLBB**). Subsequently, the *Home Owners' Loan Act of 1933* (*HOLA*) granted the FHLBB the authority to charter and regulate federal thrifts.
- The US Congress also moved to establish a federal charter for credit unions, passing the *Federal Credit Union Act in 1934*, making it possible to charter a credit union anywhere in the United States.
- The *Banking Act of 1933* also created the **Federal Deposit Insurance Corporation (FDIC)** to regulate participants in the commercial bank deposit insurance system, while the *National Housing Act of 1934* created **the Federal Savings and Loan Insurance Corporation (FSLIC)** to regulate participants in the thrift deposit insurance system.
- The *Bank Holding Company (BHC) Act of 1956*: Although prohibiting affiliations between commercial and investment banks, the **Glass–Steagall Act** did not explicitly prohibit affiliations between banks and other types of commercial entities. As a result, many nonfinancial companies began acquiring commercial banks under a holding company structure. Consequently, the US Congress enacted the *BHC Act of 1956*, explicitly prohibiting BHCs controlling multiple US commercial

(*Box 3.2 continued*)

(Box 3.2 continued)

banks from engaging in activities other than banking, managing banks, or activities "closely related" to banking through affiliates.

The *Savings and Loan Holding Company (SLHC) Act of 1967*: When concerns emerged regarding the thrifts' enjoyment of competitive advantages in comparison with commercial banks due to these *BHC Act* requirements, the US Congress responded by enacting the similar *SLHC Act of 1967*.

The Savings and Loan Crisis in the 1980s and Related Legislations—A number of legislations related to the deregulation of interest rate ceilings in the wake of the savings and loan crisis were enacted during the 1980s:

- The *Depository Institutions Deregulation and Monetary Control Act of 1980* eased the deposit rate ceilings imposed upon banks and thrifts during the 1930s.
- The *Garn-St Germain Depository Institutions Act of 1982* removed certain business and investment restrictions imposed on thrifts, permitting them to invest some funds in commercial real estate.
- The *Financial Institutions Reform, Recovery, and Enforcement Act of 1989 (FIRREA)* terminated the FSLIC and the FHLBB. It created the **Office of Thrift Supervision (OTS)**. The OTS was modeled after the OCC and designated as an office within the US Treasury.
- The *Federal Deposit Insurance Corporation Improvement Act (FDICIA)* was passed in 1991, which established a system of capital-based prompt corrective action (PCA), and eliminated various discretionary powers granted to regulators and instead imposed requirements on regulators to act upon regulated institutions' failure to meet certain prescribed tests.
- The *Riegle-Neal Interstate Banking and Branching Efficiency Act (Riegle-Neal Act)* was passed in 1994, repealing the prohibitions on interstate bank and branch acquisitions, thereby providing banks more of the advantages already enjoyed by thrifts.

The *Gramm-Leach-Bliley (GLB) Act of 1999*: The *GLB Act of 1999* relaxed the activity restrictions for commercial banking organizations. The GLB Act repealed the Glass–Steagall Act's prohibitions on certain affiliations and management interlocks between banks and securities firms, and significantly expanded the permissible activities of BHCs by establishing a financial holding company (FHC) structure, allowing qualifying institutions to participate in commercial banking, full-scale securities underwriting and dealing, insurance underwriting, and merchant banking all under one holding company.

Source US Treasury (2008a).

TABLE 3.4

Systemic Crises and the Financial Regulators in the US

Systemic Event	Perceived Problem	Solution	New Regulator	Created in
Panic of 1857	Failure of Private Clearing houses that Processed State Bank Notes (circulated as currency)	Single National Currency through System of Federally Chartered and Regulated Banks	Office of the Comptroller of the Currency (OCC)	1863
Panic of 1907	Series of Runs on Banks and Financial Trusts with Inadequate Reserves	Lender of Last Resort with Power to Regulate a National System of Bank Reserves	Federal Reserve System (Fed)	1913
Great Depression	Series of Runs on Banks by Small Depositors who Feared Full Value of Deposits Would Not be honored	Limited Deposit Insurance to Maintain Depositor Confidence and Prevent Bank Runs	Federal Deposit Insurance Corporation (FDIC)	1933
	Sharp decline in stock prices along with widespread belief that some investors had an information advantage reduced confidence in securities markets	Restore Confidence in Securities Markets by Standardizing Disclosures and Requiring Regular Reporting	Securities and Exchange Commission (SEC)	1934

Source Jickling and Murphy (2009).

TABLE 3.5
Structure of the US Federal Financial Regulators

Regulatory Agency	Institutions Regulated
(1)	*(2)*
1. Federal Reserve	Bank holding companies, financial holding companies, state banks that are members of the Federal Reserve System, US branches of foreign banks, and foreign branches of US banks
2. Office of the Comptroller of the Currency (OCC)	National banks, US federal branches of foreign banks
3. Federal Deposit Insurance Corporation (FDIC)	Federally insured depository institutions, including state banks that are not members of the Federal Reserve System
4. Office of Thrift Supervision (OTS)	Federally chartered and insured thrift institutions and savings and loan holding companies
5. National Credit Union Administration (NCUA)	Federally chartered or insured credit unions
6. Securities and Exchange Commission (SEC)	Securities exchanges, brokers, and dealers; mutual funds; and investment advisers
7. Commodity Futures Trading Commission (CFTC)	Futures exchanges, brokers, pool operators, and advisers
8. Federal Housing Finance Agency (FHFA)	Fannie Mae, Freddie Mac, and the Federal Home Loan Banks

Source Jickling and Murphy (2009).

market, there was considerable presence of non-bank entities like hedge funds. Besides, the notion of capital charge or the imposition of Basel-type capital adequacy ratios was limited to banking institutions, while the credit risks were quite spread out over the insurance firms or investment banks. Another major weakness of the existing regulatory policies is a pro-cyclical bias. For example, regulatory capital requirements tend to increase during downturns, when financial institutions are particularly capital constrained; and they tended to decrease in booms when financial institutions have healthy capital positions. The key issue, therefore, is how to make regulatory frameworks more countercyclical. While these issues are addressed in Chapter 6 on the policy response, the key message is best summed up as:

> Our financial system operated with large gaps in meaningful oversight, and without sufficient constraints to limit risk. Even institutions that were overseen by our complicated, overlapping system of multiple regulators put themselves in a position of extreme vulnerability. These failures helped lay the foundation for the worst economic crisis in generations. (Geithner 2009)

Systemic Institutions

Investment Banks

In some sense, investment banks are seen as both the source and the major victims of the current crisis. Had the foundation of the investment banking sector become so fragile? Is the basic model of investment banking inherently faulty?

At this point, it may be useful to explore the genesis of the investment banks. The modern concept of the investment bank was created in the *Glass–Steagall Act* (*Banking Act of 1933*) which separated commercial banks, investment banks, and insurance companies.[7] While it was repealed consequent to President Clinton's signing the *Graham-Leach Bill* in November 1999 into law, it is often asked whether such a separation was successful in avoiding such crisis. So far, not much clarity has emerged with regard to these questions, answers to which would determine the form of the appropriate policy response.

Investment banks assist public and private corporations and governments in raising funds in the capital markets (both equity and debt) as well as in providing strategic advisory services for mergers, acquisitions, and other types of financial transactions. They also act as intermediaries in trading for clients. While investment banks differ from commercial banks which take deposits and make commercial and retail loans, in recent years the line of demarcation between the two types of structures has blurred, especially as commercial banks have increasingly offered more investment banking services. Investment banks may also differ from brokerages which in general assist in the purchase and sale of stocks, bonds, and mutual funds. However, some firms operate as both brokerages and investment banks; this includes some of the best known financial services firms in the world. Nevertheless, the major investment banks were key players in handling MBSs and held massive amounts of such securities.

In fact, the two incidents that defined the current financial crisis have been the takeover of Bear Sterns and the fall of Lehman Brothers. Furthermore, one of the many striking consequences of the crisis for the US financial system is that none of the five large investment banks (Goldman Sachs, Morgan Stanley, Merrill Lynch, Lehman Brothers, and Bear Stearns) that existed in 2007 remain today. Two have been absorbed into existing BHCs, one has been merged with a bank and the remaining two have been converted into new BHCs, which made them eligible for emergency government liquidity and guaranty assistance. In effect, government assistance was made available *ex post* to protect the counterparties of four of the five firms. Yet none was subject to a statutory *ex ante* framework for prudential regulation. The source of all of this is of course the over-leveraged nature of investment banks. At the end of 2007, Lehman Brothers was leveraged 30:1—they turned US$1 into US$30 through the magic of leverage (Table 3.6).

Government Sponsored Enterprises (GSEs)

Another set of institutions that played a key role in the genesis and propagation of the crisis are the GSEs like Fannie Mae and Freddie Mac. The GSEs are essentially a group of financial services corporations created by the US which enhance the availability of and reduce the cost of credit to the three major targeted borrowing sectors, viz., agriculture, home finance, and education. The largest GSEs operate in the residential mortgage borrowing sector. Apart from the US government-owned corporation within the Department of Housing and Urban Development, the Ginnie Mae, the Fannie Mae, and Freddie Mac are the major GSEs in the housing finance market. While Ginnie Mae, backed by the full faith and credit of the US government, guarantees that investors receive timely payments, Fannie Mae and Freddie Mac also provide certain guarantees and, while not backed by the full faith and credit of the US government, have special authority to borrow from the US Treasury.[8]

Fannie Mae and Freddie Mac stand behind mortgages in two ways. First, they purchase mortgages, bundle them together, and then sell

TABLE 3.6
Leverage Ratios of Six Major Investment Banks

		Assets (Million US$)	Leverage Ratio (Debt–Equity Ratio)
Lehman Brothers	2003	312,061	22.7
	2004	357,168	22.8
	2005	410,063	23.4
	2006	503,545	25.2
	2007	691,063	29.7
Bear Sterns	2003	212,168	27.4
	2004	255,950	27.5
	2005	292,635	26.1
	2006	350,433	27.9
	2007	395,362	32.5
Merill Lynch	2003	480,233	15.6
	2004	628,098	19.0
	2005	681,015	18.1
	2006	841,299	20.6
	2007	1,020,050	30.9
Goldman Sachs	2003	403,799	17.7
	2004	531,379	20.2
	2005	706,804	24.2
	2006	838,201	22.4
	2007	1,119,796	25.2
Morgan Stanley	2003	603,022	23.2
	2004	747,578	25.5
	2005	898,835	29.8
	2006	1,121,192	30.7
	2007	1,045,409	32.4

Source   Annual Reports of Respective Banks.

claims on the cash flows to be generated by these bundles. These claims are known as MBS. Second, they buy mortgages or their own MBS outright and finance those purchases by selling debt directly in the name of the GSE (Greenspan 2004). Thus, the GSEs can either sell the MBS to other investors or retain the securities for themselves. In the 1990s, Freddie Mac gradually shifted from a strategy of selling most of its secur-ities to a strategy of retaining most of its securities. Fannie has always predominantly held its securities in its portfolio. Whether it retains or sells the security, the GSE bears the default risk of the mortgages, which is the source of the recent crisis. Although both Fannie Mae and Freddie Mac are private companies, as "government-sponsored enterprises" established by federal law, they receive special privileges. The most important of these privileges is the notion of an implicit guarantee so that the investors tend to believe that if these GSEs are threatened with failure, the federal government will come to their rescue. The presence of "implicit government guarantees" for the GSEs is succinctly captured by the then US Secretary of State, Henry Paulson:

> Congress established Fannie and Freddie decades ago to meet a public policy goal—to increase the funding available for home mortgage financing. The GSEs achieve this through providing liquidity to the secondary market for a limited range of home mortgages, either through credit guarantees on mortgage-backed securities (MBS) or by directly investing in mortgages and mortgage-related securities through their retained mortgage portfolios. To further this mission, their congressional charters grant the GSEs several benefits which together created a perception that the GSEs were backed by the U.S. government, even though this was not the case. This "implicit" government guarantee provided the GSEs with a funding advantage over other mortgage market participant. (Paulson 2009)

Over time, the GSEs grew at a phenomenal pace so that their outstanding obligations (held by investors in the US and around the world) grew to nearly US$5.4 trillion in 2008, which is almost 40 percent the size of the entire US$14 trillion US economy. The systemic risk posed by such size was heightened by the fact that investors assumed that GSE securities were backed by the US government and, therefore, were virtually risk-free. This implicit guarantee means that profits are privatized but losses are socialized. It has been aptly put: "If Fannie and Freddie do well, their stockholders reap the benefits, but if things go badly, Washington picks up the tab. Heads they win, tails the public lose" (Krugman 2008).

As mortgages started collapsing, the share prices of the GSEs plummeted from mid-2008 and on September 7, 2008 the Federal Housing Finance Agency (the regulator in the housing finance market) placed Fannie and Freddie into conservatorship, enabling Treasury to take creative steps to support their obligations. Thus, the implicit guarantee turned into an explicit one and was invoked.

Insurance Companies

While the crisis originated and developed in the banking sector, the insurance sector has been far from immune. The insurance companies played a major role in the booming market for CDSs. In fact, non-bank institutions shouldered at least US$180 billion of losses till October 2008—some US$100 billion of credit-related losses were reported by insurance companies, of which US$20 billion is by monoline insurers.[9] Thus, while banks are expected to bear about two-thirds of the write-downs on account of toxic assets, their financial institutions, including pension funds and insurance companies, also have significant credit exposures.

The story of the insurance giant, the AIG, is a case in point. AIG had significant exposures to CDSs and suffered from a liquidity crisis. In fact, after the collapse of Lehman Brothers investors started to compare the valuation of toxic assets in the balance sheet of AIG with those of Lehman Brothers. Consequently, its credit ratings were downgraded below "AA" levels in September 2008. As the failure of AIG would have had systemic ramifications, the US Fed created a US$85 billion credit facility on September 16, 2008. This enabled AIG to meet increased collateral obligations consequent to the credit rating downgrade in exchange for the issuance of a stock warrant to the Federal Reserve Bank for 79.9 percent of its equity. Subsequently, the AIG borrowed an additional US$37.8 billion via a second secured asset credit facility created by the Federal Reserve Bank of New York on October 9, 2008. As the crisis spread and asset prices fell, life insurance companies and reinsurers suffered substantial falls in shareholder equity, leading to rating downgrades and rises in CDS spreads that endangered their business models.

Credit Rating Agencies

Credit rating agencies provide evaluations of the likelihood that obligations will be repaid. There are three major credit rating agencies in the United States: Moody's, Standard & Poor's (S&P), and Fitch. The agencies issue ratings on individual issues such as structured finance offerings and corporate, government, and municipal bonds. The three major agencies are responsible for 96 percent of outstanding structured finance ratings and 98 percent of all outstanding ratings issued by agencies recognized by the US Securities and Exchange Commission (SEC).

They follow more or less a uniform rating scale (Box 3.3). The leading credit rating agencies grew rich rating MBS and CDOs, with the total revenues for the three firms doubling from US$3 billion in 2002 to over US$6 billion in 2007. At Moody's, profits quadrupled between 2000 and 2007. In fact, Moody's had the highest profit margin for any company in the S&P 500 for five years in a row.

BOX 3.3
Rating Scales of the Major Rating Agencies

S&P and Fitch use the same scale:
Investment Grade

AAA:	the best quality borrowers, reliable, and stable
AA:	quality borrowers, a bit higher risk than AAA
A:	economic situation can affect borrower's ability to pay
BBB:	medium class borrowers, satisfactory at the moment

Speculative Grade	("High Yield" or "Junk")
BB:	borrower's ability to pay is more prone to changes in the economy
B:	borrower's financial situation varies noticeably
CCC:	borrower is currently vulnerable and dependent on favorable economic conditions to meet its commitments
CC:	borrower is highly vulnerable
C:	borrower may be in bankruptcy but is still paying its obligations
D:	borrower has defaulted on obligations and the Rating Agency believes that it will generally default on most or all obligations

Moody's scale varies slightly:

From Aaa to Baa3:	Investment Grade
From Ba1 to C:	Speculative Grade, C being in default

Source   Bahena (2008).

The recent crisis has also illustrated the limitations of credit ratings in the case of structured credit products, the potential conflict of interest of credit rating agencies as well as the injudicious use of credit ratings by investors. As foreclosures in the US mortgage markets started increasing from end 2007, the structured products started crumbling. The rating agencies failed to adequately assess the credit risks in residential mortgage-backed securities (RMBS) and CDOs. Various factors can be ascribed to this. First, the rating agencies tended to hold an overoptimistic view of the housing market with the assumption that housing prices would continue to increase generally. Second, while MBSs and CDOs contained individual mortgages, the rating agencies knew little about the creditworthiness of individual borrowers behind the mortgages at the time of rating. When rating MBSs and CDOs, the rating agencies relied heavily on historical statistical data, not on personal information about each borrower. Finally, the rating agencies seemed to have underestimated the complexity of the MBSs and CDOs.

The US President's Working Group on Financial Markets, which submitted its report in March 2008, found flaws in credit rating agencies' assessments of subprime RMBs and other complex structured credit products, especially CDOs that held RMBs and other ABSs:

> Faulty assumptions underlying rating methodologies and the subsequent re-evaluations by the credit rating agencies (CRAs) led to a significant number of downgrades of subprime RMBS, even of recently issued securities. Downgrades were even more frequent and severe for CDOs of ABS with subprime mortgage loans as the underlying collateral. The number and severity of negative ratings actions caused investors to lose confidence in the accuracy of the ratings of a wide range of structured credit products. This loss of investor confidence caused many structured finance markets to seize up and caused markets for asset-backed commercial paper (ABCP), some of which was backed by RMBS and CDOs of ABS, to contract substantially. (US Treasury 2008b)

Other Factors

Valuation and Accounting Norms

Insofar as the subprime crisis is concerned, much of the discussion on the valuation and accounting appears to be somewhat confusing.[10] IAS 39, formulated by the International Accounting Standards Board (IASB), relates to "Financial Instruments: Recognition and Measurement." It was adopted by the European Union (EU) in 2004. Subsequently, the EU also introduced the fair value and hedging provision of the amended version of IAS 39 in 2005. On the other hand, FAS 133, formulated by Financial Accounting Standards Board (FASB) in 1998, relates to "Accounting for Derivative Instruments and Hedging Activities." Furthermore, the FASB issued Statement of Financial Accounting Standards (SFAS) 134 ("Accounting for Mortgage-based Securities retained after the securitisation of mortgage loans"), which was preceded by SFAS 65 ("Accounting for certain Mortgage Banking Activities"), SFAS 115 ("Accounting for certain investments in debt and equity securities"), and SFAS 125 ("Accounting for transfers and servicing of financial assets and extinguishment of liabilities").

As per the current accounting standards (such as IAS 39 or FAS 133), all derivatives must be recognized in the balance sheet at their *fair value*. As per the US Generally Accepted Accounting Principles (GAAP), fair value is defined as "the price that would be received to sell an asset or paid to transfer a liability in an orderly transaction between market participants at the measurement date." International Financial Reporting Standards (IFRS), on the other hand, defines fair value as "the amount for which an asset could be exchanged, or a liability settled, between knowledgeable, willing parties in an arm's length transaction."[11]

The changes or the variations of fair value need to be recognized in the profit and loss statement, excepting for the derivatives that may qualify for hedge accounting. In some way, fair value accounting may be seen as an offshoot of the accounting scandals of early 2000s and from this standpoint good corporate governance and fair value accounting can be seen as two sides of the same coin. Since historical cost accounting masked the problem of balance sheet erosion by allowing it only to show up gradually through negative annual net interest income, one could even argue that the absence of such accounting norms worsened the S&L crisis of the 1980s in the US. Thus, while there could be elements of pro-cyclicality in these accounting norms, valuing the assets at their historical/acquired value would clearly be erroneous.

How is "fair value accounting" responsible for the global financial crisis? The FASB standard requires fair value accounting for derivatives, as does the EU since 2005. This suffered from three major limitations. First, market measures of asset values are current, not historical. Second, true prices are hard to discover when markets' functioning is impaired. Third, when prices fall, realized asset values can trigger sales creating a downward spiral. As a result of these problems, when the structured mortgage market products became toxic and their markets collapsed, the balance sheets of the banks suffered a great deal.

Nevertheless, blaming "fair value accounting" for the global financial crisis is perhaps overstating its importance. We would rather go with the view of the US SEC that complaints over fair value accounting are like "shooting the messenger."

Compensation Norms in the Financial Services Industry

Another factor that is often highlighted in the context of the global financial crisis is the compensation structure in the financial services industry. In fact, it was widely believed that the new generation of executives of publicly held companies, such as investment banks or insurance companies, were gambling on long-term economic stability in order to achieve short-term financial goals. In a 2007 statement by the Research and Development Committee of the Committee for Economic Development (CED), a distinguished panel of business, academic, and policy leaders lamented the focus of corporate executives on short-term financial results rather than on long-term value and stability. The panel suggested that "decision making based primarily on short-term considerations damages the ability of public companies and, therefore, of the US economy to sustain superior long-term performance."

The existing compensation structure had many limitations. First, compensation plans failed to reward performance. Second, compensation was not structured to account for the time horizon of risks. Third, compensation practices were not aligned with sound risk management. Finally, the practices did not promote transparency and accountability in the process of setting compensation.

Admittedly, the short-term horizon of the decision-making process and the prevalence of bonuses linked to current yearly performance, encouraged excessive risk-taking amongst portfolio managers and other executives. This would have played a significant role in an otherwise ripe environment waiting for the crisis to be brewed.

Conclusion

Over the past three decades, there occurred a sea change in the volume, composition, and conduits of extension of bank credit. At the heart of the financial crisis lies the complex, opaque derivative securities created perhaps with the passive complicity of regulators. The process was exacerbated by rating agencies and insurance firms. Fair value accounting and presence of perverse and short-term incentives in the compensation practices of many Wall Street investment banks significantly contributed to the evolution of this crisis. Moving forward, dealing with these factors is going to shape the regulatory regime as well as the behavior of global financial firms, especially in risk-taking and risk-reward trade-offs. As the global economy emerges from the crisis, there is an implicit risk of the financial sector going back to a model of "business as usual." At the other extreme, there is also the risk that overkill in re-regulation in response to these factors may choke the appetite for risk that is vital for financial innovation and progress.

Notes

1. See *World Economic Outlook* of the IMF for the years 2007 and 2008 for a detailed discussion on the origin of the global financial crisis.
2. There was also a rapid expansion in the shadow banking and broader financial systems although, importantly, this was part of a trend which can be traced back to the early 1980s.
3. This apart, their evidence suggests that high levels of capital served large banks well around banking crises. High-capital listed banks enjoyed significantly higher abnormal stock returns than low-capital listed banks during banking crises. In contrast, high-capital ratios appear to have helped small banks improve their liquidity creation market share during banking crises, market-related crises, and normal times alike, and the gains in market share were sustained afterwards. Their profitability improved during two crises and subsequent to virtually every crisis. Similar results were observed during normal times for small banks.
4. Leverage refers to the degree to which a firm is utilizing borrowed money. Firms with high leverage may be at risk of bankruptcy if they are unable to make payments on their debt. Financial leverage is not always bad, however; it can increase the shareholders' return on their investment and often there are tax advantages associated with borrowing. See for details http://www.investorwords.com/1952/financial_leverage.html
5. See Box 3.1 for the definition of CDS.
6. However, this is not intended to belittle the importance of the originate-to-distributive model. It is instructive to turn to the then Bank for International Settlements (BIS) General Manager, Malcolm Knight, who in a conference in 2008 commented: *"I do believe that the originate-to-distribute model provides the avenue for both increased diversification and financial innovation."*
7. Carter Glass, senator from Virginia, reportedly believed that commercial banks securities operations had contributed to the crash of 1929, that banks failed because of their securities operations, and that commercial banks used their knowledge as lenders to undertake insider trading of securities.

8. Some private institutions, such as brokerage firms, banks, and homebuilders, also securitize mortgages, known as "private-label" mortgage securities.

9. A monoline insurance company provides guarantees to issuers, often in the form of credit wraps, and enhances the credit of the issuer. While these insurance companies first began providing wraps for municipal bond issues, then started providing credit enhancement for other types of bonds such as MBS and CDOs.

10. There are two major accounting standard setting bodies:

    • First, the accounting standards of the London-based IASB are known as the IFRS (also known by the old name of International Accounting Standards, IAS).

    • Second, the US-based FASB formulates US GAAP or GAAP. While the GAAP is for private and public companies, for governments, GAAP is determined by the Governmental Accounting Standards Board (GASB). Financial reporting in federal government entities is, however, regulated by the Federal Accounting Standards Advisory Board (FASAB).

11. Note that while the two definitions of "fair value" under the two accounting standards are generally consistent, there are subtle differences between them. First, the definition in FAS 157 is explicitly an exit price, whereas the definition in IFRS is neither explicitly an exit price nor an entry price. Second, while FAS 157 explicitly refers to market participants, IFRS simply refers to knowledgeable, willing parties in an arm's length transaction.

4
Impact of the Crisis[1]

Introduction

The subprime crisis that unfolded in 2007 morphed into a credit crisis in September 2008, causing a seizure of financial markets and intense solvency panic for the largest US-based and European financial institutions in the United States and Europe, pushing the global financial system to the brink of systemic meltdown. Asphyxiating credit conditions became a serious threat to the ability of nonfinancial firms and a number of emerging economies to raise capital. The US and European authorities responded with extraordinary measures, including massive liquidity provision, intervention to restore weak institutions, extension of guarantees, and brought to bear changes in regulatory provisions as well as in legislation to use public funds to buy troubled assets from banks. Soon it became evident that these measures were not sufficient to stabilize markets and bolster confidence. The outbreak of the crisis was in a setting in which prices of oil and basic commodities had reached historically high levels in the months just gone by.

By October 2008, it was clear that the world economy was entering a major downturn in the face of the most dangerous financial shock to mature financial markets since the 1930s. The immediate policy challenge at that juncture was to stabilize financial conditions, but policy authorities were already bracing up to deal with real economic activity going down quickly. Many advanced economies were already in or soon moved into recession, while growth in emerging and developing economies weakened sharply. The future of the world economy hinged around the ability of policy authorities to restore financial stability and since confidence in this ability was low, global growth prospects turned bleak and appeared to be poised on the shoulder of a steep and prolonged downturn. A protracted period of deleveraging, balance sheet cleansing, resolution of troubled institutions and markets, bottoming out of the housing collapse, and resuscitation of demand lay ahead. Furthermore, the horizon was clouded with substantial downside risks from very high levels of financial stress, credit constraints that could turn deeper and more protracted than envisaged if confidence and stability did not return soon enough, and muted but lurking deflation. Disruptions to capital flows and the risks of rising protectionism represented additional risks.

This chapter deals with the impact of the global crisis, although some overlaps with earlier chapters is unavoidable in the interest of preserving the continuity of narration. Nevertheless, the focus of this chapter is on the actual unfolding of events. It begins by tracing the metamorphosis of events between September 2008 and the last quarter of 2009. Regional dimensions of the mutation of the crisis are set out subsequently. As firm data and information are still in the formative stages, the narrative is essentially in terms of assessments at the specific stages that are delineated rather than actual outcomes. This is followed by a stylized assessment of the impact of the crisis against broad macroeconomic metrics—growth, inflation, financial markets—as is evident in the available data and projections. The chapter then turns to some key issues and challenges that have emerged in the context of the crisis which are likely to shape not only the recovery but also the contours of future policy responses. An important issue here is the specific features of the downturn, especially in the context of its association with financial turbulence and implications therefrom.

Morphology

Between 2003 and 2007, global GDP (on a purchasing-power-parity weighted basis) rose at an average of about 5 percent, its highest sustained rate since the early 1970s. About three-fourths of this growth was attributable to a broad-based surge in the emerging and developing economies. Inflation remained generally contained, albeit with some upward drift. From the second half of 2007, the global economy was affected by the deepening turmoil in financial markets, major corrections in housing markets in a number of advanced economies, and by surges in commodity prices. In early 2008, the Federal Reserve engineered the emergency sale of a major US investment bank (Bear Stearns) and increased broker–dealer access to emergency liquidity. Banks had also made progress in recognizing their losses on subprime–mortgage-related exposures, rebuilding their capital, and reducing their leverage. Nevertheless, financial market strains intensified over the ensuing months on solvency concerns and the prolonged process of balance sheet repair that lay ahead. There were growing fears that as the financial stress fed into the real economy, credit losses would begin to pile up. Banks as purveyors of credit were increasingly facing high funding costs, reduced revenue streams from fee-based securitization business, and forced accumulation of assets from off-balance sheet entities. Falling equity prices made raising new capital increasingly expensive, often prohibitively so. Starting in August, Fannie Mae and Freddie Mac, the two giant GSEs, came under heavy pressure over concerns about the adequacy of their capital bases in the face of rising losses, which were not relieved by assurances from the US authorities that these two institutions would have access to federal funding to meet their liquidity and capital needs. In the light of the crucial role of these agencies in the US housing market and the global financial system, the two institutions were placed under the conservatorship of the US Federal Housing Finance Agency, with the US government pledging additional financial support as needed to maintain adequate capital and funding. This nutshell description of the crisis is intended as a chapeau for the narrative in the chapter. An extensive treatment of the evolution of the crisis has already been provided in Chapter 3. The extent of the downturn and the slow pulling out that is now underway is best captured in the quarterly profile of the economies that have been at the epicenter of the crisis (Table 4.1).

Fourth Quarter, 2008

The sudden outbreak of the crisis in mid-September 2008 was dramatic, to say the least, defying expectations and even imagination, uprooting confidence in global financial institutions and markets, and starting off a drastic reshaping of the financial landscape.

Global financial markets plunged and froze in mid-September following the bankruptcy of the second largest US investment bank, Lehman Brothers. In the next few days, markets were shocked by the merger of

TABLE 4.1
Quarterly Real GDP Growth in Major Advanced Economies

(percentage change on the previous quarter)

Country	2007	2008				2009				2010	
	Q4	Q1	Q2	Q3	Q4	Q1	Q2	Q3	Q4	Q1	Q2
OECD—Total	**0.7**	**0.3**	**-0.2**	**-0.7**	**-2.0**	**-2.2**	**0.2**	**0.6**	**0.8**	**0.7**	**0.7**
OECD—Europe	0.6	0.6	-0.3	-0.5	-2.0	-2.5	0.0	0.5	0.4	0.4	1.1
European Union	0.5	0.6	-0.3	-0.5	-1.9	-2.5	-0.3	0.3	0.2	0.3	1.0
Euro Area	0.4	0.7	-0.4	-0.5	-1.8	-2.5	-0.1	0.4	0.2	0.3	1.0
G7	**0.5**	**0.2**	**-0.2**	**-0.9**	**-1.9**	**-2.2**	**0.2**	**0.3**	**0.9**	**0.8**	**0.7**
Canada	0.5	-0.2	0.0	0.1	-0.8	-1.8	-0.7	0.2	1.2	1.4	0.5
France	0.2	0.5	-0.7	-0.2	-1.6	-1.5	0.1	0.3	0.6	0.2	0.7
Germany	0.2	1.4	-0.7	-0.4	-2.2	-3.4	0.5	0.7	0.3	0.5	2.2
Italy	-0.4	0.4	-0.7	-1.1	-2.0	-2.9	-0.3	0.4	-0.1	0.4	0.5
Japan	0.4	0.2	-0.7	-1.2	-2.7	-4.4	2.3	-0.1	0.9	1.2	0.4
United Kingdom	0.3	0.5	-0.3	-0.9	-2.1	-2.3	-0.8	-0.3	0.4	0.4	1.2
United States	0.7	-0.2	0.1	-1.0	-1.7	-1.2	-0.2	0.4	1.2	0.9	0.4

Source OECD Stat database, available at www.Oecd.org /statsportal

another investment bank (Merrill Lynch) with a large commercial bank and the effective acquisition by the Federal Reserve of the world's largest insurance company (AIG) to avoid a disorderly bankruptcy. All of these institutions were heavily exposed to mortgage-related losses. As confidence vanished, interbank markets effectively seized up, despite coordinated injections of massive liquidity by major central banks and agreement on foreign exchange swaps of unprecedented magnitude. Subsequently, a number of other US and European banks needed to be resolved through closure, nationalization, or merger with public support.[2]

Soon, market segments that had been less affected by the turmoil came under substantial increased pressure, including the nonfinancial corporate sector and emerging markets. With government securities regarded as a safe haven, US Treasury bill yields were driven down close to zero. The financial strains permeated into a tightening of lending standards affecting credit. Actual credit growth was sustained for a while by the reintermediation of off-balance sheet exposure and prior lending commitments, but credit growth soon started slowing visibly. Local money markets across the world experienced a tightening of funding constraints, prompting central banks in a number of countries to ease reserve requirements and to take other actions to reduce strains on liquidity. Equity prices fell sharply, and spreads on both sovereign and corporate paper widened markedly. Countries with large external financing needs and commodity exporters came under increasing pressure from the reversal/drying up of capital flows (Box 4.1).

The advanced economies grew at a collective annualized rate of only 1 percent during the period from the fourth quarter of 2007 through the second quarter of 2008, down from 2.5 percent during the first three quarters of 2007. The US economy suffered most, managing to grow by only 1.3 percent on average since the fourth quarter of 2007. Activity in Western Europe also slowed appreciably, dampened by high oil prices, tightening credit conditions, housing downturns in several economies, the US slowdown and the appreciating euro. Japan's economy initially showed more resilience but was soon affected by slowing exports and the impact of deteriorating terms of trade on domestic demand. In the third quarter of 2008, the downturn in the advanced economies continued to deepen. Business and consumer confidence indicators fell to lows experienced during the 2001–02 recession. In the emerging and developing economies, growth eased from 8 percent in the first three

---

BOX 4.1
The Interplay of Finance and Housing

An important aspect of the current crisis is the interaction of financial factors with the housing downturn, amplifying it. Largely as a consequence, the downswing in the US housing market accentuated in the third quarter of 2008 into the largest in the post-World War II period. The virtual disappearance of the subprime market was effectively exacerbated by a general tightening of lending standards, increasing spreads on conventional mortgages despite monetary easing (due to the deteriorating financial situation of the GSEs), and sharply rising foreclosures.

In Western Europe, housing cycles also turned down sharply as lending standards tightened and credit became more expensive. The most severe downswings were concentrated in a few national markets—Ireland, Spain, and the United Kingdom—which had experienced the most rapid house price appreciation or the greatest building booms in the years preceding the crisis. The housing downturns produced a strong negative impact on growth through a range of channels—directly, through the contraction of residential investment as well as indirectly via heavy losses from mortgage-related assets.

As has been underscored in this crisis, declining house prices generally constrict opportunities for borrowing by using housing collateral, with associated negative wealth effects, all of which cause private consumption to turn down. In 2008–09, this knocked out the principal engine of growth in advanced countries.

Sources   Authors.

---

quarters of 2007 to 7.5 percent in the subsequent three quarters, as both domestic demand—particularly business investment—and net exports moderated. Countries with the strongest trade links with the United States and Europe slowed markedly, while some countries that relied on bank-related or portfolio inflows to finance large current account deficits were hit hard by an abrupt tightening of external financing. Global output and trade plummeted in the final months of 2008. Plunging asset values across advanced and emerging economies decreased household wealth and put strong downward pressure on consumer demand. In addition, the associated high level of uncertainty prompted households and businesses to postpone expenditures, reducing demand for consumer and capital goods. At the same time, widespread disruptions in credit constrained household spending and curtailed production and trade.

Against this uncertain backdrop, output in the advanced economies was for the first time expected to decline in 2009, the first annual contraction during the post-war period, with a cumulative output loss (relative to potential) comparable to the 1974–75 and 1980–82 periods. The only hope was that financial policy actions as well as sizable fiscal stimulus and large interest rate cuts in many advanced economies would cushion the fall in late 2009. Growth in emerging and developing economies was also expected to slow sharply in 2009 under the drag of falling export demand and financing, lower commodity prices, and much tighter external financing constraints, especially for economies with large external imbalances. Stronger economic frameworks in many emerging economies provided more room for policy support to growth than in the past, helping to cushion the impact of this unprecedented external shock. Accordingly, although these economies faced serious slowdowns, their growth was expected to remain at or above rates seen during previous global downturns. Developing countries in Africa and elsewhere were also better prepared this time to face policy challenges because of improved macroeconomic policy implementation, but high poverty levels and reliance on commodity exports were attendant risks (actual outcomes are given in Table 4.3 onwards).

Despite the deceleration of global growth, headline inflation remained round the world at the highest rates since the late 1990s, pushed up by the surge in fuel and food prices. In the advanced economies, 12-month headline inflation registered 4.3 percent in August 2008, down modestly from a peak in July in the wake of some commodity price easing. The persistence in inflation was particularly visible in the emerging and developing economies, with headline inflation reaching 8.3 percent in the aggregate in August and with a wide swath of countries experiencing double-digit inflation due to the considerably greater weight of food prices in consumption baskets in these economies—typically in the range of 30–45 percent as opposed to 10–15 percent in the advanced economies. Although central banks in these economies had raised interest rates and reserve ratios earlier in 2008 against inflation, some of these steps had to be reversed in the third quarter of 2008 in the face of intense liquidity strains related to the financial turmoil.

The financial crisis led to a flight to safety and rising home bias. Gross global capital flows contracted sharply in the fourth quarter of 2008.

In net terms, flows favored countries with the most liquid and safe government securities markets. Consequently, net private flows to emerging and developing economies collapsed. These shifts affected the world's major currencies. Since September 2008, the euro, US dollar, and yen appreciated notably. The Chinese renminbi and other currencies pegged to the dollar (including those in the Middle East) also appreciated in real effective terms. Most other emerging economy currencies weakened sharply, despite use of international reserves for support.

First Quarter, 2009

By January 2009, it was evident to even the most optimistic forecasters that, contrary to earlier expectations of resilience in the global economy, world growth could at best be flat at around zero in 2009 in purchasing-power-parity terms, its lowest rate since World War II. Despite wide-ranging policy actions, financial strains remained acute, pulling down the real economy. It was also widely recognized that a sustained economic recovery will not be possible until the financial sector's normal functioning is restored and credit markets are unclogged. Also, growing realization since November 2008, when the G-20 ministers first met, began to gain momentum that international cooperation will be critical in designing and implementing these policies.

Attendant macroeconomic and financial conditions clearly pointed to a bleak period ahead. Financial market conditions remained extremely difficult for a longer period than envisaged, despite measures to provide additional capital and reduce credit risks. Spreads in funding markets only gradually narrowed despite government guarantees, and those in many credit markets remained close to their September–October 2008 peaks. In emerging economies, sovereign and corporate spreads were still elevated in spite of some moderation. With the deterioration in economic prospects, equity markets in both advanced and emerging economies made little or no gains. Currency markets were volatile. These indications seemed to suggest that financial markets would remain strained through 2009. According to the IMF's estimates in April 2009, expected write-downs on US-based assets suffered by all financial institutions over 2007–10 were placed at US$2.7 trillion (up from the estimate of US$2.2 trillion in January 2009). Total expected write-downs on global exposures were estimated at US$4 trillion, of which about two-thirds were expected to fall on banks, with the remainder distributed among insurance companies, pension funds, hedge funds, and other intermediaries. By that time, banks had recognized less than one-third of estimated losses. It was estimated that additional capital would be required (measured as tangible common equity) amounting to US$275 billion–US$500 billion in the United States, US$475 billion–US$950 billion for European banks (excluding those in the United Kingdom), and US$125 billion–US$250 billion for UK banks.

Industrial production and merchandize trade fell rapidly in early 2009 across both advanced and emerging economies, as purchases of investment goods and consumer durables such as autos and electronics were hit by credit disruptions and rising anxiety; inventories started to build rapidly. Employment continued to drop fast, notably in the United States. Overall, global GDP, which was estimated to have contracted by 6.3 percent (annualized) in the fourth quarter of 2008, fell almost as fast in the first quarter of 2009. All economies around the world were seriously affected, although the direction of the blows varied. The advanced economies experienced an unprecedented 7.5 percent decline in the fourth quarter of 2008, and most suffered deep recessions in the first quarter of 2009. While the US economy may have suffered particularly from intensified financial strains and the continued fall in the housing sector, Western Europe and advanced Asia were hit hard by the collapse in trade as well as rising financial problems of their own and housing corrections in some national markets. Emerging economies too suffered badly in the first quarter of 2009, over and above the contraction of 4 percent in the fourth quarter of 2008. The damage was inflicted through both financial and trade channels. Activity in East Asian economies with heavy reliance on manufacturing exports fell sharply, although the downturns in China and India were somewhat muted, given the lower shares of their export sectors in domestic production and more resilient domestic demand. Emerging Europe and the Commonwealth of Independent States (CIS) were badly affected because of heavy dependence on external financing as well as on manufacturing exports and, for the CIS, commodity exports. Countries in Africa, Latin America, and the Middle East suffered from plummeting commodity prices as well as financial strains and weak export demand.

As the vicious loops between the real and financial sectors intensified, global economic prospects deteriorated further in the first quarter of 2009. In April 2009, accordingly, the IMF projected global activity to decline by 1.3 percent in 2009, the deepest global recession since the

Great Depression. Growth was projected to re-emerge in 2010, but at 1.9 percent would still be well below potential. It judged that the key factor determining the course of the downturn and recovery will be the rate of progress toward returning the financial sector to health. There was also recognition that financial stabilization will take longer than previously envisaged, given the complexities involved in dealing with bad assets and restoring confidence in bank balance sheets. Thus, financial strains in the mature markets were expected to remain heavy until well into 2010 with deleveraging balance sheets, and stress on market institutions protracted. Private credit in the advanced economies was projected to contract in both 2009 and 2010. Continuing stress and balance sheet adjustment in mature markets were expected to have serious consequences for financing to emerging economies. Overall, emerging markets were expected to experience net capital outflows in 2009 of more than 1 percent of their GDP. Monetary policy interest rates would remain near the zero bound in the major advanced economies and central banks would continue to seek ways to use their balance sheets to ease credit conditions. The projections built in fiscal stimulus plans in G-20 countries amounting to 2 percent of GDP in 2009 and 1.5 percent of GDP in 2010, as well as the operation of automatic stabilizers in most of these countries, with implications for fiscal deficits in developed and developing economies alike.

Advanced economies were projected to suffer deep recessions. Overall output was projected to contract by 2.6 percent (measured on the basis of fourth-quarter-over-fourth-quarter) during 2009. In 2010, output was expected to increase gradually over the course of the year—by 1.0 percent—still well below potential, implying a continuing rise in unemployment to over 9 percent. Among the major economies, the United States and the United Kingdom were expected to continue to suffer most heavily from credit constraints, given the direct damage to their financial institutions and major housing corrections. The Euro Area would experience an even deeper decline in activity than the United States on account of the sharp contraction in export sectors. In Japan, the downturn was expected to be exceptionally severe, driven largely by the heavy reliance on manufacturing exports and by spillovers to domestic investment. Emerging and developing economies as a group were projected to eke out a modest 1.6 percent growth in 2009, rising to 4 percent in 2010. The biggest output declines were projected for the CIS countries due to reversal of capital flows and dwindling commodity export revenues.

Countries in emerging Europe were confronted with adjustment to a sharp curtailment of external financing, as well as a drop in demand from Western Europe. While export-oriented economies of East Asia would suffer loss of manufacturing exports, countries like Japan, China, and India were expected to achieve lower but positive rates of growth, given the momentum of domestic demand. Middle Eastern oil exporters used financial reserves to maintain government spending plans to cushion the impact of lower oil prices. In Latin America, prudent macroeconomic management in many countries provided buffers, but economies were heavily affected by declines in export volumes, weak commodity prices, and tight external financing conditions. African economies were also squeezed by declines in commodity export prices and export markets, but most were less reliant on external financing.

The slump in global demand led to a collapse in commodity prices in the first quarter of 2009. Despite production cutbacks and geopolitical tensions, oil prices declined by over 60 percent since their peak in July 2008. Metals and food prices were also markedly softer, reflecting dampened demand as growth headed into negative territory. Sluggish real activity and lower commodity prices dampened inflation pressures. In the advanced economies, headline inflation entered a period of very low or even negative increases. In emerging and developing economies also, inflation subsided quite dramatically. At the same time, rising economic slack contained wage increases and eroded profit margins. As a result, 12-month headline inflation in the advanced economies fell below 1 percent in February 2009, although core inflation remained in the 1.5–2 percent range with the notable exception of Japan. Inflation also moderated significantly across the emerging economies, although in some cases falling exchange rates moderated the downward momentum.

Central banks in the advanced economies took strong actions to cut policy rates and improve credit provision. Policy interest rates were brought down substantially to or close to zero. Central banks in emerging economies also moved to much easier policy stances with determined efforts to improve market liquidity. To combat the downturn, many governments announced fiscal packages to boost their economies.

Thus, by the first quarter of 2009, there was a strong sense that downside risks had increased and dominated the outlook, and that the global financial crisis had taken the global economy into uncharted waters. There was considerable apprehension that unless financial strains and uncertainties are forcefully addressed, there would be more toxic effects on global growth. In addition, the risks of deflation had increased substantially in a number of advanced economies and in some emerging economies too. Corporate defaults and even sovereign credit risks became a clear and present danger. Furthermore, with fiscal policy in full play, the sharp increase in the issuance of public debt threatened to generate adverse market reactions and crowding out of the private sector, pushing out the recovery of demand even further. Nevertheless, the focus was on financial sector policies—forceful and credible loan loss recognition; public support to the viable financial institutions; measures to resolve insolvent banks and set-up public agencies to dispose of the bad debts. With interest rates at or approaching zero in several major countries, central banks were forced to explore alternative policy approaches, relying on using their balance sheets to ease monetary conditions further and unlock credit markets.

Second Quarter, 2009

Until the end of June 2009, the outlook remained exceptionally uncertain, with risks still weighing on the downside. A dominant concern all around was that policies continue to be insufficient to arrest the negative feedback between deteriorating financial conditions and weakening economies in the face of limited public support for policy action. The threat of rising corporate and household defaults seemed to imply still-higher risk spreads, further falls in asset prices, and greater losses across financial balance sheets. Additional stress in the financial sector was a persisting risk in the form of greater deleveraging and asset sales, tightening of access to credit, greater uncertainty, higher saving rates, and even more severe and prolonged recessions. Deflation risks were also seen, but muted and mainly in advanced economies.

Notwithstanding these dark clouds on the horizon, however, there were green shoots wanly in evidence in the second quarter of 2009 extending into July, indicating that the global economy was beginning to pull out of the unprecedented recession, helped by unprecedented macroeconomic and financial policy support. Yet, it was also clear that stabilization would be uneven and the recovery sluggish. Financial conditions improved more than expected, owing mainly to public intervention, and lead indicators on consumer and business confidence suggested that the rate of decline in economic activity was moderating, although in varying degrees among regions. In the United States, high-frequency indicators pointed to a diminishing rate of deterioration, including in the labor and housing markets. Industrial production seemed close to bottoming out; the inventory cycle was turning; and business and consumer confidence improved. These developments were consistent with stabilization of output during the second half of 2009 and hopes of a gradual recovery emerging in 2010. In Japan, following a dismal first quarter, there were signs that output was stabilizing. Improved consumer confidence, progress in inventory adjustment, aggressive fiscal policies, and strong performance by some other Asian economies was expected to lift growth in the coming quarters. In the Euro Area, consumer and business survey indicators began recovering but data on real activity showed few signs of stabilization. Macroeconomic policies provided support but much of the adjustment in the labor market still lay ahead. Rising unemployment weighed on consumption and activity, as also the economy's heavy dependence on a still-ailing banking sector.

There were also welcome positive signs of regenerating activity in the emerging and developing economies. In China and India, economic prospects showed improvement reflecting substantial macroeconomic stimulus and a faster-than-expected turnaround in capital flows. In Latin America, activity was benefiting from rising commodity prices, but Central and Eastern Europe and the CIS economies continued to suffer from a combination of adverse factors such as the reversal of capital flows and contracting commodity exports, with the recent recovery of commodity prices providing a silver lining. For both Africa and the Middle East, activity continued to be dragged down by the drop in global trade, though in the latter this was somewhat cushioned by drawing on foreign exchange reserves.

In its July update of the *World Economic Outlook* (*WEO*), the IMF expected the global economy to contract by 1.4 percent in 2009 and to expand by 2.5 percent in 2010. On a fourth-quarter-over-fourth-quarter basis, real GDP growth was projected at 2.9 percent in 2010, compared with 2.6 percent in the April 2009 *WEO* forecast. Real GDP in the advanced economies was projected to decline by 3.8 percent in 2009 before growing by 0.6 percent in 2010, but still short of potential in view of the continuing increases in unemployment. Emerging and developing economies were projected to regain growth momentum during the second half of 2009, albeit with notable regional differences. Growth projections in emerging Asia were revised upward while those for Latin America, Central and Eastern Europe, the CIS and Africa, and the Middle East have been lowered by differing degrees.

Inflation pressures continued to ease with the weakness of the global economy. Year-over-year inflation moderated to 1.7 percent in May, down from around 6 percent one year earlier. In the advanced economies, headline inflation fell below zero percent in May as oil prices remained far below levels one year earlier, despite some pickup in recent months. Similarly, headline and core inflation in the emerging markets moderated, falling below 4.3 percent and to around 1 percent in May, respectively. However, developments were uneven, with inflation falling more in China and the Middle East than elsewhere. According to the IMF, global inflation was expected to remain subdued through 2010, held back by significant excess capacity. Risks for sustained deflation were seen small as indicated in core inflation and inflation expectations still holding in the 1–2 percent range. Unemployment rates were expected to reach double digits in some countries, holding back wages and household spending and presenting significant policy challenges. In the emerging economies, stronger disinflationary forces set in, notwithstanding the upward revisions to output growth.

Third Quarter, 2009

In the third quarter of 2009, there were strengthening indications that the global economy was expanding again, pulled up by the strong performance of Asian economies and stabilization or modest recovery elsewhere. Growth was led by a rebound in manufacturing and a turn in the inventory cycle. There were also some signs of gradually stabilizing retail sales, returning consumer confidence, and firmer housing markets. Commodity prices staged a comeback from lows reached earlier this year, and world trade began to pickup. The triggers for this rebound were strong public policies across advanced and many emerging economies supporting aggregate demand.

Global activity was estimated by the IMF to have risen by about 3 percent during the second quarter of 2009, following a 6 percent contraction in the first quarter. High-frequency indicators pointed to stronger growth in the second half of the year, with the nascent recovery most evident in financial markets. Equity markets posted strong gains, corporate risk spreads declined, and spreads in interbank markets fell to levels fairly close to those prevailing before the bankruptcy of Lehman

Brothers in September 2008. Investors began allocating an increasing amount of funds away from government bonds in search of higher yields. Confidence in advanced economy banking systems received a fillip from better-than-expected earnings results and a series of successful bank capital raisings. In addition, stress-testing exercises completed and published in the United States and in various other countries helped to rebuild trust in banks. International capital flows recovered, including to emerging markets. Compared with levels in the beginning of 2009, sovereign spreads were down and sovereign issues up for both advanced and emerging economies, consistent with a noticeable pickup in portfolio flows, particularly in Asia and Latin America. Since June 2009, emerging market corporate and sovereign deals were oversubscribed and refinancing risks fell sharply, although less so in emerging Europe and the CIS. The return of some appetite for risk in international markets contributed to depreciation of the dollar and yen and appreciation of emerging market currencies. This followed sharp movements in the opposite direction at the height of the crisis. The euro also strengthened against both the dollar and the yen, although it held more or less steady at the level prevailing before the crisis in nominal effective terms. The renminbi moved in line with the dollar over the past year.

The rebound in activity in the real sector lagged the financial sector, especially in advanced countries in which saving rates stayed high and investment rates low. Public policies and the pickup in financial market conditions helped industrial production to stabilize and even to increase in a growing number of countries, notably in Asia. As a result, demand for commodities increased, boosting international trade. However, in major advanced economies, spare capacity was high and still rising. The labor market remained weak. In the US, the unemployment rate climbed to a 26-year high of 10.2 percent in October 2009 (10.8 percent in 1982) and although there was a marginal ebbing to 9.6 percent, it was projected to stay over 10 percent through 2010. Starting from a higher level, the rate in the Euro Area rose to 9.7 percent in September 2009 and further to 10 percent in December 2010. Countries that experienced particularly large real estate-related shocks, e.g., Ireland and Spain, saw much larger increases in unemployment because of the sharp contraction in construction jobs. House prices declined at a slower rate or began to stabilize in some advanced economies, such as the United States and the United Kingdom, but many markets faced the risk of further price declines.

Furthermore, the fall in activity was yet to bottom out for commercial real estate, which lagged the residential sector but kept going through a severe downturn. Growth dynamics were somewhat stronger in emerging economies. Domestic demand was relatively robust, particularly in China and India, helped by strong macroeconomic policy support. In addition, many economies benefited from the rebound in commodity prices. Limited information on unemployment in emerging economies pointed to less difficult although still challenging conditions, with economies in emerging Europe and the CIS suffering large job losses

Questions remained about the sustainability of bank earnings and the implications of elevated credit risks, with loan delinquencies continuing to increase and delays by banks in recognizing loan losses. In particular, bank loans to the private sector were still stagnating or contracting in the United States, the Euro Area, and the United Kingdom. In its October 2009 assessment, the IMF estimated that global bank write-downs could reach US$2.8 trillion, of which US$1.5 trillion was yet to be recognized. The bulk of these losses were attributable to US, UK, and Euro Area banks. Furthermore, these banks face a wall of maturing debt, which will reach US$1.5 trillion by 2012. Deleveraging was thus likely to continue for a considerable period in the United States, the Euro Area, and the United Kingdom. Securitization markets remained heavily impaired, which severely limited banks' capacity to originate (and distribute) credit. More generally, the risk of a reversal was a significant market concern, and a number of financial stress indicators remained elevated. In emerging Europe and other countries heavily dependent on external financing, cross-border funding was vulnerable to deleveraging while refinancing and default risks in the corporate sector continued to be relatively high.

According to the IMF's October 2009 forecasts, global growth was projected to reach about 3 percent in 2010, following a contraction in activity of about 1.1 percent in 2009. Advanced economies were projected to expand sluggishly through much of 2010 with average annual growth in 2010 only modestly positive at about 1 percent, following a contraction of 3 percent during 2009. In emerging economies, real GDP growth was forecast to reach 5 percent in 2010, up from 1 percent in 2009. The rebound was expected to be driven by China, India, and a number of other emerging Asian economies. Economies in Africa and the Middle East were also expected to post solid growth of close to 4 percent, helped by recovering commodity prices, whereas Latin America would benefit from higher commodity prices and rising global trade. In emerging Europe and the CIS, the recovery was expected to lag because of tighter external financial constraints. The gradual pace of recovery pointed to a prolonged period of subdued inflation—close to zero in advanced economies in 2009 and a modest acceleration to about 1 percent in 2010, largely reflecting rising commodity prices, and around 5 percent in emerging economies in 2009–10, down from more than 9 percent in 2008. An interesting study of the swiftness of the deterioration in the global economy and the sluggishness of the recovery is captured in the evolution of the IMF's growth projections. Illustratively, global growth for 2009 was projected at 3.8 percent in April 2008. In the span of a year, i.e., this projection underwent a 510 basis point downward revision, which was followed by a 50 basis point upward revision over the next 10 months (Table 4.2).

In the IMF's January 2010 projections, a degree of cautious optimism relative to the assessment in October 2009 is discernible although the balance of risks still remains slanted to the downside. It is useful to observe the shift in sentiment (Box 4.2).

TABLE 4.2
Evolution of IMF's Projections of World Output Growth

(percent)

Date of projection	2008	2009	2010
January 2008	4.1		
April 2008	3.7	3.8	
July 2008	4.1	3.9	
October 2008	3.9	3.0	
November 2008	3.7	2.2	
January 2009	3.4	0.5	3.0
April 2009	3.2	−1.3	1.9
July 2009	3.1	−1.4	2.5
October 2009	3.0	−1.1	3.1
January 2010	3.0	−0.8	3.9
April 2010	3.0	−0.6	4.2
July 2010	3.0	−0.6	4.6
October 2010	2.9	−0.6	4.6

Source *World Economic Outlook*, IMF, various issues/releases, Washington D.C.

BOX 4.2
Key Sentiments in the IMF's January 2010
***World Economic Outlook* Update**

- The global recovery is off to a stronger start than anticipated earlier but is proceeding at different speeds in the various regions—in most advanced economies, the recovery is expected to remain sluggish, whereas in many emerging and developing economies, activity is expected to be relatively vigorous.
- Financial markets have recovered faster than expected, but financial conditions are likely to remain more difficult than before the crisis—bank lending to remain sluggish, sovereign debt under pressure, and cross-border bank financing still contracting in most regions.
- Commodity prices are expected to rise strongly, despite generally high inventories, largely due to the buoyant recovery in emerging Asia.
- Still-low levels of capacity utilization and well-anchored inflation expectations are expected to contain inflation pressures in advanced economies, but emerging and developing economies may face growing upward pressures due to more limited economic slack and increased capital flows.
- Risks to the outlook are significant—premature and incoherent exit from supportive policies; impaired financial systems and housing markets; rising unemployment in key advanced economies; worsening budgetary positions and fiscal sustainability.
- At the same time, credible strategies for unwinding policy support need to be prepared and communicated.
- Emerging market countries will have to manage a surge of capital inflows—some fiscal tightening to ease pressure on interest rates; exchange rate appreciation; macro-prudential policies limiting asset price bubbles; some buildup of reserves, and some capital controls on inflows.
- Policymakers face major structural policy challenges—closing output gaps, rebalancing, demography, restoring competitiveness, and flexibility are some of them.

Sources   Authors.

Thus, as 2009 drew to a close and 2010 began with hopes of renewal and recovery, a balanced assessment suggested that there are continuing risks and that the worst may not entirely be behind us. In the advanced economies, these risks relate mainly to rising unemployment and a loss of confidence in the stability of the financial sector. A number of emerging economies remained vulnerable to the global downturn, besides intensified financial stress. At the same time, commodity prices rebounded in a broad-based manner ahead of the recovery, particularly international crude prices. Expansionary macroeconomic policies and inventory adjustment supported global activity but these are temporary forces. Accordingly, there is a need for policy frameworks to develop beyond the short-term to laying the foundations for a return to strong medium-run growth. Financial, monetary, fiscal, and structural policies all have a role to play in this regard. The overarching policy priority remains restoring financial sector health—restoring bank solvency; stopping the deleveraging; raising capital; and continuous monitoring including through stress tests. It is vital that the financial sector resumes its role of allocating savings to competing projects and thereby sustain productivity growth. Monetary policy should remain supportive until growth resumes and deflationary risks dissipate. At the same time fiscal policy should stay supportive through 2010. Simultaneously, plans should be made for rebuilding fiscal balances and ensuring sustainable debt paths after growth is firmly re-established. Relevant reforms should aim at strengthening fiscal rules and institutions and reducing the buildup of future pension and health liabilities.

Looking ahead, the crisis is likely to have reduced the global economy's sustainable output, both level and the rate of growth. There is also the danger that rising cyclical unemployment may translate into higher structural unemployment. Policymakers will also need to engage in a rebalancing of demand—public demand will have to recede and private demand increase. In countries running persistent large current account deficits in the recent past, this may require a shift from internal to external demand. By implication, the reverse will be required in countries that posted large current account surpluses.

Impact of the Crisis

As the onslaught of the crisis progressed as chronicled in the foregoing section, the assessment was that despite wide-ranging policy actions the real economy would be badly affected. The outlook remained uncertain. Sustaining policy intervention was seen as critical to securing a recovery in 2010, conditional upon world trade picking up, an improvement in credit conditions, and a steadying of the housing market in various parts of the world (Table 4.3).

TABLE 4.3
World Growth: Shifting Perspectives

(percent)

	2007	2008	2009	2010 projections
World output	**5.3**	**2.9**	**-0.6**	**4.6**
Advanced economies	**2.7**	**0.3**	**-3.2**	**2.6**
United States	*2.1*	*0.0*	*-2.6*	*2.9*
Euro Area	*2.7*	*0.6*	*-4.1*	*1.1*
Germany	2.5	1.2	-4.9	1.6
France	2.3	0.1	-2.5	1.5
Italy	1.6	-1.3	-5.0	0.9
Spain	3.6	0.9	-3.6	-0.4
Japan	2.3	-1.2	-5.2	2.9
United Kingdom	2.6	0.1	-4.9	1.6
Canada	2.5	0.5	-2.5	3.3
Other advanced economies	*4.7*	*1.7*	*-1.1*	*5.0*
Emerging and developing economies	**8.3**	**6.0**	**2.5**	**6.9**
Sub-Saharan Africa	7.0	5.5	2.3	4.9
Central and eastern Europe	5.5	3.1	-3.6	3.1
Commonwealth of Independent States	8.6	5.5	-6.5	4.5
Russia	8.1	5.6	-7.9	4.3
Excluding Russia	9.9	5.4	-3.2	5.0

Developing Asia	10.6	7.7	6.9	9.3
China	13.0	9.6	9.1	10.5
India	9.4	6.4	5.7	9.4
ASEAN-5	6.3	4.7	1.7	6.5
Middle East and North Africa	6.2	5.0	2.1	4.1
Latin America and the Caribbean		4.3	-1.7	5.1
Brazil	5.7	5.1	-0.2	7.1
Mexico	3.3	1.5	-6.5	4.5
Memorandum				
European Union	3.1	0.8	-4.1	1.2
World Growth on Market Exchange Rates	3.8	1.6	-2.1	3.6

Source IMF, *World Economic Outlook*, IMF, various issues, Washington D.C.

Regional Impact

Countries and regions have exhibited differentiated effects as well as responses in the context of the crisis and its attendant intense financial strains. While a detailed analysis follows, the current state of the regional economies can be captured in a nutshell at the outset. The United States, the epicenter of the crisis, is emerging out of a severe recession. Asia had little exposure to US mortgage-related assets but has been badly affected by the slump in global trade, given its heavy dependence on manufacturing exports. In Europe, as in the United States, the financial system has been dealt a heavy blow, housing corrections have been intense, and industrial production is only recently recovering from a sharp drop in durables demand. Heavy reliance on capital inflows translated into heightened pain for the emerging European and CIS economies, the latter also suffering from the slump in commodity prices. In Latin America and the Caribbean, the fallout from the crisis moved through both trade and financial channels, intensified by the drop in commodity prices. The Middle Eastern economies suffered mainly because of the decline in energy prices, and hard-won gains in African economies were threatened by slumping commodity prices and potentially lower aid inflows.

North America

As discussed earlier, the United States has been at the center of the biggest global financial storm since the Great Depression which pushed it into a severe recession. The US economy had expanded at an annualized 2.8 percent in the second quarter of 2008 as surging net exports and tax rebate checks buoyed consumption and outweighed the drag from financial turmoil and housing correction. Thereafter, there was a sharp slowdown. Real GDP contracted by 6.3 percent in the fourth quarter of 2008 and by 6.4 percent in the first quarter of 2009. Since then, there have been signs of improving business sentiment and firming consumer demand. The contraction of real GDP slowed to 1 percent in the second quarter of 2009 and thereafter there has been a return to positive growth; but employment has continued to fall rapidly pushing the unemployment rate to 9.7 percent in January and February 2010.

The key issue facing the US economy is the effectiveness of policy action to stabilize financial conditions and the housing sector. The process of balance sheet repair will be long and arduous and it will take considerable time before losses are fully recognized, banks are recapitalized, leverage is reduced, and market confidence is regained. The strategy for banks has two aspects. First, banks with more than US$100 billion in assets have been subjected to a mandatory stress test to assess whether their existing levels of capital are robust. Banks that cannot raise additional capital from private investors to fill identified capital shortfalls will receive additional government funds. Second, the Public–Private Investment Program (PPIP) is in place to enable the purchase of distressed assets, potentially allowing purchases of US$500 billion to US$1 trillion. Bank participation in the plan, however, is entirely voluntary, as banks are not required to sell their assets. Moreover, recognizing that further declines in the price of MBS will also hurt banks, the administration is applying US$75 billion in public funds toward curbing foreclosures by offering cash incentives for lenders to modify loans, allowing borrowers with high LTV mortgages to refinance into new, government-backed mortgages with a lower interest rate, and by increasing the capacity of Fannie Mae and Freddie Mac to buy mortgages.

Despite large cuts in policy interest rates and credit easing measures, credit is still not flowing easily for many households and firms, reflecting severe strains in financial institutions. Households are hit by large financial and housing wealth losses, much lower earnings prospects, and elevated uncertainty about job security, all of which has affected consumer confidence. These shocks have depressed consumption; the household saving rate, which had been falling for two decades, rose sharply to more than 4.5 percent in January 2010, up from about 0.25 percent a year earlier.

Fiscal policy played an important part in supporting demand, providing 2.0 percent of GDP stimulus in 2009 and 1.8 percent expected in 2010. This is projected to bring the federal budget deficit to about 10 percent of GDP in 2010. A key issue that is drawing both heat and light is the sustainability of the public finances going forward, with debt ratios set to touch 100 percent of GDP by 2014 (Table 4.4).

In Canada, economic activity slowed sharply from mid-2007 and the global downturn accentuated the slowdown. Although the resource-intensive sectors benefited in the first half of 2008 from high commodity prices, the lagged effect of past real appreciation of the Canadian dollar, together with the US slowdown, adversely impacted manufacturing. Growth returned to positive territory (0.1 percent) in the third

TABLE 4.4
US Gross Debt

Year	Gross debt in US$ billion	as % of GDP
1940	60.6	52.4
1950	256.8	94.0
1960	290.5	56.0
1970	380.9	37.6
1980	909.0	33.4
1990	3,206.3	55.9
2000	5,628.7	58.0
2005	7,905.3	64.6
2009	12,311.4	86.1
2010 (Estimate)	14,456.3	98.1
2014 (Estimate)	18,350.0	99.8

Source US Congressional Budget Office.

quarter of 2009 after contracting continuously through the previous three quarters. The Bank of Canada eased interest rates by 150 basis points between December 2007 and April 2008 but held rates steady since then. Inflation generally remained well anchored, in part owing to the rising currency. Banks generally weathered the financial strains well so far, reflecting conservative regulation and low exposure to structured products, but risks remain, given the strong economic and financial linkages with the United States.

Europe

Since early 2007, European banks had been struggling with a confluence of adverse shocks—losses on their holdings of US mortgage-related assets and deteriorating overall credit quality, apart from an evaporation of confidence in the face of rising creditor concerns about balance sheet risk. Beginning September 2008, Western Europe was hit by extraordinary financial stress. In the ensuing period, financial systems suffered a much larger and more sustained shock than expected, macroeconomic policies were slow to react, confidence plunged as households and firms drastically scaled back their expectations about future income (Table 4.5).

Fears about growing losses on US-related assets at major European banks caused wholesale markets to freeze in September 2008, with a number of failing banks requiring state intervention. Initially, problems

TABLE 4.5
European Countries: Real GDP Growth and CPI Inflation, 2007–10

	Growth				Inflation			
	2007	2008	2009	2010	2007	2008	2009	2010
Europe	**3.9**	**1.6**	**-4.5**	**1.6**	**3.6**	**5.7**	**2.7**	**2.7**
Advanced European economies	2.9	0.7	-4.0	1.0	2.1	3.4	0.7	1.5
Emerging European economies	6.8	4.3	-6.1	3.3	7.8	12.0	8.5	6.3
European Union	3.1	0.9	-4.1	1.0	2.4	3.7	0.9	1.5
Euro Area	2.8	0.6	-4.1	1.0	2.1	3.3	0.3	1.1
Austria	3.5	2.0	-3.6	1.3	2.2	3.2	0.4	1.3
Belgium	2.8	0.8	-3.0	1.2	1.8	4.5	-0.2	1.6
Cyprus	5.1	3.6	-1.7	-0.7	2.2	4.4	0.2	2.7
Finland	4.9	1.2	-7.8	1.2	1.6	3.9	1.6	1.1
France	2.3	0.3	-2.2	1.5	1.6	3.2	0.1	1.2
Germany	2.5	1.2	-5.0	1.2	2.3	2.8	0.1	0.9
Greece	4.5	2.0	-2.0	-2.0	3.0	4.2	1.4	1.9
Ireland	6.0	-3.0	-7.1	-1.5	2.9	3.1	-1.7	-2.0
Italy	1.5	-1.3	-5.0	0.8	2.0	3.5	0.8	1.4
Luxembourg	6.5	0.0	-4.2	2.1	2.3	3.4	0.8	1.0
Malta	3.8	2.1	-1.9	0.5	0.7	4.7	1.8	2.0
Netherlands	3.6	2.0	-4.0	1.3	1.6	2.2	1.0	1.1
Portugal	1.9	0.0	-2.7	0.3	2.4	2.7	-0.9	0.8

(Table 4.5 continued)

(Table 4.5 continued)

(percent)

	Growth				Inflation			
	2007	2008	2009	2010	2007	2008	2009	2010
Slovak Republic	10.6	6.2	-4.7	4.1	1.9	3.9	0.9	0.8
Slovenia	6.8	3.5	-7.3	1.1	3.6	5.7	0.8	1.5
Spain	3.6	0.9	-3.6	-0.4	2.8	4.1	-0.3	1.2
Other EU advanced economies								
Denmark	6.1	2.5	-4.3	1.7	2.9	6.3	1.0	1.6
Sweden	1.7	-0.9	-5.1	1.2	1.7	3.4	1.3	2.0
UK	2.6	-0.2	-4.4	1.2	1.7	3.3	2.2	2.4
New EU countries	2.6	0.5	-4.9	1.3	2.3	3.6	2.2	2.7
Bulgaria	6.0	4.4	-3.0	1.4	4.6	6.5	3.9	2.6
Czech Republic	6.2	6.0	-5.0	0.2	7.6	12.0	2.5	2.2
Estonia	7.2	-3.6	-14.1	0.8	6.6	10.4	-0.1	0.8
Hungary	1.0	0.6	-6.3	-0.2	7.9	6.1	4.2	4.3
Latvia	10.0	-4.6	-18.0	-4.0	10.1	15.3	3.3	-3.7
Lithuania	9.8	2.8	-15.0	-1.6	5.8	11.1	4.2	-1.2
Poland	6.8	5.0	1.7	2.7	2.5	4.2	3.5	2.3
Romania	6.3	7.3	-7.1	0.8	4.8	7.8	5.6	4.0

Non-EU advanced economies								
Iceland	6.0	1.0	-6.5	-3.0	5.0	12.4	12.0	6.2
Israel	5.2	4.0	0.7	3.2	0.5	4.6	3.3	2.3
Norway	2.7	1.8	-1.5	1.1	0.7	3.8	2.2	2.5
Switzerland	3.6	1.8	-1.5	1.5	0.7	2.4	-0.4	0.7
Other emerging economies								
Albania	6.0	7.8	2.8	2.3	2.9	3.4	2.2	3.5
Belarus	8.6	10.0	0.2	2.4	8.4	14.8	13.0	7.3
Bosnia and Herzegovina	6.5	5.4	-3.4	0.5	1.5	7.4	-0.4	1.6
Croatia	5.5	2.4	-5.8	0.2	2.9	6.1	2.4	2.3
Macedonia	5.9	4.8	-0.7	2.0	2.3	8.3	-0.8	1.9
Moldova	3.0	7.8	-6.5	2.5	12.4	12.7	0.0	7.7
Montenegro	10.7	6.9	-7.0	-1.7	3.5	9.0	3.6	-0.6
Russia	8.1	5.6	-7.9	4.0	9.0	14.1	11.7	7.0
Serbia	6.9	5.5	-2.9	2.0	6.5	12.4	8.1	4.8
Turkey	4.7	0.7	-4.7	5.2	8.8	10.4	6.3	9.7
Ukraine	7.9	2.1	-15.1	3.7	12.8	25.2	15.9	9.2

Source IMF, *Regional Economic Outlook: Europe*, May 2010, Washington D.C.

were concentrated in a few banks, and their causes varied. The macroeconomic implications were generally not considered large, and thus fiscal and monetary policy responses were initially limited. But the problems quickly caused broad repercussions because of the close linkages between Europe's major financial institutions and their high leverage. With funding markets frozen, the financial crisis rapidly transformed into a crisis for the real economy during the fourth quarter of 2008. Remedial financial policies were put in place quickly but, as elsewhere, were not sufficiently comprehensive and coordinated, undermining rather than reinforcing their cross-country effectiveness. Equity prices took a steep fall, and business investment was slashed.

Residential investment fell sharply in countries with housing booms (e.g., Ireland, Spain, and the United Kingdom). Despite significant support from the large fall in oil prices, consumption declined from end-2008 as unemployment spread. Households and firms operating in real estate had to struggle under growing debt burdens, particularly in countries such as Ireland, Spain, and the United Kingdom, as in real terms, residential property prices fell sharply. Real GDP growth stalled after a noticeably weaker outturn in the first half of 2008. In fact, the European economies suffered sharp contractions since mid-2008. Real GDP fell by 1.9 percent during the fourth quarter of 2008 for the European Union as a whole and by 2.2 percent in the first quarter of 2009, before turning around to positive growth of an average of 0.5 percent during the rest of 2009. In the United Kingdom, real GDP declined by 1.8 percent in the fourth quarter of 2008 followed by a contraction of 2.5 percent in the first quarter of 2009 and by 0.2 percent in the second quarter. In the second half of 2009, real GDP growth averaged 1.0 percent with most of the improvement in the fourth quarter.

Growth is expected to have picked up to 1.5 percent in 2010; on a fourth-quarter-to-fourth-quarter basis, the turnaround is more apparent, from a decline of 1.8 percent in 2009 to an increase of about 1.1 percent in 2010. The depth of the recession ranges—particularly severe in Ireland, as its construction boom is painfully reversed, exceptionally deep in Iceland, both of which are receiving IMF support following the collapse of their overextended financial sectors, and quite severe in the United Kingdom, which is hit by the end of the boom in real estate and financial activity. As a result of the broad-based fall in output, unemployment rates in the advanced economies are projected to climb above 10 percent through 2011.

Economic activity took a particularly sharp turn for the worse in many emerging European economies. Heavy reliance on all kinds of capital inflows—notably funding from Western banks to sustain local credit booms—caused these economies to be much more severely affected by the financial crisis than emerging economies in Asia. As Western export markets contracted and the flight from risk became generalized during the third quarter of 2008, the outlook for local exports, growth, and government revenues worsened drastically, causing sovereign spreads to jump from levels of about 50–100 basis points to 150–900 basis points. Several economies in the region received IMF support to sustain their balance of payments including access to a Flexible Credit Line from the IMF (by Poland). Accordingly, real GDP in the emerging economies is projected by the IMF to have contracted by about 4.3 percent in 2009 and could recover to about 2 percent in 2010.

Advanced economies outside the Euro Area are projected to record small deficits or surpluses, with the exception of Iceland and the United Kingdom. The UK's fiscal deficit is projected to have reached 11 percent of GDP in 2010, reflecting mainly automatic stabilizers and asset-price related revenue shortfalls rather than discretionary stimulus. In emerging Europe, countries are faced with an unprecedented widening of their sovereign risk premiums. With access to funding heavily restricted, most are not allowing automatic stabilizers to play freely, and none are implementing major stimulus packages.

Financial policies have generally been forceful and innovative in addressing liquidity strains but have lagged with respect to addressing solvency concerns and cross-country coordination. Central banks are providing liquidity at longer maturities and are accepting a wide range of collateral in repurchase operations, including assets for which markets have essentially ceased to operate. In addition, most countries have adopted measures to guarantee wholesale funding and provide support for recapitalizing banks deemed viable.

Asia

The impact of the global crisis on economies in Asia has been surprisingly heavy. There were many reasons to expect Asia to be relatively shielded from the crisis: unlike Europe, the region was not heavily exposed to US securitized assets; improved macroeconomic fundamentals and relatively sound bank and corporate balance sheets were expected to provide buffers. Nevertheless, since September 2008, the crisis spread quickly to Asia and dramatically affected its economies.

Japan's economy contracted at a 12 percent (annualized) rate in the fourth quarter and by 9.7 percent in the first quarter of 2009. The newly industrialized economies (Hong Kong SAR, Korea, Singapore, and Taiwan Province of China) declined at rates between 10 percent and 25 percent in the last quarter of 2008, and Southeast Asian emerging economies were badly damaged. These falls resulted mostly from the collapse in demand for consumer durable goods and capital goods in (non-Asian) advanced economies and, to a lesser degree, the deterioration in global financial conditions. Similar order of contraction was recorded in the first quarter of 2009 although growth in South Asia and China held on to positive territory. There was a strong turnaround in economic activity in China in the first quarter of 2009 with real GDP growth at 6.1 percent followed by 7.9 percent in the second quarter, 8.9 percent in the third quarter, and a robust 10.7 percent in the fourth quarter of 2009. In India, real GDP growth was placed at 5.8 percent in the first quarter of 2009, followed by 6.0 percent in the second quarter, 8.6 percent in the third quarter, and 6.5 percent in the fourth quarter.

Spillovers from the global financial crisis to domestic financial markets across Asia have also been substantial. Equity and bond prices plummeted, sovereign and corporate spreads increased, and interbank spreads rose. Real estate markets remained under pressure in a number of economies (Singapore, China). Currencies depreciated in most of the region's emerging economies, although the yen appreciated considerably since September 2008 (as carry trades have been unwound), and the renminbi remained broadly unchanged relative to the dollar. Portfolio and other flows dwindled in the fourth quarter of 2008 and early 2009, implying tighter domestic credit conditions. As a result, many banks and firms experienced serious stress (Table 4.6).

The exact channels of transmission of the external shocks and the severity of their impact varied considerably across economies. The advanced economies in the region were the hardest hit, given their greater exposure to the decline in external demand in other advanced economies, especially for automobiles, electronics, and investment goods. Given their openness and high dependence on external demand, the other advanced economies in the region—Hong Kong SAR, Korea, Singapore, Taiwan—also suffered. Among these economies, Singapore and Hong Kong SAR were particularly exposed, given their importance as

TABLE 4.6
Real GDP Growth in Asia and the Pacific

	(year-on-year percent change)		
	2008	2009	2010 *(Projections)*
Industrial Asia	**–0.2**	**–4.1**	**2.1**
Japan	–0.7	–5.2	1.9
Australia	2.4	1.3	3.0
New Zealand	0.2	–1.6	2.9
Emerging Asia	**6.8**	**5.7**	**8.5**
Newly Industrialized Economies	*1.5*	*–0.9*	*5.5*
Hong Kong	2.4	–2.7	5.0
Korea	2.2	0.2	4.5
Singapore	1.1	–2.0	8.9
Taiwan	0.1	–1.9	6.5
China	9.0	8.7	10.0
India	7.3	5.7	8.8
ASEAN-5	*4.8*	*1.7*	*5.4*
Indonesia	6.1	4.5	6.0
Malaysia	4.6	–1.7	4.7
Philippines	3.8	0.9	3.6
Thailand	2.6	–2.3	5.5
Vietnam	6.2	5.3	6.0
Emerging Asia excluding China	**4.8**	**2.6**	**6.8**
Emerging Asia excluding China and India	**3.1**	**0.4**	**5.5**
Asia	**5.1**	**3.4**	**7.1**

Source IMF, *Regional Economic Outlook: Asia and the Pacific*, April 2010, Washington D.C.

global financial centers. Vulnerable corporate and household balance sheets exacerbated the impact of external shocks in Korea.

Economies of the Association of Southeast Asian Nations (ASEAN) were severely affected by the combined effects of lower global demand and tighter credit conditions, although not as harshly as the advanced economies. Although these economies were also hurt by the drop in global trade, the composition of their exports is less concentrated in the durable goods that have been most affected by the global downturn.

Faced with a quickly deteriorating outlook, most economies aggressively loosened monetary conditions. In Japan, to address the slowdown in growth and the tightening financial conditions, the central bank cut rates to virtually zero, increased liquidity provision, broadened the range of eligible collateral, and started purchasing commercial paper and bonds to ease corporate funding pressures. In China, the central bank reduced interest rates and reserve requirements and loosened credit ceilings. In India, the policy rate and reserve requirements were cut and large liquidity injections eased pressure in money markets; foreign exchange liquidity shortages were alleviated by easing controls on capital inflows and introducing foreign exchange swaps for banks. Other central banks in the region—in Cambodia, Korea, Malaysia, the Philippines, Singapore, and Thailand—also cut policy (or other relevant) rates or decreased reserve requirements. In addition, they injected liquidity into strained money markets, drew on reserves, and boosted available liquidity buffers. Notably, Korea arranged for foreign exchange swaps with the United States, Japan, and China. Most economies in Asia had already implemented expansionary fiscal policies. The most ambitious plans had been announced in China and Japan. In Japan, the government announced a substantial new stimulus package in early April 2009 to support activity in 2009 and 2010. With the deficit projected to be close to 10 percent of GDP in 2009 and net debt to exceed 100 percent of GDP, room for additional stimulus was close to being exhausted. To preserve financial stability, some economies extended deposit guarantees (Hong Kong SAR, Malaysia, Singapore, and Thailand) or raised deposit insurance limits (Indonesia, Philippines). A number of economies announced measures to boost capital in the financial system (India, Japan) and credit support to the corporate sector (China, Korea).

Latin America and the Caribbean

The global financial crisis spread quickly to Latin American and Caribbean markets after mid-September 2008. Local equity markets sold off heavily, with the largest losses (about 25 percent) in Argentina. Domestic currencies depreciated sharply, especially in Brazil and Mexico, which are large commodity-exporting countries with flexible exchange rate regimes. Local banks' funding costs increased, particularly for small and medium-size banks. The cost of external borrowing also rose, since higher spreads on sovereign and corporate debt were only partially offset by lower yields on US Treasury bills, and capital flows to the region dwindled in the last quarter of 2008. Nonetheless, financial markets differentiated between borrowers: the cost of financing increased substantially for some countries (e.g., Argentina, Ecuador, and Venezuela) but remained relatively low for other countries with better initial positions and larger policy buffers, including Brazil, Chile, Colombia, Mexico, and Peru. Some of the latter successfully issued foreign debt in recent months.

As in the other emerging regions, financial sector stress and dele-veraging in advanced economies raised borrowing costs and reduced capital inflows across Latin America and the Caribbean. In addition, the decline in commodity prices badly affected large economies in the region—Argentina, Brazil, Chile, Mexico, and Venezuela, which are among the world's major exporters of primary products. Moreover, the economic slump in advanced economies—especially the United States, the region's largest trading partner—depressed external demand and lowered revenues from exports, tourism, and remittances. Public and private balance sheets were, however, relatively strong at the outset of the crisis in these economies, which were also less financially linked to advanced economies' banking systems.

Adverse effects on real activity did not take long to surface. The slump in commodity prices dampened growth prospects for the region's com-modity producers (mainly Argentina, Bolivia, Brazil, Chile, Colombia, Ecuador, Mexico, Peru, Trinidad and Tobago, Uruguay, and Venezuela), although it helped commodity importers in the Caribbean and Central America. Furthermore, the collapse in growth in advanced economies, particularly in the United States, lowered demand for exports, weak-ened tourism, and reduced workers' remittances—key supports in the Caribbean and Central America. With all these factors playing out, credit growth slowed abruptly, industrial production and exports collapsed, and consumer confidence plummeted across the region.

Considering the very challenging external environment, most coun-tries weathered the storm well relative to earlier experiences with global turbulence, thanks to improvements in policy frameworks and balance sheet positions. Nonetheless, real GDP contracted in 2009, before stag-ing a modest recovery in the first half of 2010. The task of monetary and exchange rate policy was particularly difficult. The region came into the crisis with relatively high inflation. For the inflation-targeting regimes, inflation was above the target ranges in all countries except Brazil. Faced with negative shocks to capital flows and demand pressure on exchange rates, central banks in these countries refrained from cutting rates until December, when Colombia's central bank lowered its policy rate. As the sharp deterioration in real activity became increasingly evident and inflation started to decelerate, the central banks of Brazil, Chile, Mexico, and Peru followed suit. Across the region, existing reserve buffers have been used to alleviate currency pressures and smooth the adjustment to the shocks.

Room for fiscal policy to mitigate the adverse effects of the external shocks differed greatly across countries with slowdowns in activity and declines in commodity prices weakening fiscal positions across the region in 2009. In countries with high external borrowing costs and large financing requirements, policymakers' ability to conduct counter-cyclical fiscal policy was limited. In other countries, existing fiscal room was already being partly used, with stimulus packages announced in a number of countries with lower debt levels, including Brazil, Chile, Mexico, and Peru.

Many countries also took steps to provide liquidity and support credit flows, especially to the corporate sector (notably in Brazil and Mexico). Several have sought IMF support, including under precautionary arrangements (Costa Rica, El Salvador), and Mexico secured access to the new Flexible Credit Line.

Commonwealth of Independent States (CIS)

Among all the regions of the global economy, the CIS experienced the largest reversal of economic fortune. Their economies were badly hit by three major shocks: the financial turbulence, which greatly curtailed access to external funding; slumping demand from advanced economies; and the related fall in commodity prices, notably for energy.

The large direct impact of the financial market turmoil on CIS economies reflected the abrupt reversal of foreign funding to their largest nonfinancial firms and, more importantly to their banking systems. Prior to the crisis, all but a few economies with less externally linked financial sectors (Azerbaijan, Tajikistan, Turkmenistan, and Uzbekistan) relied significantly on external funding to sustain domestic borrowing that far outstripped domestic demand for bonds or deposits. Soon after the crisis struck, both nonfinancial firms and banks found it very difficult to renew funding from investors, who steered clear of anything but the safest assets. Adding to the pressure, households began to switch from domestic- to foreign-currency-denominated assets. Russia, Kazakhstan, Belarus, and Ukraine were badly impacted, with the first two drawing down large amounts of foreign currency reserves to buffer the impact of the shock on the exchange rate. These economies face severe constraints on access to external financing over the near term, with the exception of Russia, which should be able to better sustain rollover rates. Belarus and Ukraine have faced difficulties meeting their external obligations and have received IMF financing; Armenia and Georgia are also receiving IMF support, although Georgia's arrangement predates the financial crisis.

The beginning of the financial crisis coincided with slumping prospects for exports and commodity prices because of rapidly weakening activity in the advanced economies. This added to the pressure faced by CIS economies with open banking systems and severely undercut growth prospects for the commodity exporters, including Russia, Kazakhstan, and Ukraine, but also the less open economies, e.g., Turkmenistan. Other countries, including the Kyrgyz Republic, Tajikistan, and Uzbekistan suffered from falling foreign remittances, particularly from migrant workers in Russia.

Prospects differ noticeably between energy exporters and importers: the former are projected to see large current account surpluses evaporate because of falling commodity prices, while the latter see a sharp narrowing of their external deficits because of tightening financing conditions. Although many CIS economies are better positioned to weather a crisis than they were in the aftermath of Russia's 1998 debt default, the fallout will nonetheless be severe. Real GDP in the region, which expanded by 8.5 percent in 2007, is expected to have contracted by 7.5 percent in 2009 before recovering to a growth of 3.8 percent in 2010. With currencies under pressure, inflation is expected to remain close to double digits in the net energy exporters, despite slowing activity. Inflation pressures are expected to recede more quickly for the net energy importers.

With most countries operating under pegged exchange rate regimes, monetary policymakers have had to choose between drawing down reserves, raising policy rates to defend pegs, and allowing exchange rates to depreciate. Countries that could afford to, including Russia and Kazakhstan, initially drew down foreign exchange reserves. Faced with very strong pressures, however, they changed their tack: Russia allowed the ruble to depreciate substantially below its earlier band and raised interest rates, while Kazakhstan opted for a step devaluation of some 18 percent. Other countries, including Ukraine and Belarus, experienced large currency depreciations early in the crisis.

Rapid currency depreciation raises the effective debt burden on nonfinancial firms that have borrowed in foreign currency. In fact, the share of foreign-currency-denominated credit in domestic bank credit stretches from close to 30 percent in Belarus and Russia, to about 50 percent in Kazakhstan and Ukraine, and to some 70 percent in Georgia. As exchange rates depreciated, meeting these foreign currency obligations required major cutbacks in investment and employment in several of these economies. By the same token, defaults further exacerbated already intense strains on bank balance sheets and diminished prospects for renewed credit growth.

Countries whose banking sectors struggled with the need to rollover foreign debt—e.g., Belarus, Georgia, Kazakhstan, Russia, and Ukraine—deployed remedial measures. These include provision by the central banks of ample liquidity, public guarantees, funding for recapitalization (including from international financial institutions), and nationalization. It will be crucial to carefully assess bank balance sheets with a view to writing off bad assets in a proactive manner, determining which banks have sound medium-run prospects, and replenishing their capital as needed, drawing on budgetary resources rather than central bank support.

With significant public support needed for banks and difficult conditions in capital markets, room for fiscal policy stimulus is limited in most CIS countries. Belarus and Ukraine have needed to tighten. Georgia and the Kyrgyz Republic can afford to let automatic stabilizers work, provided sufficient donor support is forthcoming. Azerbaijan, Kazakhstan, Russia, and Uzbekistan—all of which posted fiscal surpluses ahead of the crisis—have allowed automatic stabilizers to operate and have eased fiscal policy to sustain growth.

Africa

Relatively weak financial linkages with advanced economies did not shield African countries from the global economic storm. The main shock buffeting the continent was severe deterioration in external growth, which reduced demand for African exports and curtailed workers' remittances. The sharp fall in commodity prices also hurt the resource-rich countries in the region. Moreover, the tightening of global credit conditions adversely affected FDI and reversed portfolio flows, especially to emerging and frontier markets (Ghana, Kenya, Nigeria,

South Africa, and Tunisia). These external shocks caused a severe slow-down in economic activity. For the region as a whole, growth declined from 5.5 percent in 2008 to 1.1 percent in 2009, but picked up to 4.3 percent in 2010 as the global environment improves. On average, the downturn was most pronounced in oil-exporting countries (Angola, Equatorial Guinea) and in key emerging and frontier market economies (Botswana, Mauritius, South Africa), which suffered from all three shocks that affected the continent. South Africa's economy, e.g., con-tracted by about 0.25 percent in 2009, its lowest growth rate in a decade, with capital outflows forcing a sharp adjustment in asset prices (mainly in equity, bond, and currency markets) and in real activity.

The deep downturn in economic activity across the region and the sharp decline in food and fuel prices tempered inflation pressures and will likely continue to do so in the months ahead. Nevertheless, for the region as a whole, inflation is projected to decrease only gradually, since the pass-through of commodity price changes to consumer prices is more limited than in advanced economies.

Fiscal and external balances deteriorated substantially and are likely to remain weak. As commodity-based revenues dwindled, the overall fiscal position of the region deteriorated by about 5.8 percentage points to a deficit of 4.5 percent of GDP in 2009. This is mainly as a result of a large swing in the fiscal balances of some oil-exporting countries (Angola, Republic of Congo, Equatorial Guinea, and Nigeria). The cur-rent account balance of the region worsened to a deficit of 6.5 percent of GDP in 2009. Again, the deterioration was most pronounced for many commodity exporters (Algeria, Angola, Gabon, Equatorial Guinea, and Nigeria), as both export volumes and prices suffer. With global credit conditions remaining tight, the financing of external deficits is expected to remain strained in a number of emerging and frontier markets (Ghana, Nigeria, South Africa, and Tanzania) going forward.

Against this backdrop, the key priority for policymakers is to contain the adverse impact of the crisis on economic growth and poverty, while preserving the hard-won gains of recent years, including macroeconomic stability and debt sustainability, through fiscal policy to the extent pos-sible with monetary and exchange rate policy playing a supportive role. Even in countries with less exchange rate flexibility—in the West African Economic Monetary Union (WAEMU)[3] and the Economic Union of Central African Countries (CEMAC),[4] for instance—there could be some limited room for policy easing, falling inflation, weakening demand, and existing reserve buffers. In this regard, the new facility set up by the central bank in the WAEMU area has been helpful in alleviating the liquidity squeeze in domestic markets.

In the financial sector, given the potential for knock-on effects from the slowdown in real activity, monitoring closely the balance sheets of financial institutions and preparing to act promptly if necessary assumes importance. Although a number of countries have policy room to maneuver, others face very tight external and domestic financing constraints. For the latter group, additional donor support is critical to limit the social fallout of the crisis and preserve the hard-won gains in macroeconomic stability.

Middle East

The global crisis did not spare the Middle East. The extremely large fall in the price of oil was the main shock. The deterioration in external financing conditions and reversal of capital inflows took their toll: local property and equity markets came under intense pressure across the region, domestic liquidity conditions deteriorated, credit spreads soared for some firms, financial system strains emerged in a number of countries, and sovereign wealth funds suffered losses from investments in global markets. Furthermore, the substantial decline in external demand (including from countries in the Gulf region) dampened export growth, workers' remittances, and tourism revenues (Egypt, Jordan, and Lebanon).

Although highly expansionary policies were set to mitigate the impact, these adverse shocks are expected to have prolonged severe negative effects on economic activity. In the region as a whole, growth declined from 5.3 percent in 2008 to 2.2 percent in 2009. The slowdown in growth was broadly similar in oil-producing and non-oil-producing countries, even though the forces behind it were quite different. Among the oil-producing countries, the sharpest slowdown was in the United Arab Emirates (UAE), where the exit of external funds (which had entered the country on speculation of a currency revaluation) contributed to a large contraction in liquidity, a sizable fall in property and equity prices, and substantial pressure in the banking system. A major financial center, UAE also suffered from the contraction in global finance and merger and acquisition activity. At the other end of the spectrum is Qatar, which grew by an estimated 18 percent in 2009 (up from 16.5 percent in 2008), since its production of natural gas doubled. Among the non-oil-producing countries, Lebanon experienced the steepest slowdown, as difficult external liquidity conditions raised the cost of debt servicing and the downturn in the Gulf reduced remittances.

For the region as a whole going forward, inflation pressures are contingent upon commodity prices, rents, and economic activity. The current account balance of the region is expected to swing into a small deficit in 2009–10. With dwindling surpluses in oil producing countries, fiscal balances are set to deteriorate substantially, as revenues decline and governments use the buffers accumulated during the recent boom to sustain domestic demand by maintaining ongoing investment projects.

In many countries, high government expenditures filled the void left by the retrenchment of private sector activity (Kuwait, Libya, Oman, Qatar, and Saudi Arabia) and will be essential for growth in the entire region. Regarding monetary policy, central banks across the region reacted appropriately by providing liquidity, cutting reserve requirements, and lowering interest rates (Egypt, Jordan, Kuwait, Saudi Arabia, and UAE). In this respect, countries with pegged exchange rates (Bahrain, Kuwait, Libya, Oman, Qatar, Saudi Arabia, Syrian Arab Republic, and UAE) benefited from the continued monetary easing in the United States. In the financial sector, pressures built to varying degrees across the region, owing to banks' credit exposure to slumping property and stock markets and tightening external liquidity conditions. In countries that were most affected, policy responses were relatively swift, with authorities implementing a myriad of measures to shore up confidence and prevent a systemic banking crisis. These included introducing blanket deposit insurance (Kuwait and UAE), providing liquidity, and injecting capital into banks (Qatar, Saudi Arabia, and UAE).

Estimates of Losses from the Crisis

The estimation of the financial loss from the banking crisis has been a difficult task. Besides, with the unfolding of the crisis, the loss estimates too underwent significant revision. Looking first at the banking system, the IMF staff estimates, reported in the April 2008 *Global Financial Stability Report*, suggested that potential losses to banks from exposure to the US subprime mortgage market and from related structured securities, as well as losses on other US credit classes such as consumer and corporate loans, could be on the order of US$440–510 billion out of total potential losses of US$945 billion. Subsequently this underwent significant revision. The April 2010 *Global Financial Stability Report* (*GFSR*) of the IMF estimated that losses on US-based loans and securities may rise to some US$1.2 trillion. Including assets originated in other mature market economies, total write-downs could reach US$2.3 trillion (down from US$2.8 trillion as estimated in October 2009) over the period 2007–10 (Table 4.7). Subsequently, in October 2010, IMF's estimate of total bank write-downs and loan provisions between 2007 and 2010 underwent further revision and falling from US$2.3 trillion in the April 2010 to US$2.2 trillion, driven mainly by an 11 percent fall in securities losses.

The crisis generated a process of deleveraging[5] which led to a credit crunch and with the potential to exacerbate the global recessionary trend. Two immediate implications of the crisis may be noted in particular. First, raising new capital for the banking sector became important to repair troubled balance sheets. Second, the most serious risk going forward is an intensifying adverse feedback loop between the financial system and the real economy. Through this process, financial institutions' distress leads to impaired credit intermediation and slower economic growth which, in turn, leads to further credit deterioration.

Inflation Scenario

The slump in global demand led to a collapse in commodity prices in the peak of the crisis. Despite production cutbacks and geopolitical tensions, oil prices declined by over 60 percent since their peak in July 2008. Commodity prices rose strongly during the early stages of the recovery in 2009, despite generally high inventories. To a large extent, this was due to the buoyant recovery in emerging Asia, the onset of recovery in other emerging and developing economies more generally, and the improvement in global financial conditions. Looking ahead, commodity prices are expected to rise further, supported by the strength of global demand, especially from emerging economies. However, this upward pressure may be cushioned by the above-average inventory levels and substantial spare capacity in many commodity sectors. In the advanced economies, headline inflation was expected to pick up from 0.1 percent in 2009 to 1.3 percent in 2010, as rebounding energy prices more than offset

TABLE 4.7
Estimates of Global Bank Write-downs by Domicile (2007–10)

(in billions of US dollars)

	Estimated holding (billions of US$)	Estimated write-downs in Oct 2009 (billions of US$)	Estimated write-downs in April 2010 (billions of US$)	Share of total write-downs in April 2010 (%)
1 US Banks				
1.1 Loans	8,059	654	588	66.5
1.2 Securities	4,502	371	296	33.5
1.3 Total for Loans and Securities	**12,561**	**1,025**	**885**	**100.0**
2 UK Banks				
2.1 Loans	6,744	497	398	87.5
2.2 Securities	1,625	107	57	12.5
2.3 Total for Loans and Securities	**8,369**	**604**	**455**	**100.0**
3 Euro Area Banks				
3.1 Loans	15,994	480	442	66.4
3.2 Securities	6,907	333	224	33.6
3.3 Total for Loans and Securities	**22,901**	**814**	**665**	**100.0**
4 Other Mature Europe Banks				
4.1 Loans	3,241	165	134	86.0
4.2 Securities	729	36	22	14.0
4.3 Total for Loans and Securities	**3,970**	**201**	**156**	**100.0**

(Table 4.7 continued)

(Table 4.7 continued)

(in billions of US dollars)

	Estimated holding (billions of US$)	Estimated write-downs in Oct 2009 (billions of US$)	Estimated write-downs in April 2010 (billions of US$)	Share of total write-downs in April 2010 (%)
5 Asian Banks				
5.1 Loans	6,150	97	84	73.5
5.2 Securities	1,728	69	30	26.5
5.3 Total for Loans and Securities	**7,879**	**166**	**115**	**100.0**
6 Grand Totals				
6.1 Grand Total for Loans	40,189	1,893	1,647	72.4
6.2 Grand Total for Securities	15,491	916	629	27.6
6.3 Grand Total for Loans and Securities	**55,680**	**2,809**	**2,276**	**100.0**

Source IMF, *Global Financial Stability Report*, April 2010, Washington D.C.

slowing labor costs. In emerging and developing economies, inflation is expected to have edged up to 6.2 percent in 2010 from 5.2 percent a year ago, as some of these economies faced growing upward pressures due to more limited economic slack and increased capital flows. These inflation prospects are best evaluated against the backdrop of trends in pre-crisis years (Chart 4.1).

CHART 4.1
Global Trends in Inflation

HeadLine Inflation

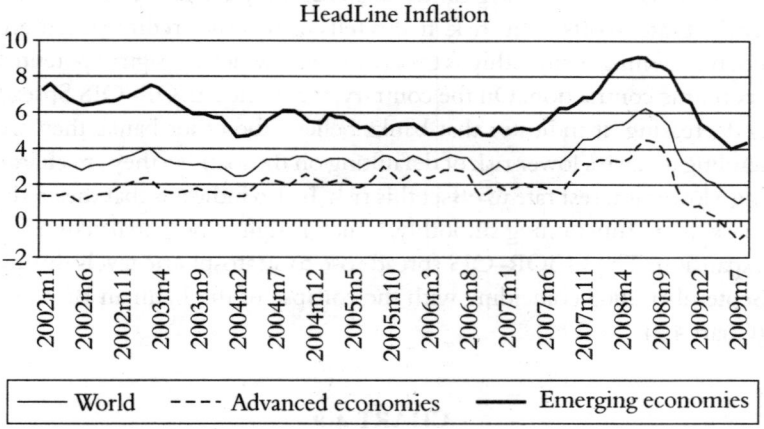

Core Inflation

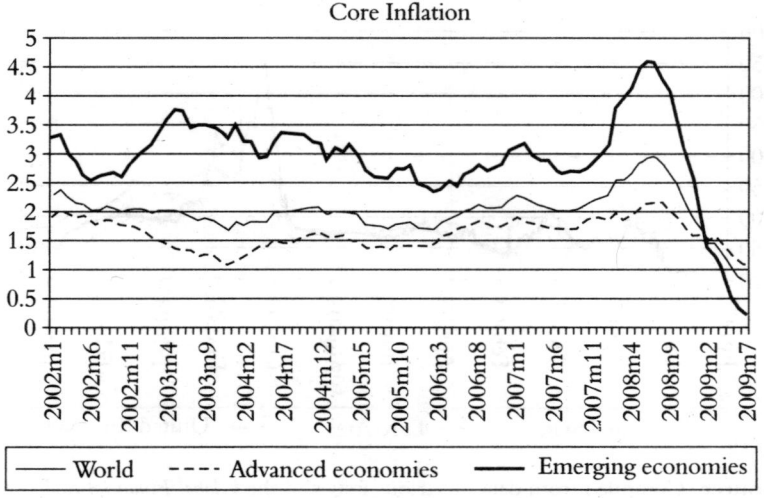

Source Compiled from IMF, *World Economic Outlook* database, Washington D.C.

Impact on Financial Markets

Money Markets

The LIBOR–OIS spread (difference) is a comparison between the London Interbank Offered Rate (LIBOR) and the overnight index swap (OIS) rate. When the LIBOR–OIS spread is increasing, it is indicative of the fact that banks believe the other banks they are lending to have a higher risk of defaulting on the loans so they are charging a higher interest rate to offset this risk. It also tells us that the credit markets are not functioning as smoothly as they could be—which is a sign of potential economic contraction. On the contrary, when the LIBOR–OIS Spread is decreasing, it indicates that banks believe the other banks they are lending to have a lower risk of defaulting on the loans so they are charging a lower interest rate to offset this risk. It also indicates that the credit markets are functioning smoothly, which is sign of potential economic expansion. The LIBOR–OIS spread rose to stratospheric levels during September 2008 coinciding with the collapse of the Lehman Brothers (Chart 4.2).

CHART 4.2
LIBOR–OIS Spread (Three-month, Basis Points)

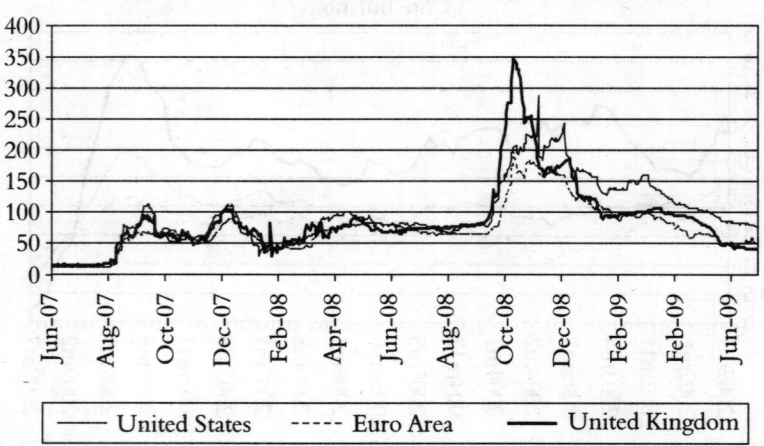

Source Compiled from data in various issues of the *Global Financial Stability Report*, IMF, Washington D.C.

Credit Default Swap (CDS) Spreads

Another way to assess the status of the credit market is through the "spread" on a CDS.[6] This spread indicates the annual amount the protection buyer must pay the protection seller over the length of the contract, expressed as a percentage of the notional amount. All things being equal, at any given time, if the maturity of two CDSs is the same, then the company with a *higher* CDS spread is considered *more likely* to default by the market, since a higher fee is being charged to protect against this happening. However, factors such as liquidity and estimated loss given default can impact the comparison. Credit spread rates and credit ratings of the underlying or reference obligations are considered among money managers to be the best indicators of the likelihood of sellers of CDSs to have to perform under these contracts. While the CDS spreads seem to have come down from the abnormal levels witnessed during September 2008, they are still elevated relative to normal levels (Chart 4.3).

Bank Lending Conditions

The crisis became almost synonymous with the process of deleveraging, whereby the commercial banks almost stopped lending due to its fear of counterparty risks and the resultant loss of faith. While there have

CHART 4.3
10-year Median Bank Credit Default Swap (CDS) Spreads
(in basis points)

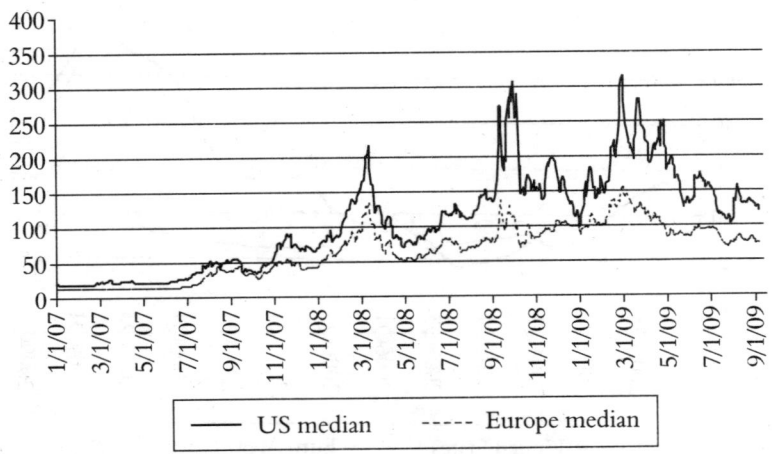

Source IMF, *World Economic Outlook*, October 2009, Washington D.C.

been steep declines in credit growth in bank credit to private sector since mid-2008 in the advanced economies, this is perhaps best captured in terms of lending market conditions in terms of the survey data. Chart 4.4 depicts the percentage of respondents describing lending standards as tightening "considerably" or "somewhat" minus those indicating standards as easing "considerably" or "somewhat" over the previous three months.[7] There has been sharp decline in the lending conditions since mid-2008—the turnaround is protracted.

Equity Markets

As expected, the impact of the global financial crisis was felt most in the equity market with equity prices all over the world fell steeply. New securities issues came to a virtual stop with curtailing of bank-related flow (Chart 4.5).

Key Issues and Challenges

In order to understand the magnitude of the crisis, its pervasiveness and, therefore, its uniqueness across space and time, it is worthwhile sifting

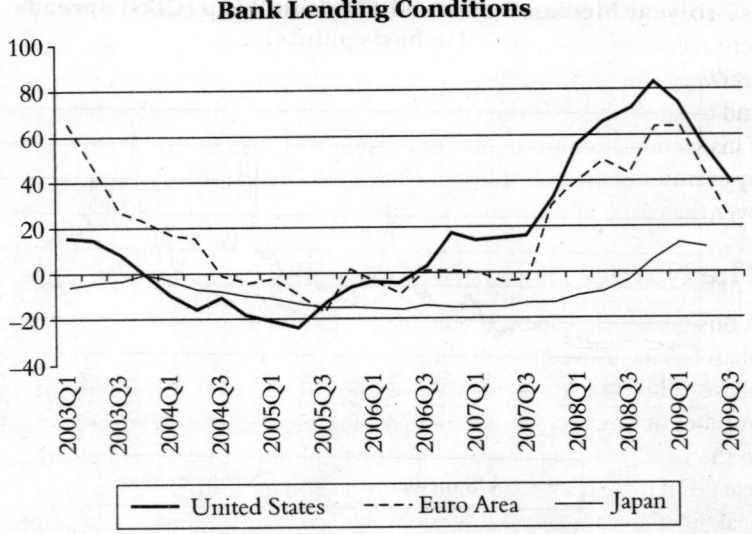

CHART 4.4
Bank Lending Conditions

——— United States   - - - - Euro Area   ——— Japan

Source IMF, *World Economic Outlook*, October 2009.

CHART 4.5
Performance of the Equity Markets (1/1/2007=100)[8]

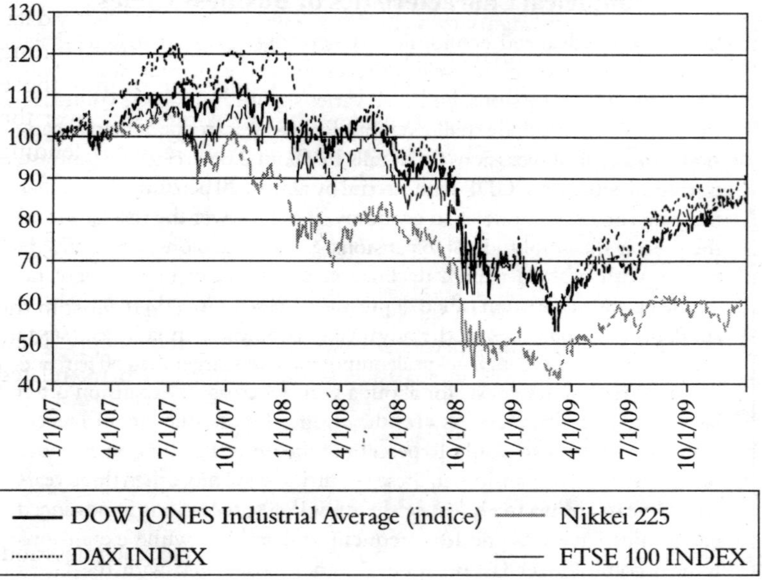
130
120
110
100
90
80
70
60
50
40
1/1/07
4/1/07
7/1/07
10/1/07
1/1/08
4/1/08
7/1/08
10/1/08
1/1/09
4/1/09
7/1/09
10/1/09
DOW JONES Industrial Average (indice)
Nikkei 225
DAX INDEX
FTSE 100 INDEX

Source Bloomberg.

through some of the key aspects that set it apart. This crisis is a downturn associated with a financial crisis. It is globally synchronized. The current recession is widely regarded as unusually long and severe and the recovery sluggish. Countercyclical policies have been unconventional and as spectacular as the crisis itself. So is this crisis different or not? This section attempts to put the current cycle in a historical perspective by examining the available evidence on the dynamics of business cycles over the past half century.[9]

The Nature of Business Cycles

A business cycle is typically divided into two main phases: a recession phase, characterized by a decline in economic activity, and an expansion phase. There are three main properties of the cycle: (*a*) duration: the number of quarters from peak to trough in a recession, or from trough to the next peak in an expansion; (*b*) amplitude: the percent change in real GDP from peak-to-trough in a recession, or from trough to the next peak in an expansion; and (*c*) slope: the ratio of amplitude to duration, which indicates the steepness of each cyclical phase (Box 4.3).

BOX 4.3
Empirical Characteristics of Business Cycles

On average, advanced economies—where this crisis emanated—have experienced six complete cycles of recession and expansion since 1960. The number of recessions, however, varies significantly across countries. Recessions are distinctly shallower, briefer, and less frequent than expansions. In a typical recession, GDP falls by about 2.8 percent. In contrast, during an expansion, GDP tends to rise by almost 20 percent. The higher the long run growth rate of an economy, the shallower the recession and the greater the amplitude of expansions. Some recessions, however, are severe, with peak-to-trough declines in output exceeding 10 percent. These episodes are often called depressions. Since 1960, there have been six depression episodes in the advanced economies. In contrast, some expansions witness trough-to-peak output increases larger than 50 percent. A typical recession persists for about a year, whereas an expansion often lasts more than five years. As a result, advanced economies are in a recession phase of the cycle only 10 percent of the time. The longest episodes of recessions and expansions in these countries lasted more than three years and 15 years, respectively. Since the mid-1980s, recessions in advanced economies have become less frequent and milder, while expansions have become longer lasting, a development associated with the Great Moderation. A host of factors may explain this, including global integration, improvements in financial markets, changes in the composition of aggregate output toward the service sector and away from manufacturing, and better macroeconomic policies (Blanchard and Simon 2001). An economy typically recovers to its previous peak output in less than a year. Recoveries are also typically steeper than recessions—the average growth per quarter during a recovery exceeds the rate of contraction during a recession by more than 25 percent.

Recessions associated with financial crises are observed to be typically severe and protracted, whereas recoveries from recessions associated with financial crises have typically been slower, held back by weak private demand and credit. In addition, highly synchronized recession episodes are longer and deeper than other recessions, and recoveries from these recessions are typically weak. Moreover, developments in the United States are found to play a pivotal role both in the severity and duration of these highly synchronized recessions. Although recessions have become less common overall during the Great Moderation, those associated with financial crises have become more common.

Financial crises have often been associated with credit booms involving overheated goods and labor markets, house price booms, and, frequently, a

(Box 4.3 continued)

(Box 4.3 continued)

loss of external competitiveness. Relative to other expansions, labor market participation is high, nominal wage growth is high, and unemployment is low. Credit booms have frequently followed financial deregulation. There is some evidence of asset price bubbles. Rapid credit growth has typically been associated with shifts in household saving rates and a deterioration of the quality of balance sheets. However, after a financial crisis strikes, saving rates increase substantially, especially during recessions. These stylized features suggest that expansions associated with financial crises may be driven by overly optimistic expectations for growth in income and wealth. Turning to the recovery phase, the weakness in private demand tends to persist in upswings that follow recessions associated with financial crises. Private consumption typically grows more slowly than during other recoveries. Private investment continues to decline after the recession trough; in particular, residential investment typically takes two years merely to stop declining. The unemployment rate continues to rise by more than usual. Credit growth is faltering, whereas in other recoveries it is steady and strong.

Source   Reinhart and Rogoff (2009).

The downturn was global and highly synchronized. Evidence from past synchronized recessions suggests that they are longer and deeper than others: the average duration (amplitude) of a synchronous recession is 40–45 percent greater than that of other recessions. There are other distinctive features of highly synchronized recessions as well. They are severe and recoveries are, on average, very slow, with output taking 50 percent longer to recover to its previous peak than after other recessions. Credit growth is also weak in contrast to recoveries from non-synchronous recessions, during which credit and investment recover rapidly. As with financial crises, investment and asset prices continue to decline after the trough in GDP. However, a key difference from the recoveries following localized financial crises is that net trade is much weaker. When compared with non-synchronous recessions, exports are typically more sluggish in synchronous recessions. The United States has often been at the center of synchronous recessions, causing significant contractions in world trade and strong external effects on credit and equity prices. Recessions that are associated with both financial crises and global downturns have been unusually severe and long-lasting.

Across all types of recessions, there is evidence that expansionary monetary policy is typically associated with shorter recessions, whereas expansionary fiscal policy is not. However, during recessions associated with financial crises, both expansionary fiscal and monetary policies tend to shorten the duration of recessions. In particular, increases in government consumption, and reductions in both nominal and real interest rates. The stronger impact of fiscal policy in these events is consistent with evidence that fiscal policy is more effective when economic agents face tighter liquidity constraints. However, the aggressive use of discretionary fiscal policy raises concern about the sustainability of public finances. The degree of public indebtedness reduces the effectiveness of fiscal policy. The effectiveness of monetary and fiscal policies is substantially reduced without the implementation of prompt and well-targeted financial policies. Financial sector support typically entails fiscal costs. However, a substantial part of the upfront gross cost is usually recovered, through asset sales, over the medium-term.

Lessons from the Recession and Prospects for Recovery

The global crisis was caused by a breakdown in the financial system in the wake of a massive housing and credit bubble. As observed in the foregoing, downturns caused by financial crises play out differently. The machinery of the financial system grinds to a halt; people cannot get credit to buy things and businesses cannot borrow money to expand. An analysis of 14 financial crises around the world has shown that the unemployment rate rises an average of seven percentage points in a downturn (Reinhart and Rogoff 2009). Moreover, downturns driven by financial crisis have been found to last an average of 4.8 years—this one is at the two-year point. Growth spurts can emerge, and it appears increasingly likely that the US economy will grow at a solid pace in the first half of 2010, as companies restock depleted inventories. But it is unclear what would come after that. Given the ongoing restrictions on credit, US banks have sustained massive losses already, and a wave of soured commercial real estate loans threatens to further limit their ability to lend in the year ahead. A bigger problem looms outside of banks—in credit markets, which account for vast chunks of mortgage lending, consumer loans, and commercial real estate loans. This shadow banking system remains dysfunctional—notwithstanding a slew of programs the Fed put in place to get it going again. All that makes it more expensive for people or businesses to borrow money—if they can get a loan at all—which could serve as a powerful brake on any recovery. Credit fuels housing and consumer durable goods. It fuels business investment. It is in every part of the economy. Credit makes recessions after a financial crisis longer, and all the signs are that it is happening this time as well.

The financial crisis and recession reversed a 30-year trend, carrying Americans toward a high point in debt. The ratio of consumer debt to the nation's total economic output rose to 97 percent in the first quarter of 2009 from 45 percent in 1975. Currently, Americans are saving more and paying down debt; the saving rate was 1.2 percent of disposable income in early 2008. By the second quarter of 2009, that rose to 5.2 percent. Savings has to go much higher, and that is going to slow growth of consumption even once incomes start growing (Roubini and Mihm 2010). Every dollar that Americans save is one fewer dollar for consumption, which means less economic output. When the saving rate goes up by a percentage point, spending decreases by more than US$100 billion, according to the McKinsey Global Institute. What held Japan back in the 1990s was that firms there wanted to pay down debts and so they saved more.

When nations in financial crisis defied the trend and experienced a rapid recovery, it was often because of strength elsewhere in the world. East Asian economies rebounded nicely from their 1997–98 financial crisis, for example, on the back of exports to the United States—which had a booming economy at the time. The silver lining is that the US economy has proven its resilience in the past, emerging out of deep downturns with force. There is only one reliable regularity in business cycle history in the United States—"deep recessions are followed by steep recoveries and economic forecasts almost never take account of this regularity" (Mussa 2009).

Will US Recovery Go Global?

The economic collapse has been global. No recovery can succeed unless it, too, is global (Samuelson 2009). The world can no longer rely for growth on free-spending Americans, who are overburdened by debt and sobered by trillions of dollars of losses on homes and stocks. Without a substitute for American buying, any global revival will be feeble, because the United States needs export-led growth and other countries must somehow offset their lost sales to the US market. Developing countries would seem to be the obvious replacement for American spending as the world's economic motor. These countries already account for nearly half of global economic output, according to the IMF—China (11.4 percent), India (4.8 percent), and Brazil (2.9 percent) alone represent nearly a fifth. By comparison, the United States is also a fifth. All these societies have huge needs for housing, consumer goods, health care, and more. Logically, these countries should produce more for themselves and less for export. Stronger domestic spending would also increase their demand for imports. As a result, the United States would export more and import less. What economists call "global imbalances"—big US trade deficits matched by big surpluses in China and elsewhere—would shrink. World economic growth would revive.

Just possibly, this transformation is starting. Other countries have stimulated their economies, most conspicuously China. Government spending increased; credit eased. China expanded at an impressive 7.7 percent rate in 2009. Fast growth has also re-emerged in Indonesia and South Korea. India grew by 7.2 percent in 2009 and expects even faster growth in 2010. Brazil's long-term prospects are good with a strong industrial base and energetic and creative entrepreneurs. Government debt has dropped from 85 percent of GDP in 2002 to 65 percent now. Even France and Germany have shown signs of recovery.

If Americans are spending less and saving more, then a balanced global economy requires people elsewhere to spend more and save less. That is the permanent fix, not repeated bursts of temporary economic stimulus. The large trade imbalances fundamentally stemmed from high saving rates, especially in Asia, that dampened domestic spending and encouraged export-led growth. In 2008, China's saving rate was an astounding 54 percent of GDP, Hong Kong's 35 percent, and Taiwan's 28 percent. The US saving rate, including both households and businesses, was 12 percent of GDP. In theory, these vast savings could be absorbed by equal amounts of investment spending—on factories, machinery—but for most Asian countries (an exception: India), there was an investment shortfall. The surplus savings were then invested abroad, exchange rates were artificially depressed, and exports substituted for domestic demand. China is the key country in any transition. It is trying to boost domestic spending by decreasing household saving and by rebuilding the social safety nets. Since 2005, spending on health insurance, pensions, and education has roughly doubled. There are, undoubtedly, mixed sentiments on the role of exchange rate adjustment in this rebalancing effort.

The Main Risks

Prospects for the global economy remain exceptionally uncertain at this stage even with the recovery visible. The overarching risk is that of further delays in implementing policies to stabilize financial conditions, intensifying the negative feedback loops between the real economy and the financial system. With policy rates already near the zero bound in many instances, monetary authorities have limited capacity to counteract deflationary pressures. Second, there is a serious risk that emerging economies will be unable to secure external financing. Risks are largest for emerging economies that rely on cross-border flows to finance current account deficits or to fund the activities of their financial or corporate sectors. Third, trade and financial protectionism is a rising concern. It is, therefore, useful to balance the analysis with recognition of the key risks and challenges.

Financial market risks

Financial market risks remain acute. Notwithstanding forceful policy efforts, markets remain under stress and the threat of disorderly deleveraging remains a serious risk to the outlook. Concerns remain high about the solvency of financial institutions in mature markets faced with rising losses, tight funding conditions, and dwindling capital bases. Low bank capital remains a serious issue, especially because asset sales could imply greater loss recognition and because weakening activity is likely to push up losses on a broad range of assets in the United States and Europe. A related concern is that the process of deleveraging and balance sheet repair could be deeper and more extended than projected, implying that credit constraints on growth could be greater than currently envisaged. Moreover, prospects for raising capital are highly uncertain, particularly in light of the large losses suffered by equity holders in recent resolutions and continuing uncertainty over valuation. Emerging economies are highly vulnerable to turbulence in advanced financial markets. Intensified or extended deleveraging in US or European banks or growing risk aversion among investors could prompt a further scaling back of bank and portfolio flows to emerging economies.

Risks to domestic demand

Downside risks to domestic demand in advanced economies remain clearly evident. Related to the financial risks just discussed is the threat of deeper and more prolonged housing corrections. The real possibility remains that US housing prices and activity will not find the projected bottom in 2010–11, and instead will overshoot, in the context of still-depressed sentiment. In Western Europe, housing market prospects are uncertain, and dynamics could be affected by financial deleveraging that restricts the supply of mortgage financing. Thus, existing downturns could intensify, and a broader range of countries could experience house price declines, a sharp reduction in residential investment, and greater strains on household balance sheets.

Risks to domestic demand in the emerging economies are now distinctly to the downside. The principal concerns for these economies are external—exposure to slower global trade, tighter external financing conditions, and adverse terms-of-trade shocks—but domestic demand also could be adversely affected by deteriorating conditions in financial markets and by corrections in housing markets. Countries that have allowed easy access to external financing and buoyant commodity-related revenues to drive rapid growth in domestic credit and strong growth in government spending are at particular risk of a "sudden stop" in capital inflows that could have a damaging impact on domestic financial conditions and apply a sharp knock to domestic demand.

Inflation risks

Inflation risks initially receded as commodity prices retreated and slowing growth reduced pressure on capacity. Concern remains, however, that wages could accelerate in response to the loss in purchasing power from higher food and fuel prices if activity does not slow as projected, particularly in Western Europe, where employment remains low by recent standards. Inflation risks are manifesting themselves in a number of emerging and developing economies, amid signs that higher commodity prices and increasing pressure on local supply conditions are already spilling into wage demands and inflation expectations. The concern is that once inflation expectations become unanchored, central banks may be forced to tighten abruptly to generate a "hard landing"—a period of sub-trend growth—in order to bring inflation back in line. Besides, there could be differing inflation risks as between advanced and emerging/developing countries, with the start of monetary exit in some of the latter.

Risks from oil prices

Given the likely continued volatility, oil prices are an important source of two-way risks to the projections. Option market data suggest that market participants are operating with an unusually wide band of uncertainty about the future price, with outcomes from US$60 a barrel to US$165 a barrel falling within the 90 percent confidence band. On the upside, oil prices could decline, providing some stabilizing benefit to the global economy, although such an occurrence would most likely be associated with weakening global demand rather than a positive supply shock, with a correspondingly lower multiplier. The more likely scenario is that further supply shocks could again push oil prices up, in the context of continued limited spare capacity, keeping pressure on consumer purchasing power, particularly in oil-importing countries, and limiting the relief to headline inflation from stabilizing oil prices built into the baseline.

Risks from global imbalances

Global imbalances remain an issue, even as the sources of risk are shifting. In the past, the central concern was the possibility of a disorderly unwinding of the imbalances driven by a discontinuous shift in foreign investors' willingness to continue financing the large US current account deficit and add to the share of US assets in their wealth portfolios. Such risks have moderated somewhat as the US dollar's depreciation has brought it closer in line with medium-term fundamentals and the US current account deficit is moving onto a more sustainable trajectory. Still, rising oil prices have slowed the adjustment process as the US oil deficit has jumped, and US net foreign liabilities are still projected as a rising share of global GDP. Moreover, reduced confidence in the liquidity and risk-return characteristics of US assets in the wake of the financial crisis mean that the risk of disorderly unwinding cannot be discounted. At the same time, three other types of concern have become salient. The first is that the adjustment of the dollar has been concentrated in a number of flexibly managed currencies while certain major currencies continue to be tightly managed or pegged to the US dollar. This situation could create new imbalances over time, for example, in the Euro Area, whose currency is now somewhat overvalued. Second, the sustained rise in international oil prices has increased the need to ensure the stable recycling of exporters' large surpluses. Allowing current account surpluses to increase is a reasonable response by oil exporters, reflecting their desire to save some of the additional revenues. The third concern is that continuing large trade deficits combined with weakening employment prospects in some advanced economies could prompt rising trade protectionism. Such concerns are heightened by the recent deadlock in the Doha Round of multilateral trade negotiations.

According to current projections made by the IMF, global imbalances are expected to ease moderately over 2010–14 with the US current account deficit projected to decline to 0.6 percent of GDP. On the other hand, deficit running countries could contribute more to global imbalances than before, especially China, oil exporters, and surplus running European countries (Table 4.8).

Policy Challenges

Policymakers around the world today face the imperative of stabilizing global financial markets, while nursing their economies through a global downturn and tight credit and ensuring that the recent rise in inflation is reversed. While these are the immediate priorities, work must also progress on tackling the market and regulatory flaws that have contributed to recent stresses. Financial markets and institutions must be placed on a healthier footing and supply–demand responses in commodity markets strengthened. Continued commitment to trade and financial integration of the global economy remains essential to underpin longer-term growth prospects.

For *financial sector policies*, the restoration of financial sector stability and market trust is crucial, based on: (i) credible loss recognition, particularly the valuation of troubled assets; (ii) provision of necessary public support for resolution of distressed assets and recapitalization; (iii) greater international cooperation; and (iv) a long-term vision of a healthy, efficient, and dynamic financial system. In the context of rapidly rising financing constraints, steps to ensure adequate provision of liquidity would help to reduce risks that a shortfall of foreign capital generates

TABLE 4.8
Average Current Account Balances: Past, Present, and Future

(as % of world GDP)

	1996–2000	2001–04	2005–08	2009 (Forecast)	2010–14 (Forecast)
United States	-0.8	-1.4	-1.4	-0.6	-0.6
Europe Deficit (Peripheral Europe)	-0.1	-0.4	-0.8	-0.5	-0.5
Rest of the World	-0.3	0.0	-0.3	-0.4	-0.4
China	0.1	0.1	0.6	0.6	0.9
Emerging Asia	0.1	0.2	0.2	0.3	0.2
Japan	0.3	0.3	0.3	0.2	0.2
Oil Exporters	0.2	0.4	1.0	0.3	0.7
Europe Surplus (Core Europe)	0.2	0.4	0.7	0.4	0.5
Discrepancy	-0.3	-0.3	0.4	0.2	0.9

Source Blanchard and Milesi-Ferretti (2009).

Notes 1. Europe surplus: Austria, Belgium, Denmark, Finland, Germany, Luxembourg, Netherlands, Sweden, and Switzerland.

2. Europe deficit: Greece, Ireland, Italy, Portugal, Spain, United Kingdom, Bulgaria, Czech Republic, Estonia, Hungary, Latvia, Lithuania, Poland, Romania, Slovak Republic, Turkey, and Ukraine.

3. Emerging Asia: Hong Kong S.A.R. of China, Indonesia, Korea, Malaysia, Philippines, Singapore, Taiwan province of China, and Thailand.

4. Oil exporters: Algeria, Angola, Azerbaijan, Bahrain, Republic of Congo, Ecuador, Equatorial Guinea, Gabon, Iran, Kazakhstan, Kuwait, Libya, Nigeria, Norway, Oman, Qatar, Russia, Saudi Arabia, Sudan, Syria, Trinidad and Tobago, United Arab Emirates, Venezuela, and Yemen.

5. Rest of the world: remaining countries.

solvency problems. Emerging economies should prepare, on a contingent basis, plans to address the growing risks of large-scale corporate failures with a strengthening of corporate workout frameworks.

The conduct of *monetary policy* and clear communication should assure markets of continued accommodation in stance until sustained recovery takes hold. This would be critical to guide expectations of future rates and inflation, and reduce deflation risks. With credit intermediation impaired, central banks will need to increasingly rely on unconventional measures to stimulate economic activity—direct central bank support of funding markets such as for commercial paper and asset backed securities or extending loans directly to the nonfinancial sector. In emerging economies, monetary authorities face a sharp dilemma. While slumping demand justifies monetary easing, increasing risks to external stability in the context of rising external financial constraints and inflation pressures argue for a halt in rate cuts and even for a tightening of monetary policy in some cases.

With constraints on the effectiveness of monetary policy, *fiscal policy* must play a central role in supporting demand, while remaining consistent with medium-term sustainability. The overall stimulus being provided by G-20 countries is placed at 1.8 percent of GDP in 2009 and 1.3 percent in 2010, well short of the 2 percent of GDP recommended by the IMF. At current levels, there is a negative discretionary impulse of 0.5 percent of GDP over both years. Differences in the size of the stimulus across countries are on account of the size of automatic stabilizers, fiscal multipliers, and the availability of fiscal space. The largest overall fiscal deficits (including stabilizers) are expected to appear in the US, Japan, and the UK. For the G-20, the growth effect from the total fiscal expansion is estimated between 0.8 and 3.2 percentage points in 2009 and 0.1 to 0.9 percentage points in 2010. The unemployment rate would correspondingly be lowered by about 0.75 to 1 percentage point. Including China and India, the total jobs saved or created would be nearly 19 million. Fiscal support to the financial sector by the G-20 is estimated at 2 percent of GDP. Public finances will remain under significant pressure in the short and medium run with debt to GDP ratios projected to rise sharply in advanced economies.

Corporate and banking sector vulnerabilities are becoming mutually reinforcing in several emerging economies. Relatively high rollover needs in the year ahead could rise further. Emerging market banks, especially in Europe and the CIS, may need to be recapitalized. Preliminary analysis suggests a capital shortfall of about US$250 billion. In Latin America, bank balance sheets are also beginning to weaken due to the combined effects of market losses and repatriation of capital by subsidiaries of foreign banks. In Asia, banks have been broadly less reliant on external funding, but the funding costs have risen substantially. Combined with the deterioration in earnings and asset quality, bank lending activity has declined markedly. For some banks, additional capital may be needed.

Policy responses across emerging economies have included: (i) extending deposit insurance and guarantees on other banks liabilities; (ii) capital injections into banks (and, in some cases, nationalization of problem institutions); (iii) provision of foreign currency liquidity to domestic banking systems; (iv) tighter rules on foreign currency lending to domestic residents; and (v) direct and indirect support for corporate borrowers, especially those facing difficulties accessing foreign exchange for external debt repayment. Many emerging economies eased monetary policy, but others have raised rates due to intensified exchange rate pressures and in most recent months' inflation fears. Most countries in Asia cut rates.

Conclusion

Looking ahead, it is expected that bank credit expansion will remain sluggish through the middle of the next decade and recovery in other market segments even more gradual. Capital flows to emerging economies are expected to regain momentum over the next five years but would remain well below the levels of 2007 and 2008. Fiscal deficits in advanced economies will fall to about 4 percent of GDP only by 2014 and public debt will have risen to above 100 percent of GDP. Private savings, both household and corporate, could enter a protracted period of increase, translating to moderation in the prospects for increases in investment in emerging economies.

Accordingly, setting the path to recovery will hinge around macro-economic policies continuing to be geared to supporting demand while remaining vigilant to reinforcing the long-term commitment to avoiding inflation. This calls for blending stimulus with sustainability—short-term effectiveness of macroeconomic policies will depend on medium-term credibility. Globally coordinated responses will be critical to the restoration of financial viability so as to reduce cross-border spillovers with better early-warning systems and more open communication of risks. Furthermore, creeping trade and financial protectionism should be avoided. Ideally, the provision of fiscal stimulus to sustain global demand should have been a joint effort, with countries with the most fiscal room playing the lead role. Monetary and credit policies should avoid seeking to engineer competitive currency depreciation. Sources of official financing support should be strengthened, including increasing the availability of international financial resources that can be tapped flexibly in adverse market conditions, aid flows to low-income countries need to be protected and built up, and the task of rebuilding the financial regulatory framework must be a multilateral endeavor.

Beyond the crisis, effective exit strategies from exceptional policy actions will be central to ensure a smooth return to normal market functioning—communication is the key to allay fears of premature withdrawal. As the recovery sets in, plans should be made for rebuilding fiscal balances and ensuring sustainable debt paths—strengthening fiscal rules and institutions; reducing the buildup of future pension and health liabilities; commitments to raise statutory retirement ages in line with life expectancies; slowing down health services costs through efficiency improvements. Central banks will need to devise plans to exit from unconventional measures to ensure a smooth return to private inter-mediation and to forestall concerns about inflation—appropriate se-quencing is important. Monetary policy frameworks will also need to pay renewed attention to the role of asset prices and financial stability. Restoring healthy and innovative financial systems capable of providing credit for investment and growth while avoiding exces-sive buildup of risk in the future will be the major objective—it will take time. Regulation of financial markets and institutions will need to be overhauled—broadening the regulatory perimeter to bring systemically important institutions and markets under regulatory oversight; stricter control over leverage; more robust risk management; macro-prudential approach to mitigate pro-cyclical effects; strengthening of market disci-pline through improved transparency and more incentive-compatible compensation structures—international cooperation and coordination is essential. For national economies, policy frameworks should adjust to allow for stronger growth in private demand in economies with sub-stantial external surpluses and large reserve positions. Policies to extend and strengthen social safety nets—including health care, pensions, and social assistance—would help reduce the need for precautionary saving in some emerging economies. Supply-side policies and structural reforms will be important to support potential growth which may have been damaged by the crisis.

Notes

1. This chapter draws on the contemporaneous assessments of global economic and financial developments made by supranational entities such as the IMF and the World Bank as well as independent evaluations by analysts and research institutions.
2. The authorities in the United States and Europe responded to this firestorm with a series of new initiatives. Many of these initiatives are discussed in Chapter 6.
3. Members of the West African Economic and Monetary Union (also known by its French acronym, UEMOA) are Benin, Burkina Faso, Cote d'Ivoire, Guinea–Bissau, Mali, Niger, Senegal, and Togo.
4. Six countries in Western Central Africa are members of CEMAC: Cameroon, Central African Republic, Chad, Equatorial Guinea, Gabon, and Republic of Congo.
5. Deleveraging, in this context, covers a range of strategies. On the liabilities side of bank balance sheets, these strategies entail raising fresh capital, as well as ensuring diversified, longer-maturity, and durable sources of funding. On the assets side, the strategies are to avoid concentrated exposures to illiquid or risky assets, dispose of non-core assets, and adopt hedging strategies that accurately mirror exposures.
6. A CDS is a swap contract in which the *buyer* of the CDS makes a series of payments to the *seller* and, in exchange, receives a payoff if a credit instrument (e.g., a bond or loan) goes into default.
7. Sources of data are as follows: (i) For Euro Area: survey of changes to credit standards for loans or lines of credit to enterprises; (ii) for the US: average of surveys on changes in credit standards for commercial/industrial and commercial real estate lending for the United States; diffusion index of "accommodative" minus "severe"; (iii) for Japan: Tankan survey of lending attitude of financial institutions.
8. The Dow Jones Industrial Average, also referred to as the Industrial Average, is the index of equity price in the New York Stock Exchange; Nikkei 225 is a stock market index for the Tokyo Stock Exchange (TSE); The DAX (*Deutscher Aktien IndeX*, that is, the German stock index) is a blue chip stock market index consisting of the 30 major German companies trading on the Frankfurt Stock Exchange; The FTSE 100 Index is a share index of the 100 most highly capitalized UK companies listed on the London Stock Exchange.
9. In this effort, the section draws heavily from Reinhart and Rogoff (2009) and IMF's *World Economic Outlook*, various issues, Washington D.C.

5

Impact on India

Introduction

The loss of confidence in the global financial markets set off waves of deleveraging, declining asset values, falling income, contracting demand, and rising unemployment that ravaged a broad swath of emerging economies including India. The rapidly deteriorating global economic situation and the heightened turbulence in the global financial system since September 2008 impacted domestic financial markets in India on a scale and duration not experienced earlier. The spillover to the real economy, already moderating in a cyclical downturn that started in the beginning of 2007, was also deeper than expected. The initial hope that the crisis could be contained in the financial sector was belied.

How did the crisis get transmitted to India? Let us turn to an influential view:

> The impact on India can be both direct and indirect. The direct impact comes from the exposure to the "toxic" or "distressed" assets by the Indian banks and other financial institutions. This is expected to be minimal. Indian banks, in general, have very little exposure to the asset markets of the developed world. Indian banks have very few branches abroad. The indirect impact will be through trade and capital flows. (Rangarajan 2009a)

The actual outturn of events broadly followed this sequence.[1]

Specifically, the crisis engulfed India through three major channels, viz., the trade channel, the financial channel, and the confidence channel. First, since merchandise exports account for less than 15 percent of GDP, the impact through the trade was expected to be bearable.[2] Second, once the financial channel is taken into account the scenario undergoes a

radical transformation. If one considers the ratio of total external transactions (i.e., both current and capital account flows in gross terms) to
GDP, it more than doubled from 47 percent in 1997–98 to 117 percent
in 2007–08 (Subbarao 2009a).[3] The financial channel of transmission
of the crisis to India appeared in three distinct forms: (a) reduced access
of Indian corporates to external finance, (b) reduced domestic liquidity,
and (c) falling stock prices. In fact, nearly all segments of the financial
markets, viz., money, foreign exchange, bond, and equity markets were
affected. Third, the confidence channel affected India via transmission of
the general recessionary situation in the global economy. Illustratively,
by September 11 (Thursday), 2008, the fall of Lehman Brothers became
imminent; by September 15 (Monday), with a quick jump, the money
market conditions in India became remarkably tight (Aziz, Patnaik, and
Shah 2008).

Against this backdrop, this chapter explores the impact of the crisis
on the Indian economy. For expository convenience, the discussion
follows a time line and to begin with, traces the initial conditions. This
is followed by quantitative indicators of the impact of the crisis and the
policy initiatives undertaken. The penultimate section examines the
aftermath of the crisis, followed by concluding observations.

Initial Conditions

In the quinquennium preceding the crisis (2003–08), the Indian economy moved decisively to a higher growth trajectory than in all preceding
years, emerging as the second fastest growing economy of continental
dimensions in the world. In association with this uptrend, there was an
acceleration in domestic investment and saving rates. The strength of
macroeconomic performance and building investor optimism inspired
confidence enough to set a 9 percent growth target for the Eleventh Five
Year Plan period (2007–12). The acceleration of growth expanded fiscal
revenues and enabled progress towards rule-based fiscal consolidation
under the *Fiscal Responsibility and Budget Management Act* (*FRBMA*). Yet
the strong momentum of expansion in the economy brought with it
macroeconomic challenges for which, in hindsight, policymakers were
not fully prepared. Inflation surged in the second half of 2006–07 and
was fuelled further by the global spurt in commodity prices in the first
half of 2008–09. The pickup in growth also attracted unprecedented

waves of capital inflows which produced strong appreciation pressures on the exchange rate and put to the razor's edge the setting and conduct of monetary policy. In this milieu, the underlying economic cycle began to turn in early 2007 and a slackening of pace began to be reflected in the consumer goods segment of industry and infrastructure. Political expediencies also brought a hiatus in the institution of structural reforms in the economy.

The Growth Plane

By 2007–08, India became a US$1 trillion economy (US$1.16 trillion at current market prices and exchange rates) with a per capita income of US$1,021. In purchasing-power-parity terms, India's GDP was placed at US$3.3 trillion in 2008, making it the fourth largest economy in the world after the United States, China, and Japan. Real GDP growth in 2007–08 was 9.0 percent, a modest deceleration from the average of 9.6 percent in the preceding two years but still higher than the average of 8.8 percent recorded in the period from 2003–04 to 2006–07. But the cyclical shift in the headwinds of growth was discernible in 2007–08, spread across most sectors of the economy, although sector-specific factors were also in evidence that obscured a fuller preparedness for the ebbs and tides that were to follow. The deceleration in the growth of the agriculture sector was attributed to the winter or *rabi* crop. Slower growth in manufacturing and construction was seen in the context of the base effects of double-digit growth in the previous year. The deceleration in the growth of consumer durables, however, evoked concern as it presaged a possible slowdown of manufacturing after a period of hectic growth driven in part by improvements in productivity and competitiveness. There was also a deceleration in the growth of revenue-earning freight traffic by railways, passengers handled at airports, and bank credit which was ominous, since they are regarded as lead indicators of service sector activity. Nevertheless, for the time being, the growth in the services sector continued to be broad-based, affirming its role as the main engine of India's growth. Among the sub-sectors of services, "transport and communication" were the fastest growing, followed by "construction" (Table 5.1).

The rate of growth of per capita income as measured by per capita GDP at market prices (constant 1999–2000 prices) grew by an annual average rate of 3.1 percent during the 12-year period from 1980–81 to

TABLE 5.1
Growth of Real GDP of the Indian Economy

(percent)

	2003–04	2004–05	2005–06	2006–07	2007–08
Agriculture, forestry, and fishing	10.0	0.0	5.8	4.0	4.9
Mining and quarrying	3.1	8.2	4.9	8.8	3.3
Manufacturing	6.6	8.7	9.1	11.8	8.2
Electricity, gas, and water supply	4.8	7.9	5.1	5.3	5.3
Construction	12.0	16.1	16.2	11.8	10.1
Trade, hotels, and restaurants	10.1	7.7	10.3	10.4	10.1
Transport, storage, and communication	15.3	15.6	14.9	16.3	15.5
Financing, insurance, real estate, and business services	5.6	8.7	11.4	13.8	11.7
Community, social, and personal services	5.4	6.8	7.1	5.7	6.8
Total GDP at factor cost	8.5	7.5	9.5	9.7	9.0

Source *National Accounts Statistics*, Central Statistical Organization, Government of India, various issues.

1991–92. It accelerated marginally to 3.7 percent per annum during the next 11 years, i.e., 1992–93 to 2002–03. Since then, there was a sharp acceleration to an average of 7.2 percent per annum (2003–04 to 2007–08). This laid the foundation for average income to double in a decade, well within one generation. The growth of per capita consumption accelerated from an average of 2.2 percent per year during 1980–81 to 1991–92 to 2.6 percent per year during the next 11 years and almost doubled to 5.1 percent per year during the subsequent five years (2003–04 to 2007–08). In the consumption basket, food and beverages had the lowest average growth while the growth of transport and communication, education and recreation, and miscellaneous services rose by more than 10 percent in 2002–07. The gap between the growth of per capita income and per capita consumption reflected rising saving rates.

The average rate of growth of gross capital formation during 2002–07 (the Tenth Five-year Plan) more than tripled to 17.3 percent per year from an average growth of 5.3 percent per annum in the preceding five years. Thus, this high growth phase was essentially investment driven with its contribution to overall demand being about 65 percent in the period 2002–07. Although the average growth of private consumption (PFCE) did accelerate moderately, its contribution to growth of aggregate demand declined from 59 percent to 46 percent between the two five-year periods. The contribution of net export of goods and services to overall demand also declined between the two periods to a negative 5 percent.

A notable feature of the growth experience was, therefore, the sharply rising trend in gross domestic investment and saving. The investment rate (gross domestic investment/GDP) rose to 32.1 percent in 2004–05. The investment climate was imbued with business confidence, entrepreneurial optimism, and an improvement in corporate competitiveness and profitability. This also led to an upsurge in foreign direct investment (FDI). By 2007–08, the investment rate had risen to 39.1 percent of GDP while the saving rate reached 37.7 percent. Both private and public savings contributed to the increase. The saving from the private corporate sector was particularly buoyant, supported by the turnaround in public sector saving from dissaving from 2003–04 onwards. Saving of the household sector was stable at 23 to 24 percent of GDP. The upsurge in private corporate investment was a capital expenditure boom.

Faster economic growth also generated employment and created conditions for poverty reduction. During 1999–2000 to 2004–05, employment growth accelerated to 2.6 percent. The proportion of persons below the poverty line declined from around 36 percent of the population in 1993–94 to 28 percent in 2004–05 as per the uniform recall period. Based on the mixed recall period, the number of persons below the poverty line declined to 22 percent by 2004–05 from 26 percent in 1999–2000.

Inflation

India, like several other emerging and developing countries, has to deal with multiple indicators of inflation. Illustratively, movements in the wholesale price index (WPI)—the equivalent of a producer price index—are regarded as the official measure of inflation for monetary policy purposes and are available on a weekly basis.[4] The standard consumer prices index is available in four forms, based on the category of the population whose consumption pattern is the focus—industrial workers, urban non-manual employees, agricultural laborers, and rural laborers—on a monthly basis. The implicit deflator for GDP is the most comprehensive measure of inflation on an annual basis. Overall inflation, as measured by the aggregate deflator for GDP (market prices), declined from 5.6 percent in 2006–07 to 4.1 percent in 2007–08. In terms of the deflator for private final consumption expenditures (PFCE), however, inflation rose moderately from 5.1 percent in 2006–07 to 5.5 percent in 2007–08. Thus, while there was some deceleration in investment goods prices, there appears to have been persistence in inflation at the level of the consumer (Table 5.2).

Inflation, measured by the WPI, rose from 4.4 percent in 2005–06 to 5.4 percent in 2006–07 but fell back to 4.7 percent in 2007–08. The composition of the inflation outcome reflected higher primary goods inflation than in the immediately preceding years, mainly because of primary non-food prices and lower fuel price which are administered domestically and allow low pass-through of global oil prices. Prices of primary articles and mineral oils started moderating from June 2007 onwards because of a number of reasons: (*a*) a rollback in the increase in the prices of petrol and diesel at end-November 2006 and mid-February 2007 to the pre-June 2006 levels, (*b*) improved availability of primary articles, and (*c*) fiscal and monetary measures to contain

TABLE 5.2
Key Indicators of the Indian Economy

Item	2003–04	2004–05	2005–06	2006–07	2007–08	2008–09
1. Growth of Real GDP (constant market prices)	8.4	8.3	9.3	9.7	9.1	6.1
2. Growth of Real GDP (constant factor prices)	8.5	7.5	9.5	9.7	9.0	6.7
3. Saving (% of GDP)	29.8	31.7	34.2	35.7	37.7	na
4. Capital Formation (% of GDP)	27.6	32.1	35.5	36.9	39.1	na
5. Per Capita Income(₹, constant prices)	20,871	23,198	26,003	29,524	33,283	37,490
6. Food grains (Million tonnes)	213.2	198.4	208.6	217.3	230.8	229.9
7. Index of Industrial Production (% growth)	7.0	8.4	8.2	11.6	8.5	2.6
8. Inflation (WPI—52 week average)	5.5	6.5	4.4	5.4	4.7	8.4
9. Inflation (CPI—industrial workers)	3.9	3.8	4.4	6.7	6.2	9.1
10. Export growth (% change)	21.1	30.8	23.4	22.6	28.9	3.6
11. Import growth (% change)	27.3	42.7	33.8	24.5	35.4	14.4
12. Current Account Deficit (% of GDP)	2.3	-0.4	-1.2	-1.1	-1.5	-4.1
13. Foreign Exchange Reserve ($ billion)	113.0	141.5	151.6	199.2	309.7	252.0
14. Exchange Rate (₹/$)	45.95	44.93	44.27	45.28	40.26	45.99
15. M3 Expansion (% change)	16.8	12.3	17.0	21.3	21.2	18.4
16. Bank Credit Growth (%)	15.2	30.7	37.0	28.5	22.3	17.5
17. Gross Fiscal Deficit (% of GDP)	4.5	4.0	4.1	3.5	2.7	6.2
18. Revenue Deficit (% of GDP)	3.6	2.5	2.6	1.9	1.1	4.6
19. Primary Deficit (% of GDP)	0.0	0.0	0.4	-0.2	-0.9	2.6
20. Population (million)	1,072	1,089	1,106	1,122	1,138	1,154

Source *Economic Survey*, Ministry of Finance, Government of India, various issues.

inflationary pressures. There was also some deceleration in the prices of manufactured products. These trends were reflecting the onset of the slowdown in activity, domestically and globally. The lagged adjustment of domestic energy prices to international developments played a major role in determining the headline inflation in India. In turn, this had major fiscal and quasi-fiscal implications.

Monetary Policy and Monetary Conditions

Monetary policy in India is invested with multiple objectives—sustaining high growth, price stability, and financial stability being the principal ones—with a hierarchy of priorities, depending on the prevailing macroeconomic circumstances and the Reserve Bank of India's (RBI) judgment on the evolution of the outlook. Accordingly, for policy purposes, numerical indicative projections are set for growth, inflation as well as for the intermediate variables—money supply, bank deposits, and non-food credit (food credit, i.e., credit given by banks to public sector agencies for procurement of food grains for the purpose of building stocks and subsequently selling them at subsidized prices through the public distribution system to sections of the population below the poverty line, is administered by a consortium of banks). These projections are evaluated on a quarterly basis and reset, if warranted.[5] For 2007–08, the RBI assumed a real GDP growth of 8.5 percent with inflation close to 5 percent, monetary expansion in the range of 17–17.5 percent and credit expansion in the range of 20–24 percent as consistent with envisaged growth and inflation. In its mid-term review in October 2007, the RBI retained the monetary policy stance but announced its resolve "to be in readiness to take recourse to all possible options for maintaining stability and the growth momentum in the economy in view of the unusual heightened global uncertainties, and the unconventional policy responses to the developments in financial markets." Its proximity to the financial markets was evidently providing signals of the turmoil building internationally. The average rate of money supply had been accelerating in the preceding years, reaching 19.5 percent in 2006–07 and 21.2 percent in 2007–08, reflecting the buoyancy in the growth momentum. The average growth of bank credit to the commercial sector rose strongly too, touching 28 percent in 2005–06 and 26.8 percent in 2006–07, but as the economic cycle turned down, it slowed to 22.3 percent in 2007–08 in sync with the deceleration in growth of manufacturing and construction sectors. Nominal interest rates, as measured by the cut-off yield at auctions of 91-day and 364-day Treasury Bills, followed a similar pattern. The average cut-off yield on 364-day (91-day) Treasury Bills reached a trough of 4.7 (4.6) percent in 2003–04 but rose since then. Yields averaged 7 (6.6) percent during 2006–07, and 7.5 (7) percent in April–December 2007. This also led to a widening of the interest differential between domestic and global rates. The year 2007–08 was marked by exceptionally strong reserve money expansion as net foreign assets of the RBI jumped by 25.2 percent (39.1 percent on annual basis). Capital inflows surged in and imparted large appreciation pressures upon the exchange rate and considerable volatility, necessitating sterilized intervention by the RBI. Accordingly, open market operations under the market stabilization scheme (MSS) were stepped up and the liquidity absorbed was of the order of ₹1,597,170 million. These open market operations were bolstered by the RBI's daily liquidity management operations under its Liquidity Adjustment Facility (LAF) and increases in reserve requirements.

Fiscal Policy and Fiscal Conditions

Fiscal consolidation became an integral element of the structural reforms instituted in 1991. The enactment of the *FRBMA*, 2003 provided the required mandate. Accordingly, the fiscal deficit of the central government as a proportion to GDP came down from 5.9 percent in 2002–03 to 3.4 percent in 2006–07 and further to 2.7 percent in 2007–08. States also joined the process of fiscal consolidation with 26 states enacting fiscal responsibility legislations by early 2008. The fiscal deficit of the states declined from 4.4 percent in 2003–04 to 1.5 percent in 2007–08 with a modest revenue surplus in 2007–08. The combined gross fiscal deficit of the Center and states fell from a level of 8.5 percent of GDP in 2003–04 to a level of 5.2 percent of GDP in 2007–08. The successful implementation of fiscal rectitude provided the confidence in the Budget for 2008–09 to envisage a fiscal deficit of the central government at 2.5 percent of GDP, which was lower than the 3 percent mandated level in the *FRBMA*. The other key target—elimination of the revenue deficit—was put off by a year, with the level of the revenue deficit estimated at 1.0 percent of GDP. As the year 2008–09 progressed, the fiscal situation changed dramatically in India as in the rest of the world.

The significant improvement in public finances in the five years ending 2007–08 was enabled by a prudent fiscal policy framework that targeted improvement in tax buoyancy and refocused public expenditure management on actual outcomes. As a proportion to GDP, gross tax revenues remained stagnant at around the 8–10 percent level in the 1990s in the face of reform of the tax structure that entailed reduction in indirect taxes, which was not fully compensated by the rise in direct taxes. Gross tax revenues grew at an average annual rate of 22.4 percent in the five years ending 2007–08 (post-*FRBMA* period). In 2007–08, direct tax collections exceeded indirect tax collections; within direct taxes, the main contribution came from corporate income tax. In the case of indirect taxes, while excise revenues remained less buoyant, customs revenue grew steadily, and the service tax emerged as the main driver of revenue growth. As a proportion to GDP, gross tax revenues rose from a level of 9.2 percent in 2003–04 to reach a level of 12.6 percent in 2007–08. Revenue expenditure growth was contained at 12.0 percent. Adjusted for special transactions under the National Small Savings Scheme—essentially federal transfers—there was a decline in capital expenditure in the period 2003–04 to 2007–08 from a level of 17.1 percent of GDP in 2003–04 to a level of 15.1 percent in 2007–08.

Balance of Payments

Before the outbreak of the crisis, the Indian economy had been progressively globalizing. The trade (goods and services)/GDP ratio had risen steadily to close to 50 percent by 2007–08. India accounted for 1.1 percent of world exports in 2007. There was a large (but declining) trade surplus with the United States and UAE, and a small surplus with the United Kingdom and Singapore. The largest trade deficits were with Saudi Arabia, China, and Switzerland. India is the leading remittance receiving country in the world, with workers' remittances constituting over 3 percent of GDP. India is also a world leader in IT-enabled services, which constitute a similar magnitude in terms of GDP. The surge of capital flows in 2007–08 testified to the growing influence of global developments on the Indian economy. Capital flows accounted for 9.2 percent of GDP in 2007–08. India traditionally runs a current account deficit which was of the order of 1.2 percent of GDP in 2005–06, 1.1 percent in 2006–07, and 1.5 percent in 2007–08. With the need for external financing, extremely modest even by developing country standards, there occurred a steady reserve accumulation of the order of US$15.1 billion in 2005–06, US$36.6 billion in 2006–07, and a massive US$92.2 billion in 2007–08. The level of foreign exchange reserves peaked at US$315 billion in May 2008, then the fourth largest in the world. As a consequence, the exchange rate of the Indian rupee faced persisting upward pressure over this period.

Financial Developments

Among the components of capital inflows, FDI has been a relatively stable component. In contrast, debt flows have fluctuated, primarily due to lumpy repayments. FDI inflows were broad-based and spread across a range of economic activities like financial services, manufacturing, banking services, information technology services, and construction. FDI outflows also increased steadily over the last five years reflecting the globalization of Indian enterprises and the emergence of Indian multinationals. Increased volatility in Asian and global financial markets since 2006–07 affected the flow of portfolio investment. Net portfolio flows became negative in May–July 2006 (reflecting the slump in equity markets), picked up momentum in August–November 2006, only to slow again in March 2007.

Stock markets recorded increased activity in 2007–08. Primary market issue of debt and equity increased along with private placement. The secondary market too showed a rising trend, notwithstanding intermittent ups and downs in the stock prices responding mainly to global developments. The Bombay Stock Exchange (BSE) Sensex rose from 13,072 at end-March 2007 to 15,644 as on end-March 2008, while the National Stock Exchange (NSE) index Nifty 50 rose from 3,822 to 4,734 during the same period. Both the indices gave a return of around 38 percent during this period. All the other indicators of capital market such as market capitalization, turnover, and price–earnings ratio remained strong.

India's financial sector has been regarded as stable and healthy. Even before the onset of the crisis, all indicators of financial strength such as capital adequacy, ratios of non-performing assets (NPAs), and return on assets (RoA) of publicly owned commercial banks, which account for 88 percent of banking assets, were robust. Moreover, Indian banks do not have direct financial exposure to the US subprime assets, and mark-to-market losses on the financial instruments held in the overseas portfolio of foreign branches and foreign subsidiaries of Indian banks have essentially been due to the general widening of credit spreads. The overall capital adequacy ratio of commercial banks in India was 12.7 percent, well above the regulatory minimum of 9 percent and the Basel Accord requirement of 8 percent. In fact, all commercial banks in India had a capital adequacy ratio of above 10 percent. Furthermore, the regulatory mandate of keeping more than 30 percent of net demand and time liabilities in the form of reserve requirements—Government of India securities (Statutory Liquidity Ratio or SLR) and cash (Cash Reserve Ratio or CRR) taken together—provides an inherent strength to the Indian banks.

The Pre-crisis Big Picture

Thus on the eve of the crisis, India was preparing for an acceleration of its growth trajectory on the basis of sound fundamentals and reasonable stability. While monetary policy was confronting the challenges posed by large capital flows, fiscal policy had entered into a phase of consolidation and improvement in the quality of public finances. Current account deficits were modest, despite a progressive integration into the world economy and enviable strength was building up in the form of large reserve accumulation. Significant social changes were also underway in the form of rising incomes and purchasing power, and declining poverty and inequity. A "demographic dividend" was expected to manifest itself in a rise in the working age population aged 15 to 64 years, from 62.9 percent in 2006 to 68.4 percent in 2026. Issues relating to climate change also engaged considerable attention. India is a party to the United Nations Framework Convention on Climate Change (UNFCCC) and its Kyoto Protocol. India's Clean Development Mechanism (CDM) potential represents a significant component of the global CDM market. On January 31, 2008, 309 out of total 918 projects registered by the CDM Executive Board were from India, which until then was the highest from any country in the world. The Indian National CDM Authority accorded Host Country Approval to 858 projects facilitating an investment of more than ₹711,210 million. These projects were in the sectors of energy efficiency, fuel switching, industrial processes, municipal solid waste, and renewable energy. If all these projects get registered by the CDM Executive Board, they have the potential to generate 448 million Certified Emission Reductions (CERs) by the year 2012.

The Onset of the Crisis

Until mid-September 2008, the financial system in India had been reasonably insulated from the carnage in international financial markets, including the sheer spread of the turmoil and the type of financial institutions that have plunged under, regardless of reputation or size. Nevertheless, global developments, as they unfolded, began to take their toll, initially in the form of indirect, knock-on effects. With the collapse of Lehman Brothers and the spreading crisis of confidence, money markets experienced unusual tightening of liquidity. Domestic equity markets were significantly affected by the global deleveraging of assets and the adverse sentiment from overseas markets. The foreign exchange market came under pressure on account of portfolio investment outflows and the enhanced foreign exchange requirements of oil and fertilizer companies resulting from higher international prices and import volumes. Constraints in access to external financing as also repricing of risks and higher spreads resulted in additional demand for domestic bank credit with attendant hardening of interest rates across the spectrum. The combined impact of these factors was a perception of credit pressures despite a sizeable increase in the growth of bank credit up to October 2008.

Liquidity conditions in the domestic markets were the first to react to the collapse of Lehman Brothers. The overnight call money rate in India jumped from around 9 percent on September 8 to over 13 percent on September 16. While this spurt was partly triggered by the scheduled mid-September advance tax outflows, it was soon clear that the tightness in liquidity was not solely due to local and seasonal factors as the call rate climbed to close to 15 percent on September 29. Volumes in the LAF repo auctions, which had averaged around ₹125 billion in the first half of September, rose to above ₹680 billion in the second half of the month. As the global liquidity crisis deepened, capital inflows dried up, and as domestic entities switched to credit from the domestic banking system, liquidity pressures aggravated sharply.

Timely responses by the RBI did alleviate the strains somewhat; however, liquidity conditions tightened even further after October 7 as contagion from the US financial crisis spread to Europe and Asia. Globally, money markets froze up and the stock markets turned highly volatile as even coordinated policy actions by monetary authorities in America, Europe, Asia, and Australia and currency swap lines to select central banks by the US Fed in order to enhance dollar liquidity failed to inspire the confidence of financial markets. In the fortnight ending October 10, 2008 there was a sizeable expansion in bank credit in India, of the order of ₹650 billion, which was the highest for any fortnight during 2008–09 so far. Consequently, in the domestic money market, call money rates touched a peak of 19.8 percent on October 10 with LAF repo volumes crossing ₹900 billion through the early part of October. Global financial conditions continued to remain uncertain and unsettled.

While domestic financial markets returned to fragile normalcy in response to a spectrum of monetary policy measures (discussed subsequently), early signs of a global recession were evident by late October. Globally, commodity prices, including crude, began to abate, which reduced domestic inflationary pressures. By mid-November 2008, there were indications that the global slowdown was deepening with a larger than expected impact on the domestic economy, particularly for the medium and small industry sector and export-oriented units. As the global outlook deteriorated further during December 2008, there was also increasing evidence of slackening of domestic economic activity—the demand for bank credit started moderating despite comfortable liquidity. The reduction in prices of petrol and diesel announced on December 5, 2008 further eased inflationary pressures.

By early 2009, domestic financial markets resumed functioning in an orderly manner. However, India's growth trajectory was impacted deeper and wider than earlier anticipated by the global financial crisis and the follow-on global economic downturn. Even as some public sector and private sector banks cut lending rates in response to the Reserve Bank's monetary policy stance, concerns over rising credit risk together with the slowing of economic activity moderated credit growth.

Policy Responses

In responding to the crisis, it is essential for public policy to resist the temptation to excessively focus on measures recommended by the global fora and ignore the unique features of the Indian economy (Reddy 2009). In the wake of the stress on domestic financial markets as a result of the global financial crisis, the immediate challenge for the RBI was to infuse confidence by augmenting both domestic and foreign exchange liquidity over the period mid-September through early November. As the crisis deepened, liquidity measures had to be complemented from mid-November by steps to ensure that credit requirements for productive purposes were adequately met so as to support the growth momentum of the economy. By January 2009, monetary and fiscal policies were in full stimulus mode. The measures taken since September 2008 are set out below under broad generic heads, although it is recognized that they interact as they were intended to. Indeed, the impact of policy action must be seen as the combined effect of not only monetary measures, intertwined with financial sector policies intended to ease financial stress as well as stimulate growth, but also fiscal policy action that followed in close succession. As such, the categorization given here is essentially for presentational purposes.

Enhancing Domestic Liquidity

In September 2008, banks were temporarily allowed to avail of additional liquidity support under the LAF to the extent of up to 1 percent of their net demand and time liabilities and seek waiver of penal interest. Subsequently in November, this measure was made more enduring by a reduction in the SLR by 1 percentage point to 24 percent of NDTL. A second LAF in the later half of the day was also re-introduced on a daily basis from September as an assurance to market participants of liquidity in the event of market stress.

In October 2008, these measures were augmented by a cumulative reduction of 250 basis points in the CRR, which was followed by a reduction of 100 basis points in November and a 50 basis points reduction in January 2009.

A special 14-day repo facility for a notified amount of ₹200 billion was instituted in October 2008 to alleviate liquidity stress faced by mutual funds. Banks were allowed temporary access to SLR-eligible securities of an additional 0.5 percent of NDTL exclusively for this purpose. Subsequently, this facility was expanded to include non-bank financial companies (NBFCs) and housing finance companies (HFCs) and the relaxation in the maintenance of the SLR was enhanced to the extent of up to 1.5 percent of their NDTL, with the facility remaining operational up to June 2009.

Banks and all-India term lending and refinancing institutions were allowed to lend against and buy back certificates of deposits (CDs) held by mutual funds for a period of 15 days. At the request of the government, the RBI agreed to provide the sum of ₹250 billion as the first installment under the Agricultural Debt Waiver and Debt Relief

Scheme to commercial banks, RRBs and cooperative credit institutions immediately. In order to provide further liquidity comfort, a special refinance facility for scheduled commercial banks (excluding RRBs) of up to 1.0 percent of each bank's NDTL as on October 24, 2008 was introduced under Section 17(3B) of the *Reserve Bank of India Act, 1934* up to a maximum period of 90 days. This facility was subsequently extended up to June 2009.

Buyback of MSS dated securities was announced to provide another avenue for injecting liquidity to be calibrated with the market borrowing program of the Government of India. A refinance facility was introduced for SIDBI, National Housing Bank (NHB), and EXIM Bank for ₹70 billion, ₹40 billion, and ₹50 billion, respectively, up to March 31, 2010. In January 2009, the government set up of an SPV for addressing the temporary liquidity constraints of systemically important non-deposit-taking non-banking financial companies (NBFCs–ND-SI). The total support from the Reserve Bank was ₹200 billion with an option to raise it by a further ₹50 billion.

Enhancing Foreign Exchange Liquidity

In September 2008, the RBI assured financial market participants that it would continue to sell foreign exchange to augment supply in the domestic foreign exchange market or even intervene directly to meet any demand–supply gaps at the prevailing market rates and as per market practice.

The interest rate ceilings on FCNR (B) deposits of all maturities and on deposits under the NR(E)RA for one to three years' maturity were increased by 50 basis points in September, a further 50 basis points in October, and a further 75 basis points in November.

Banks were permitted to borrow funds from their overseas branches and correspondent banks to the extent of 50 percent of their unimpaired Tier I capital or US$10 million, whichever is higher.

The RBI also announced that it would institute special market operations to meet the foreign exchange requirements of public sector oil market companies against oil bonds when they become available. The NBFCs–ND-SI were permitted to raise short-term foreign currency borrowings.

In October, external commercial borrowings (ECBs) up to US$500 million per borrower per financial year were permitted for rupee expenditure and/or foreign currency expenditure for permissible end-uses under the automatic route. Further, the all-in-cost ceiling for ECBs of average maturity period of three years and up to five years was raised to 300 basis points, and over five years, to 500 basis points above six-month LIBOR.

On November 7, 2008, Indian public and private sector banks that have foreign branches or subsidiaries were provided a foreign exchange swap facility of tenor of up to three months with the RBI. Further, for funding the swap, banks were allowed to borrow under the LAF for the corresponding tenor at the prevailing repo rate. This swap facility was extended up to June 30, 2009.

HFCs registered with the NHB were permitted to raise short-term foreign currency borrowings under the approval route. The RBI permitted Indian corporates to prematurely buy back their FCCBs at prevailing discounted rates.

Improving Credit Delivery

In November 2008, the period of entitlement of the first slab of pre-shipment rupee export credit was extended from 180 days to 270 days. The prescribed interest rate as applicable to post-shipment rupee export credit (not exceeding benchmark prime lending rate [BPLR] minus 2.5 percentage points) was extended to overdue bills up to 180 days. The period of entitlement of the first slab of post-shipment rupee export credit was extended from 90 days to 180 days.

The aggregate limit of export credit refinance (ECR) facility for scheduled banks (excluding RRBs) was enhanced from 15 percent to 50 percent of the outstanding export credit eligible for refinance. SIDBI and the NHB were allocated ₹20 billion and ₹10 billion, respectively, against banks' estimated shortfall in priority sector lending in March 2009. Banks were encouraged to use the special refinance facility under Section 17(3B) of the *Reserve Bank of India Act, 1934* for the purpose of lending to micro and small enterprises. The provisioning requirements for all types of standard assets were reduced to a uniform level of 0.40 percent, except in the case of direct advances to the agricultural and small and medium enterprises (SME) sectors which continue to attract provisioning of 0.25 percent, as hitherto. Risk weights on banks' exposures to all unrated claims on corporates, claims secured by commercial real estate, and claims on NBFCs–ND-SI were reduced to 100 percent from 150 percent.

In December, loans granted by banks to HFCs for on-lending for housing up to ₹2 million per dwelling unit were classified under the priority sector. Commercial real estate exposures restructured up to June 30, 2009 were allowed to be treated as standard assets. As a one-time measure, the second restructuring done by banks of exposures (other than exposures to commercial real estate, capital market exposures and personal/consumer loans) up to June 30, 2009 was also made eligible for concessional regulatory treatment.

Stimulating the Economy—Monetary Policy Rates

On October 20, 2008, in order to alleviate the pressures on domestic credit markets brought on by the indirect impact of the global liquidity constraint and, in particular, to maintain financial stability, it was decided to reduce the repo rate under the LAF by 100 basis points to 8.0 percent with immediate effect. The repo rate under the LAF was reduced by 50 basis points to 7.5 percent with effect from November 3, 2008. The repo rate was reduced under the LAF by 100 basis points from 7.5 percent to 6.5 percent and the reverse repo rate by 100 basis points from 6.0 percent to 5.0 percent, effective December 8, 2008. The repo rate under the LAF was reduced by 100 basis points from 6.5 percent to 5.5 percent with effect from January 5, 2009. The reverse repo rate under the LAF was reduced by 100 basis points from 5.0 percent to 4.0 percent with effect from January 5, 2009 and then to 4.75 percent and 3.25 percent, respectively, with effect from April 29, 2009.

Fiscal Stimulus

While the monetary policy measures outlined above formed the first line of defense, there has also been a sizeable fiscal stimulus. The depth and extraordinary impact of the crisis clearly indicated the need for counter cyclical public spending. Accordingly, the central government invoked the emergency provisions of the *FRBM Act* to seek relaxation from the fiscal targets and launched two fiscal stimulus packages in December 2008 and January 2009. These packages, together amounting to over 3 percent of GDP, included additional public spending, government guaranteed funds for infrastructure spending, cuts in indirect taxes, expanded guarantee cover for credit to micro and small enterprises, and additional support to exporters. These stimulus packages came on top of an already announced expanded safety net for rural poor, a farm loan waiver package and salary increases for government staff, all of which too were intended to stimulate demand. In addition to revenue losses from lower direct tax collection on account of the economic slowdown, additional revenue losses of about 0.6 percent of GDP had occurred due to cuts in excise and customs duties. The growth in expenditure, particularly in respect of revenue expenditure arising out of increase in subsidies, disbursements as well as implementation of the recommendations of the Sixth Pay Commission and the farm debt waiver scheme is estimated at 2.8 percent of GDP (₹1,503,100 million).

In addition to the expansion of the fiscal deficit of the Center from the budget estimate of 2.5 percent to 6.0 percent of GDP in 2008–09, special bonds of ₹440 billion and ₹140 billion, amounting to 1.3 percent of GDP, were issued to oil marketing companies and fertilizer companies, respectively, during 2008–09. In its *Review of the Economy* (January 2009), the Economic Advisory Council to the Prime Minister placed the consolidated fiscal deficit of the central government, including full issuances of oil and fertilizer bonds, at 8.0 percent of GDP for 2008–09. The consolidated fiscal deficit of the states rose to 2.6 percent of GDP. Although the fiscal stimulus packages meant deviation from the roadmap laid out by the *Fiscal Responsibility and Budget Management* (*FRBM*) *Act*, it was recognized that the Center and states should re-anchor to a revised *FRBM* mandate once the immediacy of the crisis ias behind us.

To sum up, both monetary and fiscal policies have been actively used along with other interventions to restore the growth momentum. It is essential in the interests of a self-sustaining and broad-based global recovery that the rest of the world also take steps to stimulate their economies (Ahluwalia 2009). This will also be beneficial to India over the medium-term.

The Impact

Liquidity Conditions and Financial Markets

Taken together, the measures taken since mid-September 2008 substantially assuaged liquidity stress in domestic financial markets arising from the contagion of adverse external developments.

The overnight interest rates, which had generally ruled above the ceiling of the LAF rate corridor at the beginning of October 2008 when the domestic money and foreign exchange markets came under pressure, eased from mid-October 2008 and remained below the upper bound of the LAF corridor since November 3, 2008. The LAF window saw a mode reversal from a net injection of ₹917,200 million on October 1, 2008 to a net absorption through reverse repos of the order of ₹277,450 million on October 22, 2008 and remained largely in absorption mode since then with average daily reverse repos in excess of ₹1 trillion (up to December 2009). Interest rates generally eased across the spectrum with the benchmark 10-year government securities yield easing from 8.80 percent on October 3, 2008 to 7.58 percent during October 22–December 2009) (Table 5.3).

TABLE 5.3
Interest Rates—Monthly Averages

(percent)

Instrument/Segment	October 2008	March 2009	July 2009	October 2009	December 2009
Call Money	9.90	4.17	3.21	3.17	3.24
Certificates of Deposit (CDs)	10.00	7.53	4.96	4.70	4.84
Commercial Papers (CPs)	14.17	9.79	4.71	5.06	5.17*
91-day Treasury Bills	8.13	4.77	3.23	3.23	3.57
10-year Govt. Security	7.80	6.57	7.01	7.33	7.57
Modal BPLR of PSBs	14.00	12.50	12.00	12.00	11.00–13.50

Source RBI (2010).
Note *Relates to November 2009. BPLR: Benchmark Prime Lending Rate.

With lower levels of capital inflows, there were some pressures in the foreign exchange market. Consistent with its policy objective of maintaining orderly conditions in the foreign exchange market, the Reserve Bank sold foreign exchange in the market. While foreign exchange sales attenuated the mismatch in the foreign exchange market, these operations drained liquidity from the rupee market and accentuated pressures on the rupee liquidity (Mohan 2009). The rupee depreciated during 2008–09 reflecting the extraordinary developments in international financial markets and portfolio outflows by foreign institutional investors (FIIs). Since early 2009, normalcy, however, was restored and sustained upside pressures on the exchange rate have been evident on the back of the revival of capital inflows.

Equity markets weakened sharply till end-October 2008 in tandem with global stock markets, particularly Asian markets, reflecting further deterioration in the global financial market sentiment, FII outflows, slowdown in industrial growth, and lower corporate profits. The BSE Sensex declined from an all-time high of 20,873 on January 8, 2008 to a low of 8,451 on November 20, 2008.

The actions of the RBI since mid-September 2008 resulted in augmentation of actual/potential liquidity of ₹5,617 billion. In addition, the permanent reduction in the SLR by 1 percent of NDTL made liquid funds of the order of ₹400 billion available for credit expansion (Table 5.4).

TABLE 5.4
Actual/Potential Release of Primary Liquidity—since Mid-September 2008

Measure/Facility	Amount (₹ million)
1. CRR Reduction	1,600,000
2. Unwinding/Buyback/De-sequestering of MSS Securities	1,555,440
3. Open Market Operations (purchases)*	800,800
4. Term Repo Facility	600,000
5. Increase in Export Credit Refinance	265,760
6. Special Refinance Facility for SCBs (Non-RRBs)	385,000
7. Refinance Facility for SIDBI/NHB/EXIM Bank	160,000
8. Liquidity Facility for NBFCs through SPV**	250,000
Total (1 to 8)	**5,617,000**
Memo: Statutory Liquidity Ratio (SLR) Reduction	400,000

Source RBI (2009).
Notes   *Include ₹334,390 million of Open Market Operations (OMO) purchases during 2009–10 so far (up to July 27) against the proposed OMO purchases of ₹800,000 million during the first half of 2009–10. **Includes an option of ₹50,000 million.

Monetary and Credit Conditions

Analytically, the various policy actions by the Reserve Bank since mid-September 2008 resulted in expansion of its domestic assets, through open market operations (OMO) and redemptions of bonds under the

MSS, among others, for creating base money to support the required monetary expansion. Liquidity expansion was consistent with the Reserve Bank's stance of ensuring a policy regime that enabled credit expansion at viable rates while preserving credit quality (Table 5.5).

TABLE 5.5
Annual Variations in Monetary Aggregates

(percent)

Item	2008–09 (January 16, 2009)	2009–10 (January 15, 2010)
Reserve Money	4.2	18.0
Reserve Money (adjusted for CRR changes)	18.0	17.5
Currency with Public	17.2	17.3
Money Supply (M3)	19.1	16.5
M3 (Policy Projection)	16.5–17.0*	16.5**
Ratio of Net Foreign Exchange Assets of RBI to Currency	183.3	169.2

Source RBI (2009).
Notes *Projection as indicated in the Annual Policy Statement 2008–09 (April 2008).
**Projection as indicated in the Third Quarter Policy Statement 2009–10 (January 2010).

There are several features of bank credit behavior that are distinguishing in relation to the past. First after three years of high growth, the year-on-year (y-o-y) growth in non-food bank credit slackened since October 2008, reflecting the slowing of the economy. Despite some expansion in bank credit, however, there was a perception of lack of credit availability. This could be attributed to reduced flow of funds from non-bank sources, notably the capital market and external commercial borrowings. Second, the expansion of bank credit appeared to have fallen short of requirements on account of substitution effects as entities sought to replace external borrowings and capital market issuances by bank credit. Third, there was noticeable variation in credit expansion across bank groups. Expansion of credit by public sector banks was much higher than in the previous year, while credit expansion by foreign and private sector banks was significantly lower. The relatively slower pace of credit expansion by foreign and private sector banks also added to the perception of inadequate credit flow in the system. There was also perceptible deceleration in growth of deposits with private and foreign banks (Table 5.6). Fourth, although bank deposit and lending rates started easing from November 2008, the magnitude of reduction by public sector banks was larger than that by foreign and private sector banks. Major public sector banks reduced their term deposit rates in the range of 50–150 basis points. BPLRs of major public sector banks came down by 150–175 basis points. Major private sector banks, on the other hand, reduced their BPLRs by 50 basis points only, while major foreign banks adjusted their rates by even less. As a result of several measures initiated by the RBI since mid-September 2008, banks' cost of funds came down.

TABLE 5.6
Bank Group-wise Deposits and Credit: Annual Growth

(year-on-year percentage change)

Bank Group	2008–09 (October 10, 2008)	2009–10 (October 9, 2009)
Deposits		
Public Sector Banks	23.6	24.4
Private Sector Banks	23.2	11.5
Foreign Banks	14.1	16.1
Scheduled Commercial Banks*	21.5	20.0
Credit		
Public Sector Banks	32.7	15.3
Private Sector Banks	32.9	(–) 15.9
Foreign Banks	19.7	2.5
Scheduled Commercial Banks*	29.5	10.8

Source RBI (2010).
Note   *Including RRBs.

Since November 2009, there was a reversal, and a pickup in non-food credit growth became visible except in the case of foreign banks. While the revival of credit has been slow and protracted, it is useful to recognize that "the role of the Reserve Bank of India is to create an environment in which additional credit can be made available" (Rangarajan 2009b).

Capital Flows and Forex Reserves

The reversal of capital flows in 2008–09 raised concerns about management of the BoP, particularly with reference to outstanding external debt with residual maturity of less than one year. India's external debt falling due in 2008–09 was estimated at around US$85 billion at end-March 2008. Sovereign debt and commercial borrowings were rolled over during 2008–09. Under NRI deposits, not only was the maturing debt rolled over, but also there were net accretions as a result of the upward adjustment in interest rate ceilings on such deposits. Of trade credits of the order of US$43.2 billion to be repaid during 2008–09, as much as US$28.1 billion had already been disbursed during April–November 2008. Additionally, there were large inflows in the pipeline on account of commitments of buyers' credit by the importers and oil companies. The foreign exchange reserves declined by US$23.4 billion from US$309.7 billion as at end-March 2008 to US$286.3 billion by end-September 2008, largely reflecting valuation effects. Excluding valuation effects, the decline was US$2.5 billion. Between October 2008 and March 2009, the foreign exchange reserves declined by US$34.4 billion to US$251.9 billion, including valuation effects.

Trade Financing

It is estimated that at the height of the crisis, US$31.4 billion of short-term trade credit was disbursed during April–December 2008 as compared with US$32.2 billion during April–December 2007. Despite tightness in the overseas markets, the monthly average disbursement of short-term credit of above US$3 billion during October–December 2008 compared well with the average disbursement of US$3.5 billion per month during April–September 2008. The repayments during April–December, 2008–09 at US$29.0 billion were higher compared to the corresponding period of the previous year (US$21.5 billion). Some difficulties in rolling over the maturing trade credits were accentuated during October–December 2008 with net inflows turning negative (Table 5.7).

Anecdotal evidence also suggested that during October–December 2008, banks were finding it difficult to arrange buyers' credit for import financing due to shortages of liquidity in overseas market and increased cost of funds. The tightness was reflected in higher approvals of buyers' credit relative to the gross disbursements. The issue was not only about the availability of the financing but that of price at which such finances could be negotiated. Press reports tended to suggest the problem of raising trade credit was more pronounced for the Indian banks as foreign banks could manage to arrange their lines of credit, though at higher cost, despite tightness in market.

TABLE 5.7
Short-term Trade Credit to India

(US$ million)

Period	Disbursements	Repayments	Net
1	2	3	4
2005–06	21,505	17,806	3,699
2006–07	29,992	23,380	6,612
Apr–Jun 2007	7,726	5,764	1,962
Jul–Sep 2007	12,469	7,842	4,627
Oct–Dec 2007	11,985	7,855	4,130
Jan–Mar 2008	16,731	10,267	6,464
2007–08	48,911	31,728	17,183
Apr–Jun 2008	10,176	7,779	2,397
Jul–Sep 2008	11,609	10,833	776
Oct–Dec 2008	9,565	10,357	–792
Jan–Mar 2008	9,234	11,828	–2,594
2008–09	41,841	43,750	–1,909
Apr–Sept 2009	21,692	22,310	–618
Apr–Sept 2008	23,892	18,986	4,906

Source RBI (2010).

The Aftermath

The Indian economy suffered a slowdown in growth in 2008–09 as the global crisis set back the buoyant performance of the period 2003–08. Double-digit export growth gave way to absolute declines from October 2008 as global demand contracted precipitously. As a consequence, domestic manufacturing also went into contraction. As the long run of profitability that began in the second half of 2002–03 halted and stalled, corporate activity was badly affected and business confidence plummeted and dented investment demand. Private consumption was damped by the overall sluggishness in demand conditions. While the financial sector remained relatively unaffected, given its negligible exposure to toxic assets and relatively high levels of capital and liquidity buffers, financial markets were strained by the loss of confidence and the severe stress caused by the global deleveraging process, which triggered capital outflows in the second half of 2008–09. The policy responses did mitigate the adverse impact of the crisis substantially—the fiscal stimulus bolstered sagging demand while massive injections of liquidity ensured that financial markets continued to function normally albeit with tighter lending conditions and higher spreads than before. By the second quarter of 2009, there were signs of an upturn in industrial production and revival of credit demand, though the delayed monsoon increased the downside risks to agricultural production.

Aggregate Supply and Demand

The Indian economy is estimated to have grown by 6.7 percent in 2008–09 after a pronounced deceleration in the second half of the year. The deceleration was spread across all sectors except mining and quarrying and community, social, and personal services (Table 5.7). The growth in per capita GDP decelerated from 8.1 percent in 2006–07 to 4.6 percent in 2008–09.

The growth in agriculture and allied activities decelerated from 4.9 percent in 2007–08 to 1.6 percent in 2008–09, mainly on account of the high base effect of 2007–08 and due to a fall in the production of non-food crops, including oilseeds, cotton, sugarcane, and jute. Food grains production was 233.9 million tonnes, an all-time high; however, the production of commercial crops such as major oilseeds, cotton, jute, and sugarcane was affected.

Manufacturing, electricity, and construction sectors decelerated to 2.4, 3.4, and 7.2 percent, respectively, during 2008–09 from 8.2, 5.3, and 10.1 percent, respectively, in 2007–08. The industrial sector decelerated sharply, recording almost no growth in the second half of 2008–09 before picking up by 6.5 percent in the first half of 2009–10 and by 11 percent in October–November 2009. The recovery of industrial output in 2009–10 was broad-based, with the pickup in growth evident in almost all major components of the IIP with the exception of consumer non-durables. It was the consistently increasing growth in consumer durables and intermediate goods that drove the industrial revival. The continuing downward movement in capital goods and consumer non-durables, and to an extent basic goods, suggested that their rate of growth was significantly below the pre-2007–08 levels. The slowdown in manufacturing could be attributed to the combined impact of a fall in exports followed by a decline in domestic demand which led to reduced margins and profitability. Infrastructural output also decelerated, affecting the growth of industry.

The economy experienced a turnaround in the second quarter of 2009–10 when real GDP grew by 7.9 percent. The economy grew at 7.4 percent in 2009–10, with the industrial and the service sectors growing at 8.2 and 8.7 percent, respectively. This recovery was impressive for at least three reasons. First, it came about despite a decline of 0.2 percent in agricultural output, which was the consequence of subnormal monsoons. Second, it foreshadowed renewed momentum in the manufacturing sector, which had been experiencing continuous decline in the growth rate for almost eight quarters since 2007–08. Indeed, manufacturing growth more than doubled from 3.2 percent in 2008–09 to 8.9 percent in 2009–10. Third, there had been a recovery in the growth rate of gross fixed capital formation, which had declined significantly in 2008–09. In the overall analysis, India is well-placed to return to high growth once the global crisis has bottomed out and the global economy returns to its upward trajectory (Virmani 2009).

As regards the components of aggregate demand, per capita consumption growth declined from 6.9 percent in 2007–08 to 1.4 percent in 2008–09. The contribution of private consumption to aggregate growth declined dramatically from 53.8 percent in 2007–08 to 27 percent in 2008–09. Although this was cushioned by an increase in the contribution to growth by government consumption expenditure from 8 percent in 2007–08 to a level of 32.5 percent in 2008–09, the overall contribution of consumption demand to growth declined (Table 5.8). While the negative contribution of net exports declined with imports falling faster than exports, government consumption, as stated earlier, rose strongly on the back of the fiscal stimulus and compensated for the deep slowdown in private consumption and investment demand. Industrial outlook surveys indicated a slow turnaround in business sentiment in key indicators such as production, order book position, capacity utilization, financial situation, and availability of finance.

In 2009–10, while the growth rates of private and government final consumption expenditure dipped, there was a pickup in the growth of private investment demand. There has also been a turnaround in merchandise export growth from November 2009, after a decline over nearly 12 continuous months.

Inflation

A positive fallout of the decline in demand and fall in commodity prices due to the crisis was a sharp decline in headline WPI inflation in 2008–09

TABLE 5.8
Growth in Real GDP and Aggregate Demand

	2007–08				2008–09				2009–10			
	Q1	Q2	Q3	Q4	Q1	Q2	Q3	Q4	Q1	Q2	Q3	Q4
1. Agriculture, Forestry, and Fishing	4.3	3.9	8.1	2.2	3.2	2.4	-1.4	3.3	1.9	0.9	-1.8	0.7
2. Mining and Quarrying	0.1	3.8	4.2	4.7	2.6	1.6	2.7	-0.3	8.2	10.1	9.6	14.0
3. Manufacturing	10.0	8.2	8.6	6.3	5.9	5.5	1.3	0.6	3.8	9.1	13.8	16.3
4. Electricity, Gas, and Water Supply	6.9	5.9	3.8	4.6	3.3	4.3	4.0	4.1	6.6	7.7	4.7	7.1
5. Construction	11.0	13.4	9.7	6.9	9.8	7.2	1.1	5.7	4.6	4.7	8.1	8.7
6. Trade, Hotels, Transport, and Communication	13.1	10.9	11.7	13.8	10.8	10.0	4.4	5.7	5.5	8.5	10.2	12.4
7. Financing, Insurance, Real Estate, and Business Services	12.6	12.4	11.9	10.3	9.1	8.5	10.2	12.3	11.8	11.5	7.9	7.9
8. Community, Social, and Personal Services	4.5	7.1	5.5	9.5	8.7	10.4	28.7	8.8	7.6	14.0	0.8	1.6
9. GDP at factor cost	9.2	9.0	9.3	8.6	7.8	7.5	6.1	5.8	6.0	8.6	6.5	8.6
10. Private Final Consumption Expenditure	8.4	7.5	8.9	9.0	4.5	2.1	2.3	2.7	2.9	6.4	5.3	2.6

(Table 5.8 continued)

(Table 5.8 continued)

(percent)

	2007–08				2008–09				2009–10			
	Q1	Q2	Q3	Q4	Q1	Q2	Q3	Q4	Q1	Q2	Q3	Q4
11. Government Final Consumption Expenditure	-2.4	10.0	2.0	18.6	-0.2	2.2	56.6	21.5	15.3	30.5	2.5	2.1
12. Gross Fixed Capital Formation	13.6	16.0	14.1	8.8	9.2	12.5	5.1	6.4	-0.7	1.6	8.8	17.7
13. Changes in Stocks	54.1	51.7	52.2	49.0	6.0	5.6	1.4	-0.9	-0.9	4.2	8.7	11.1
14. Exports	-4.0	-4.8	6.1	9.8	25.6	24.3	7.1	-0.8	-16.0	-15.8	-7.5	14.2
15. Imports	-0.7	-3.6	6.7	24.4	27.4	35.3	21.7	-5.7	-8.5	-10.5	-5.8	-3.7
16. **GDP at Market Prices**	**9.2**	**8.8**	**9.4**	**8.8**	**8.2**	**7.8**	**4.8**	**4.1**	**5.2**	**6.4**	**7.3**	**11.2**

Source Central Statistical Organization, Government of India.
Note Q1: April–June, Q2: July–September, Q3: October–December, Q4: January–March.

to as low as 0.8 percent at end-March 2009 on year-on-year basis. There were, however, wide variations in the constituents, with food prices rising by 6.8 percent while consumer prices rose in the range of 8–10.2 percent. Inflation in terms of the implicit deflator for GDPMP increased from 4.9 percent in 2007–08 to 6.2 percent in 2008–09, indicative of underlying inflationary pressures that had been muted by the drastic fall in demand. Headline inflation, measured by year-on-year variations in the WPI, turned negative in June–September 2009, adjusting to the moderation of global commodity prices from their peaks a year ago.

Since October 2009, inflation increased in terms of all indicators. At a disaggregated level, inflation on account of food articles and essential commodities was uncomfortably high. Inflation in terms of various consumer price indices (CPIs) also ruled at elevated levels (Table 5.9).

TABLE 5.9
Annual Inflation Rate

(percent)

Wholesale Price Index (WPI)	2008–09 (Till December 2008)	2009–10 (Till December 2009)
All Commodities	6.1	7.3
Primary Articles	11.1	14.9
Food Articles	10.0	19.2
Fuel Group	(–) 0.2	4.3
Manufactured Products	6.6	5.2
Manufactured Food Products	4.2	26.4
Essential Commodities*	9.4	21.9
Excluding Fuel	7.9	8.1
Consumer Price Indices (CPIs)		
Industrial Workers	9.7	15.0
Urban Non-manual Employees	9.8	15.5
Agricultural Laborers	11.1	17.2
Rural Laborers	11.1	17.0

Source RBI (2010).
Note *Essential commodities (weight in WPI: 17.8 percent) include rice, wheat, jowar, bajra, pulses, potatoes, onions, milk, fish-inland, mutton, chilies (dry), tea, coking coal, kerosene, *atta*, sugar, *gur*, salt, hydrogenated *vanaspati*, rape and mustard oil, coconut oil, groundnut oil, long cloth/sheeting, *dhotis*, sarees and voiles, household laundry soap, and safety matches.

Fiscal Developments

As stated earlier, the fiscal response to the crisis in the second half of 2008–09 included the payout of a part of the arrears to government employees (Sixth Pay Commission Award) and the debt relief (farm loan waiver) package to alleviate the debt burden of the distressed farmers. These expenditures helped to sustain domestic demand. They were supplemented by further measures during December 2008 to February 2009 consisting of increased plan expenditure, reduction in indirect taxes, sector-specific measures for textiles, housing, infrastructure, automobiles, micro and small sectors, and exports and authorization to specified financial institutions like the India Infrastructure Investment and Finance Company Limited (IIFCL) to raise tax-free bonds to fund infrastructure projects. Thus, the fiscal measures taken together provided a discretionary stimulus of about 3.5 percent of GDP. Furthermore, below the line items also contributed a stimulus of about 1.3 percent of GDP, even though they merely offset the effect of the increase in the prices of oil and fertilizer imports on domestic income and demand. The ratio of tax receipts to GDP of the central government declined from a peak of 12.6 percent of GDP in 2007–08 to 11.8 percent in 2008–09 and to 10.9 percent in 2009–10 due to the combined impact of the economic slowdown and the fiscal stimulus measures in terms of tax cuts to support growth. On the other hand, aggregate expenditure increased mainly on account of the implementation of the Sixth Pay Commission Award, the debt waiver scheme for farmers, the rural employment program, and spending on infrastructure.

In the Budget for 2010–11, which was announced on February 25, 2010, it was indicated that the fiscal deficit for 2010–11 would be pegged at 5.5 percent of GDP. The rolling targets for the fiscal deficit are pegged at 4.8 percent and 4.1 percent for 2011–12 and 2012–13, respectively. Against a fiscal deficit of 7.8 percent in 2008–09, inclusive of oil and fertilizer bonds, the comparable fiscal deficit was 6.9 percent for 2009–10. It was also indicated that conscious efforts would be made to avoid issuing bonds to oil and fertilizer companies. Returning to fiscal rectitude is essential for ensuring macroeconomic stability. In this context, "keeping the [fiscal deficit] target as a cyclical average is a good guidance in the medium term" (Rangarajan 2009b).

Monetary Conditions

Adjusted for the first round effect of the changes in CRR, reserve money growth was lower at 19.0 percent at the end of March 2009 on a year-on-year basis as compared with 25.3 percent a year ago. The contractionary impact of decline in net foreign exchange assets was offset by expansion of net domestic assets of the RBI through open market operations (OMO), unwinding MSS and other measures to augment rupee liquidity. Broad money (M3) growth was placed at 18.4 percent at end-March 2009, which was lower than 21.2 percent a year ago. The moderation in broad money growth mainly reflected a deceleration in aggregate deposits expansion during 2008–09 emanating from the downturn in economic activity. Bank credit to the commercial sector increased by 16.9 percent at end-March 2009 as compared with 21.0 percent a year ago. Non-food credit-growth was 17.5 percent at end-March 2009 as compared with 23.0 percent a year ago.

During 2009–10, reserve money registered a growth of 16.9 percent as compared with a growth of 6.4 percent a year ago. The growth in money supply (M3) moderated from 18.9 percent in 2008–09 to 16.8 percent during 2009–10, reflecting continuing deceleration in bank credit growth. Year-on-year increase in non-food bank credit to the commercial sector, at 16.9 percent in 2008–09, was lower than 17.8 percent a year ago.

Financial Markets

Liquidity conditions remained easy throughout 2009 although during October–December, 2009 the daily absorption under LAF declined in comparison with the previous quarter. The total MSS unwinding and auction-based OMO purchases during 2009–10 amounted to ₹142,824. There was some decline in the average LAF absorption, mainly on account of the absence of MSS redemptions and OMO auctions. Besides, increases in cash balances of the central government with the RBI contributed to the decline in daily absorption under LAF. The absorption through the reverse repo window declined significantly during the second half of December 2009, mainly on account of advance tax outflows. Interest rates declined across the term structure in the money and government securities markets. The overnight call money market rate remained towards the lower bound of the LAF corridor, albeit with some increase in December 2009 and January 2010, essentially reflecting temporary movements in liquidity referred to earlier. Primary yields on Treasury Bills also moderated. The secondary market yield on the 10-year government security, however, crept up from 5.82 percent in January 2009 to 6.57 percent in March 2009 and further to 7.5 percent by October–December 2009 on the back of the large market borrowing program of the government. Besides, lower yields on Treasury Bills and higher yields on longer tenor government securities steepened the yield curve (see also Table 5.3).

The foreign exchange market had remained orderly during 2009 with the rupee generally gaining against the US dollar on the back of a significant turnaround in portfolio and other inflows and weakening of the US dollar in international markets. There was steady growth in volumes, including in currency futures. By January 1, 2010, the rupee appreciated by 9.2 percent over its March 31, 2009 level against the US dollar, by 1.0 percent against the euro, and by 3.5 percent against the Japanese yen. However, it depreciated by 3.4 percent against the pound sterling. On the whole, the rupee appreciated in real terms with the six-currency trade-based real effective exchange rate (REER) (1993–94 = 100) moving up from 95.7 in March 2009 to 108.4 by January 22, 2010.

During 2009–10, the domestic equity markets rose on global cues and increased optimism regarding the Indian economy. The BSE Sensex increased from 9,709 at end-March 2009 to 17,303 on March 2010.

External Sector

The overall balance of payments (BoP) situation remained resilient in 2008–09 despite the strains due to the global crisis. India's current account deficit widened to 2.6 percent of GDP from 1.5 percent in 2007–08 reflecting deterioration in the trade balance. The adverse effect of the global financial crisis was mainly experienced in the export sector in the second half of 2008–09, initially on account of the drying up of international trade credit, followed by a fall in global demand. For the year as a whole, the growth in merchandise exports plummeted to barely 3.6 percent in US dollar terms from 28.9 percent in 2007–08. While the drivers of export growth were engineering goods and chemicals and related products, petroleum products and textile exports lost momentum substantially and exports of handicrafts, primary products, and gems and jewelry declined under the impact of the global downturn. Merchandise exports to the United States, the largest market, declined by 1.6 percent. On the other hand, exports to Asia (including ASEAN) grew by 6.9 percent and to Europe by 10.2 percent in 2008–09. A fortuitous saving came in the form of the fall in merchandise imports which began from October 2008 and continued in the following months into 2009–10 so far. Growth in POL, fertilizers, and edible oils indicated the innate strength of domestic demand. The trade deficit increased from US$88.5 billion (as per customs data) in 2007–08 to US$119.1 billion in 2008–09. A positive development was higher private transfers and software earnings which proved to be impervious to the financial crisis and the sharp retrenchment of overseas demand. On the other hand, earnings from tourism and business services were affected.

At the same time, certain elements of capital flows reflected a degree of crisis-proofing too; there was an increase in non-resident deposit flows and foreign direct investment in relation to the preceding year which pointed to the abiding confidence of expatriate Indians and foreign investors in the growth prospects of the Indian economy. Nevertheless, as other components of capital flows contracted and overall net capital inflows declined sharply from 9.2 percent of GDP in 2007–08 to 0.8 percent in 2008–09, reserves declined by US$20.1 billion (by US$58.0 billion, inclusive of valuation changes). The stress was maximum in Q3 of 2008–09 as the deteriorating current account balance was accompanied by net capital outflows, resulting in a substantial drawdown of reserves. While capital outflows persisted through Q4 of 2008–09, the trend reversed in Q1 of 2009–10.

In 2009–10, India's BoP continued to reflect the impact of the global economic downturn and deceleration in world trade witnessed since the second half of 2008–09. On a BoP basis, India's merchandise exports, which started falling in October 2008, recorded a decline of 3.6 percent in 2009–10 as against an increase of 13.7 percent during the previous year. Similarly, import payments, on a BoP basis, registered a decline of 2.7 percent during 2009–10 as compared to robust growth of 19.4 percent in the previous year. As indicated earlier, there was a revival in net capital flows across categories, which raised the level of international reserves close to US$280 billion by March 2010 (Table 5.10).

TABLE 5.10
India's Balance of Payments: Summary

(US$ million)

Sl.	Items	2007–08	2008–09	2009–10
1.	Exports	166,162	189,001	182,163
2.	Imports	257,629	307,651	299,491
3.	Trade Balance	–91,467	–118,650	–117,328
4.	Invisibles (net)	75,731	89,923	78,917
5.	Current Account Balance	–15,737	–28,728	–38,411
6.	External Commercial Borrowings (net)	22,609	7,941	2,521
7.	Foreign Investment (net) of Which	43,326	3,467	52,125
	FDI (net)	15,893	17,498	19,729
	Portfolio (net)	27,433	–14,030	32,396
8.	Total Capital Account (net)	107,901	8,648	53,597
9.	Reserves [increase (–)/decrease (+)]	(–)92,164	(+)20,080	(–)13,441
	Memo: As % of GDP			
10.	Trade Balance	–7.4	–9.8	–8.9
11.	Current Account Balance	–1.3	–2.4	–2.9
12.	ECBs	1.8	0.7	0.2
13.	FDI (net)	1.3	1.4	1.5
14.	Portfolio Investment (net)	2.2	–1.2	2.5
15.	Total Capital Account	8.8	0.6	4.1

Source   Reserve Bank of India, available at http://www.rbi.org.in

Conclusion

The global financial situation continues to be uncertain and unsettled. There are continuing concerns about the manner of and the time frame for resolution and the pace of recovery. The global crisis has reinforced the fact that no country can be immune to a storm of this intensity and reach, irrespective of where it began or how woven each economy is into the fabric of interdependence and intermeshing that is the hallmark of the global economy of the 21st century. In particular, the dark side of globalization has become evident as "globalisation spreads both prosperity and distress.... [T]he contagion works both ways" (Rangarajan 2009b).

It has highlighted two important aspects. First, that resolution of a crisis of this magnitude and complexity demands unconventional, unorthodox and swift policy actions. Second, there is need for close coordination between the government and the regulatory agencies without at the same time eroding institutional integrity and independence. India has well functioning institutional arrangements, both formal and informal, for inter-regulatory agency coordination which have been tested and found resilient and sound. There is need to constantly endeavor to build on these arrangements to further refine and strengthen them.

On balance, the worst of the crisis appears to be over. Since the beginning of 2009–10, recovery has set in, but downside risks remain. There are challenges ahead—balancing adequate liquidity and containing potential inflationary pressures; managing the large increase in the fiscal deficit and consequent market borrowings while keeping yields low and preventing crowding-out effects on private credit; ensuring that financial markets function normally and in a stable manner; and rekindling private investment demand, domestic and foreign.

In a historical perspective, the impact of the global financial crisis on India appears to have been an interruption in the secular upward drift of the economy. The experience of the year gone by has shown that the Indian economy has shock absorbers that will now facilitate early revival. The banking system is intrinsically sound and well capitalized. The high level of foreign exchange reserves and a sustainable stock of external debt are sources of comfort. Agriculture and rural demand continue to be strong and an in-built cushion against a Great Depression. As a durable pickup and a return to the pre-crisis high growth trajectory takes hold, India will have to redraw priorities toward fiscal consolidation and structural change. It has been pointed out that the recovery from the crisis will not happen by itself (Acharya 2008). Energies will have to be turned back to dealing with the underlying challenges of improving the quality of growth through enhancing the productivity in agriculture and industry, eradicating poverty, improving the physical and social infrastructure, addressing environmental concerns, education, and creating productive employment opportunities so as to accelerate the process of inclusive social development. Meeting these challenges is vital for human development and for upgrading the quality of life. At the heart of India's growth have been its growing entrepreneurial spirit and rise in productivity. These fundamental strengths continue to be in place.

To sum up, we can do no better than to quote from the Indian prime minister's address at the G-20 Leaders' Summit at Toronto:

> Thanks to an effective fiscal and monetary stimulus, we were able to contain the effect of the global crisis on our economy … We expect to grow by 8.5 percent in 2010–11 and we hope to go back to 9 percent by 2011–12 … This is an ambitious goal and we recognize that we have much to do to achieve it. We are taking steps to reverse the fiscal stimulus we had introduced to deal with the crisis. To this end we have outlined a medium term plan to halve the fiscal deficit by 2013–14. We are giving a strong push to investment in infrastructure, relying on private public partnership as much as possible to reduce the burden on scarce public resources. We have a sound and well regulated financial sector which was not affected by the crisis. We will persevere with implementing financial sector reforms to support rapid and inclusive growth in the real economy, and also to increase systemic stability in the financial sector. (Singh 2010)

Notes

1. In this chapter years are generally expressed as fiscal years (April–March).
2. Its impact on growth was expected to be less than 1 percent (Ram Mohan 2009).
3. Subbarao (2009b and 2009c) deals with these issues from an Indian perspective.
4. Up to October 2009. Since then, the overall index is available on a monthly basis while the sub-indices for primary products (including food articles) and fuel continue to be available on a weekly basis.
5. Since July 2010, monetary policy reviews are conducted on a six-weekly basis.

6

The Policy Response

Introduction

The crisis was unprecedented, to revive a cliché. Yet, after the initial shock of its sudden and severe impact, the crisis response was also unprecedented, both in terms of its unconventional forms as well as the sheer breadth of its adoption across countries. The knee-jerk reaction of each affected economy was to shore up its own financial system at any cost and protect it from contagion; go-it-alone became the order of the day. Even in this silo-based approach, similarities soon became apparent in these initial efforts—liquidity and capital injections, guarantees and deposit insurance, public takeovers. Perhaps, the delay in repairing the financial system and getting it up and running reflects these sporadic and uncoordinated initial efforts, i.e., while financial conditions have undoubtedly improved and spreads have narrowed, credit conditions remain tight, losses on tainted assets are yet to be fully recognized and the extent of capital required is not yet fully ascertained. Nevertheless, the ground for a more mature and coordinated response in the period ahead seems to have been laid by these first responses. By the time the feedback loops from the financial sector fed into the real sector and the economic downslide deepened, the policy response went beyond being just country-specific. To be candid, macroeconomic policies were undertaken nationally, but there was much greater coordination at play than at the time of the outbreak of the financial turmoil. The pan-European effort and later on the G-20 process stands out as a shining example of policy coordination in recent human history. In particular, the collective endorsement of the activation of the international financial institutions and in particular, the empowerment of the IMF in terms of resources and mandate to adapt to a central crisis-fighting role is noteworthy.

The response to the crisis is the subject of this chapter. It is broadly divided into three parts. The first part deals with country and country group responses and the most noteworthy feature of this part of the chapter is the extent of the deficiencies that the crisis revealed in country frameworks for regulation and supervision, crisis mitigation, and rescue, both in terms of institutional architecture and instruments. Against this backdrop, the speed of adaptation is truly remarkable. The second part of the chapter examines the multilateral response—the gaps and limitations in these institutions to handle a crisis of global proportions, their inability to foretell, and inadequacies in terms of lending practices and resources. Again, the sheer speed that marked the willingness to respond, to adapt strategies, to go boldly where earlier there would have been conservatism and conditionality, and, not the least, the faith of the international community in these entities in terms of endorsing their legitimacy in these extraordinary situations by committing resources are aspects that stand out in relation to the past. The crisis also spurred intense debates and introspection. The result was a proliferation of ideas on what went wrong, what could have been done better, and what should be done in the years ahead if a crisis such as this one has to be prevented. This yielded a rich body of work on a fund of policy responses for the future. This is the third and last part of this chapter.

Country-specific Policy Actions

When the crisis broke out in the US and spread across the Atlantic, it initially took the form of a financial storm, as stated earlier, affecting financial institutions that were exposed to tainted assets. Very quickly, it became more generalized—an evaporation of confidence besieged financial markets and crippled financial entities reliant on wholesale funding. The policy responses were country-specific, as drawn out in the foregoing section, intended to save national institutions and systems. We choose the US and the UK for focused attention in this section, being the most severely and immediately impacted. As the crisis broadened and covered more countries in its ambit, policy responses, impelled by peer experience, became more varied as shown in Annex II.

The US

In the US, the epicenter of the crisis, there was a swift response after the initial stunning impact of the demise of Lehman Brothers that exposed yawning gaps in the existing architecture for dealing with extreme financial stress. As was subsequently revealed, the Fed was not legislatively equipped to rescue an investment bank. Other gaps in the regulatory and lender-of-last-resort framework were also exposed, as evidenced by the failure of over 100 banks since the outbreak of the crisis. A plan to address the crisis was proposed through the *Emergency Economic Stabilization Act of 2008 (EESA)* on October 3, 2008. Under the Act, the US Department of the Treasury was granted authority/oversight of the Troubled Asset Relief Program (TARP) to resolve the financial crisis. The Treasury created the Office of Financial Stability to oversee the program.

On October 14, 2008, the US Treasury released a supplemental three-pronged plan. First, it announced a voluntary capital purchase program whereby stakes in nine large financial institutions were to be taken in an effort to help revive the banking sector and fight the global credit crunch. As much as US$250 billion from the over US$700 billion financial rescue package was earmarked to be funneled into thousands of banks potentially through the new voluntary program, whereby the government bought preferred equity stakes in Goldman Sachs, Morgan Stanley, J.P. Morgan Chase, Bank of America (including Merrill Lynch), Citigroup, Wells Fargo, Bank of New York Mellon, and State Street Corp. Second, the systemic risk exception to the *Federal Deposit Insurance Corporation (FDIC) Act* was signed, enabling the FDIC to temporarily guarantee the senior debt of all FDIC-insured institutions and their holding companies, as well as deposits in non-interest bearing deposit transaction accounts. Third, to further increase access to funding for businesses in all sectors of economy, the Federal Reserve announced an expanded Commercial Paper Funding Facility (CPFF) program as a broad backstop for the commercial paper market (Box 6.1).

In this context, it is pertinent to refer to the *Dodd–Frank Wall Street Reform and Consumer Protection Act*, which was signed into law by the US President on July 21, 2010. The major highlights of the Act are as follows:

- Consumer Protections: The Act creates a new independent watchdog (the Consumer Financial Protection Bureau) housed at the

---

BOX 6.1
Key Elements of the US Treasury's
Financial Regulatory Reform Proposals

More robust supervision and regulation of financial institutions:

- Creating a Financial Services Oversight Council (FSOC) of financial regulators, backed by force of law and chaired by the Treasury, to identify emerging risks, and improve interagency cooperation. The FSOC would have authority to gather information from any financial firm and to recommend any such firm for designation as a "Tier 1 financial holding company (FHC)."
- Introducing a new category of financial firm, the Tier 1 FHC, under consolidated supervision and regulation by the Federal Reserve, with selection criteria based on, but not limited to, size, leverage, and interconnectedness as per broad guidelines set in legislation.
- Subjecting these systemically important Tier 1 FHCs to consolidated supervision with a macro-prudential focus and stricter prudential standards, the latter linked to a prompt corrective action regime and special resolution mechanism at the holding company level.
- Eliminating the federal thrift charter and the industrial loan company exception, such that holding companies of either (or both) will be reclassified as Fed-supervised bank holding companies (BHCs).
- Merging the Office of Thrift Supervision and Office of the Comptroller of the Currency into a single National Bank Supervisor.
- Reviewing the Fed's governance structure and the supervision of all banks and BHCs, by end-September 2009; regulatory capital requirements for banks, BHCs, and Tier 1 FHCs, by end-2009; and the future of the housing GSEs, by the time of the President's 2011 budget release.

Comprehensive regulation of financial markets:

- Enhancing regulation of securitization markets, including through greater market transparency, more robust disclosure for credit rating agencies, and stronger incentives for securitizers to conduct due diligence on pooled assets and avoid excessive complexity.
- Introducing comprehensive regulation for over-the-counter derivatives and encouraging centralized clearing of standard contracts.
- Making money market mutual funds less vulnerable to liquidity pressures and credit losses through strengthened prudential requirements.
- Requiring the registration with the SEC of most hedge fund advisers and other private pools of capital.
- Mandating the Federal Reserve to oversee the payment, clearing, and settlement systems.

(Box 6.1 continued)

(*Box 6.1 continued*)

Consumer and investor protection from financial abuse:

- Creating a new Consumer Financial Protection Agency to improve the transparency, fairness, and appropriateness of financial products, services, and practices.
- Promoting higher standards for providers of consumer financial products and services through greater reliance on standardized "plain vanilla" products.

Better crisis management tools:

- Creating a new resolution regime for any firm whose disorderly unwinding would risk serious adverse effects for the economy, as determined by the Secretary of the Treasury after consulting with the President and upon the written recommendation of the Federal Reserve Board and the FDIC Board (the latter replaced by the SEC Commissioners if the largest subsidiary in the group is a broker–dealer).
- Requiring written approval from the Secretary of the Treasury for the Federal Reserve's emergency lending powers under Section 13(3) of the Federal Reserve Act.

Higher international standards:

- Encouraging a stronger capital and liquidity framework for all banks; more effective oversight of global financial markets; stronger cross-border supervision and coordination of resolution frameworks; and robust crisis management arrangements internationally.

Source   US Treasury (2008a).

Federal Reserve, with the authority to ensure that consumers get the clear, accurate information they need to shop for mortgages, credit cards, and other financial products, and protect them from hidden fees, abusive terms, and deceptive practices.

- Ends Too Big to Fail Bailouts: It seeks to end the possibility that taxpayers will bear the burden of rake-over of large financial firms by:

  - creating a safe way to liquidate failed financial firms;
  - imposing tough new capital and leverage requirements that make it undesirable to get too big;
  - updating the Fed's authority to allow system-wide support but no longer prop up individual firms; and

- establishing rigorous standards and supervision to protect the economy and American consumers, investors, and businesses.

- Advance Warning System: It creates a council (The Financial Stability Oversight Council) to identify and address systemic risks posed by large, complex companies, products, and activities before they threaten the stability of the economy.
- Transparency and Accountability for Exotic Instruments: It seeks to eliminate loopholes that allow risky and abusive practices to go on unnoticed and unregulated—including loopholes for over-the-counter derivatives, asset-backed securities, hedge funds, mortgage brokers, and payday lenders.
- Executive Compensation and Corporate Governance: It seeks to provide shareholders with a say on pay and corporate affairs with a nonbinding vote on executive compensation and golden parachutes.
- Protects Investors: It provides tough new rules for transparency and accountability for credit rating agencies to protect investors and businesses.
- Enforces Regulations on the Books: It strengthens oversight and empowers regulators to aggressively pursue financial fraud, conflicts of interest, and manipulation of the system that benefits special interests at the expense of American families and businesses.

As the financial crisis mutated into an economic downturn, the US was also among the first countries to undertake macroeconomic policy action to cushion the real sectors of the economy. Monetary policy was the first line of defense. The dropping of monetary policy rates to near zero accompanied by massive quantitative easing set the stage for a fiscal impulse which was substantial by historical standards as well as by cross-country experience (Box 6.2).

Subsequently, the US government has followed up with a number of initiatives (Annex II).

The UK

On October 8, 2008, the British Government announced its decision to put up to £250 billion into the banking system in an effort to keep banks lending. It also offered a guarantee to banks issuing medium-term debt, backing a further £250 billion of bank borrowings. Under the plan, seven

BOX 6.2
Fiscal Stimulus in the US

US President Obama and the Congress launched in February 2009 an economic stimulus package estimated to cost US$787 billion over the fiscal years 2009–11. The package included US$70 billion in alternative minimum tax (AMT) relief. Excluding the AMT patch, the stimulus totaled US$652 billion in fiscal years 2009–11.

- **Tax provisions made up 39 percent of the stimulus in the fiscal years 2009 – 11.** More than 45 percent of tax relief occurs through the Making Work Pay credit for working individuals. Other tax provisions include refunds for low-income families and families with children, credits for education and first-time home buyers, energy incentives, and business tax incentives. The FY 2010 budget blueprint proposed to make permanent a number of the tax relief provisions.
- **Aid to states and education spending take up about 29 percent.** The plan includes aid to states for Medicaid and funds to shore up state budgets, mainly for education. It also includes funds for student grants, special education, and education for the disabled.
- **Social safety spending accounts for about 15 percent** and includes help for the unemployed and struggling families, health insurance assistance for the unemployed, and nutritional assistance.
- **The remaining 17 percent comprises investment.** Of this, about one-third is spending on transport, housing, and urban development. Other items include health information technology, health research, investments in energy and water, upgrading government buildings, and homeland security and defense.

The fiscal stimulus under the *American Recovery and Reinvestment Act* of 2009—totaling about 5 percent of one year's GDP during 2009–11, with later measures adding to stimulus. Overall, stimulus added over 1 percent to growth in 2009, with a smaller effect in 2010, and negative contributions starting in 2011.

Source   IMF (2010e).

leading banks and the Nationwide Building Society would initially apply for £25 billion in permanent capital to raise their Tier I capital ratios, with a further £25 billion available as a standby and for other eligible institutions. The banks agreed to conclude their recapitalization by the end of the year. Given "extraordinary market conditions," the Bank of England (BoE) agreed to provide at least £200 billion under its special liquidity scheme—under which banks can swap illiquid loans for risk-free government securities—"until markets stabilise" (Box 6.3).

BOX 6.3
Selected Policy Measures in the UK in Response
to the Crisis since July 2008

Liquidity Support

• Expanded the size and frequency of BoE's **long-term repo** operations, and the range of eligible collateral to boost banks' access to term funding.

• Introduced the *Discount Window Facility* (DWF) as a permanent liquidity insurance facility for the banking system.

• Extended the drawdown period for the *Special Liquidity Scheme* (a Treasury bills-illiquid asset swap program), and lengthened the DWF's maximum maturity to 364 days (in addition to the standard option to draw for 30 days) upon the closure of SLS's drawdown window in January 2009. A total of £185 billion of Treasury bills were lent through the SLS.

• Established an unlimited **US dollar swap line** with the Federal Reserve to relieve pressure in the US dollar funding markets. The swap line arrangement was in place until end-October 2009.

Financial Sector Assistance

• Provided up to £78.1 billion in **capital injections** in Lloyds/HBOS and RBS (including £22.1 billion in the banks' payment of shares as fees for asset insurance). The government has taken significant voting stakes in the banks. Lloyds has since repaid £2.3 billion to the government.

• Set up *Asset Protection Scheme* to insure banks, for a fee, against excessive losses on troubled assets for at least five years. Participating banks will fully absorb the first loss, and the Treasury will absorb 90 percent of any remaining losses. So far, RBS and Lloyds have placed a total of £585 billion of assets under the scheme.

• Clarified FSA's minimum **capital ratio benchmark** and disclosed key **stress test assumptions** to increase transparency of FSA's supervisory requirements.

• Enacted temporary **short sale ban** (in the four months to January 2009) on banking and other financial firm stocks.

• Introduced *Credit Guarantee Scheme* by the Treasury to provide guarantees for unsecured bank debts for up to five years (including rollover), and *Asset-Backed Securities Guarantee Scheme* to insure investors against credit and extension risks of new issues of AAA-rated UK RMBS.

(*Box 6.3 continued*)

(Box 6.3 continued)

- Launched program to **purchase high-quality private sector assets**. Under the *Asset Purchase Facility*, the BoE may buy up to £50 billion of private assets, including investment-grade sterling commercial paper and corporate bonds.
- Reversed decision to run down Northern Rock's mortgage book in an effort to **support mortgage lending** to increase mortgage lending by up to £14 billion in 2009 and 2010.

Resolution and Prudential Measures

- **Resolved** Bradford & Bingley, promptly transferring its branch network and retail deposit book to another bank to ensure undisrupted access by depositors, while the remaining parts of the business were taken into temporary public ownership.
- Expedited a **merger** between Lloyds and HBOS.
- Raised the ceiling of retail **deposit guarantee** to £50,000 from £35,000. Pre-funding the insurance scheme (FSCS) with levies on the industry remaining an option.
- Introduced the *Special Resolution Regime*, a permanent regime to deal with failing banks. The BoE can make independent recommendations to the FSA regarding triggering the resolution regime.
- Phasing in significant **reforms to FSA's regulatory approach**, notably strengthening liquidity and capital requirements on banks.
- Strengthened through legislation the **BoE's role** in maintaining financial stability.

Monetary Policy Actions

- Reduced **policy rates** rapidly to a historical low of 0.5 percent.
- Flexibly adjusted the **operational arrangements of the standing facilities** (the width of the interest rate corridor between the facilities and of the target range of reserves balance) to allow more effective implementation of monetary policy objectives.
- Introduced **unconventional monetary policy**: In March 2009, the BoE began unsterilized purchase of assets (£125 billion planned until July). Gilts of 5–25 year maturities constitute a majority of the purchase.

Macroeconomic Stabilization Efforts

- Adopted a **fiscal stimulus** package of about 2 percent of GDP, implemented over 2008–10. Key measures included a 13-month VAT reduction (from 17.5 to 15 percent), advancing infrastructure investment, and various tax incentives for businesses. The twin fiscal rules were suspended and replaced with a more flexible temporary operating rule.

(Box 6.3 continued)

(Box 6.3 continued)

- Introduced subsidies to companies hiring jobless people ("**golden hellos**"). totaling about £500 million.
- Provided a job offer, **work-focused training** or work experience to every 18–24 year old who has been claiming unemployment benefit for 12 months.
- Encouraged banks to more widely pursue **mortgage workouts** and avoid repossessions.
- Provided **guarantees for deferred mortgage interest payments** by distressed borrowers for up to two years. Contingent liability associated with the Homeowners Support Mortgage Scheme is estimated at £1 billion.
- Extended **stamp duty holiday** for all houses up to £175, 000.
- Introduced a trade credit insurance scheme, various credit guarantee schemes (e.g., the Working Capital Scheme), and a £750 million Strategic Investment Fund to support investment.

Source   FSA (2009).

G-7 Efforts

On October 10, 2008, the G-7 finance ministers and central bank governors agreed in Washington DC that the situation called for urgent and exceptional action. While supporting the role of the IMF in assisting the countries affected by the turmoil, for stabilizing financial markets and restoring the flow of credit, and for supporting global economic growth, a five-point plan was proposed:[1]

(1) Take decisive action and use all available tools to support systemically important financial institutions and prevent their failure.

(2) Take all necessary steps to unfreeze credit and money markets and ensure that banks and other financial institutions have broad access to liquidity and funding.

(3) Ensure that banks and other major financial intermediaries, as needed, can raise capital from public as well as private sources, in sufficient amounts to re-establish confidence and permit them to continue lending to households and businesses.

(4) Ensure that respective national deposit insurance and guarantee programs are robust and consistent so that our retail depositors will continue to have confidence in the safety of their deposits.

(5) Take action, where appropriate, to restart the secondary markets for mortgages and other securitized assets. Accurate valuation and transparent disclosure of assets and consistent implementation of high quality accounting standards are necessary.

Actions in Europe

On October 12, 2008, a summit of the Euro Area countries (where UK Prime Minister Gordon Brown was also present) was held in Paris. This summit made a declaration on a concerted European action plan of the Euro Area countries. The declaration called for European Union and Euro Area governments, central banks, and supervisors to agree to a coordinated approach aiming at:

a. ensuring appropriate liquidity conditions for financial institutions;
b. facilitating the funding of banks, which is currently constrained;
c. providing financial institutions with additional capital resources so as to continue to ensure the proper financing of the economy;
d. allowing for an efficient recapitalization of distressed banks;
e. ensuring sufficient flexibility in the implementation of accounting rules, given current exceptional market circumstances;
f. enhancing cooperation procedures among European countries;
g. ensuring that respective national deposit insurance and guarantee programs are robust and consistent so that retail depositors will continue to have confidence in the safety of their deposits; and
h. taking action, where appropriate, to restart the secondary markets for mortgages and other securitized assets.

G-20 Initiatives

On October 11, 2008, the G-20 finance ministers and central bank governors held an extraordinary meeting in Washington DC and stressed their resolve to work together to overcome the financial turmoil and to deepen cooperation to improve the regulation, supervision, and the overall functioning of the world's financial markets. They emphasized that the global implications of the crisis reinforced the need for international cooperation as well as continued actions in key areas such as macroeconomic policy, liquidity provision, strengthening financial institutions, and protecting retail depositors.

These coordinated efforts to undertake macroeconomic policy support, to recapitalize the national banking systems as well as initiatives for extended coverage of deposit insurance provided a strong boost to financial markets which were then traumatized by the collapse of confidence and a resulting seizure of activity.

G-20 Leaders Summit (November 14–15, 2008)

The G-20 Leaders Summit on Financial Markets and the World Economy took place in Washington DC during November 14–15, 2008. With a view to enhancing the cooperation and working together to restore global growth and achieve needed reforms in the world's financial systems, the Summit's declaration made the following diagnosis of the global financial crisis:

> During a period of strong global growth, growing capital flows, and prolonged stability earlier this decade, market participants sought higher yields without an adequate appreciation of the risks and failed to exercise proper due diligence. At the same time, weak underwriting standards, unsound risk management practices, increasingly complex and opaque financial products, and consequent excessive leverage combined to create vulnerabilities in the system. Policy makers, regulators and supervisors in some advanced countries did not adequately appreciate and address the risks building up in financial markets, keep pace with financial innovation, or take into account the systemic ramifications of domestic regulatory actions. Major underlying factors to the current situation were, among others, inconsistent and insufficiently coordinated macroeconomic policies, inadequate structural reforms, which led to unsustainable global macroeconomic outcomes. These developments, together, contributed to excesses and ultimately resulted in severe market disruption.

The summit emphasized the following common principles for reforms: (*a*) strengthening transparency and accountability, (*b*) enhancing sound regulation, (*c*) promoting integrity in financial markets, (*d*) reinforcing international cooperation, and (*e*) reforming international financial institutions.

In terms of specifics, the leaders requested finance ministers to focus on the following specific areas:

(a) mitigating pro-cyclicality in regulatory policy;
(b) reviewing and aligning global accounting standards, particularly for complex securities in times of stress;

(c) strengthening the resilience and transparency of credit derivatives markets and reducing their systemic risks, including by improving the infrastructure of over-the-counter markets;

(d) reviewing compensation practices as they relate to incentives for risk taking and innovation;

(e) reviewing the mandates, governance, and resource requirements of the IFIs; and

(f) defining the scope of systemically important institutions and determining their appropriate regulation or oversight.

The G-20 Leaders Summit in its declaration of November 15, 2008 indicated that the IMF, in collaboration with an expanded Financial Stability Forum (FSF) and other bodies, should work to better identify vulnerabilities, anticipate potential stresses, and act swiftly to play a key role in crisis response. In particular, it emphasized the following in its menu of immediate actions:

(i) The FSF should expand to a broader membership of emerging economies.

(ii) The IMF, expanded FSF, and other regulators and bodies should develop recommendations to mitigate pro-cyclicality, including the review of how valuation and leverage, bank capital, executive compensation, and provisioning practices may exacerbate cyclical trends.

(iii) The IMF, with its focus on surveillance, and the expanded FSF, with its focus on standard setting, should strengthen their collaboration, enhancing efforts to better integrate regulatory and supervisory responses into the macro-prudential policy framework and conduct early warning exercises.

(iv) The IMF, given its universal membership and core macro-financial expertise, should, in close coordination with the FSF and others, take a leading role in drawing lessons from the current crisis, consistent with its mandate.

G-20 Leaders Summit, April and September, 2009

The second G-20 Summit concluded in London on April 9, 2009 with consensus on how to get the world out of the financial crisis, including a pledge of US$1.1 trillion to revive the world economy, a joint call to fight protectionism, and concrete actions to tighten banking regulations. In a post-summit Leaders' Statement, the G-20 leaders emphasized that "the only sure foundation for sustainable globalization and rising prosperity for all is an open world economy based on market principles, effective regulation, and strong global institutions." The G-20 leaders pledged to do "whatever necessary" to restore confidence, growth, and jobs; repair the financial system to restore lending; strengthen financial regulation to rebuild trust; fund and reform international financial institutions; promote global trade and investment and reject protectionism; and build an inclusive, green, and sustainable recovery. Among the additional funds to be injected into international financial institutions, US$500 billion was to go to the IMF for it to lend to countries hit hard by the financial crisis, US$250 billion to support a new allocation of Special Drawing Rights (SDR), US$100 billion to support additional lending by the multilateral development banks, and US$250 billion to guarantee trade finance.

However, the meeting failed to agree on any new stimulus measures, which the US had been hoping for. Meanwhile, the G-20 leaders expressed their opposition to trade protectionism and determination to promote and facilitate global trade and investment, remaining committed to a quick conclusion of the Doha Round of world trade talks as soon as possible. To ensure a "fair and sustainable recovery for all," the summit reaffirmed the commitment to meeting the UN Millennium Development Goals and to achieving official development assistance (ODA) (pledges, including commitments on Aid for Trade, debt relief, and the Gleneagles commitments, especially to sub-Saharan Africa.

The G-20 leaders agreed to take action to build a stronger, more globally consistent, supervisory and regulatory network for the future financial sector to rebuild trust in the financial system. They agreed to establish a new Financial Stability Board (FSB) with a strengthened mandate as a successor to the FSF, including all G-20 countries, FSF members, Spain, and the European Commission. The FSB would collaborate with the IMF to provide early warnings of macroeconomic and financial risks and the actions needed to address them.

The leaders agreed on extending regulation and oversight to all systematically important financial institutions, instruments, and markets, including systematically important hedge funds for the first time. They reached consensus on taking action against non-cooperative jurisdictions including tax havens, and agreed to publish a list of tax havens. They also agreed on extending regulatory oversight and registration to credit rating agencies to ensure that they meet the international code of good practice, particularly to prevent unacceptable conflicts of interest.

The broad impact of these initiatives and the resolve to collaborate on entrenching a strong and sustainable recovery while striving to prevent the recurrence of such crises is reflected in the preamble of the Leaders' Statement following the Summit at Pittsburgh, USA in September 2009 (Box 6.4).

BOX 6.4
Preamble to G-20 Leaders' Statement at the
Pittsburgh Summit (September 24–25, 2009)

1. We meet in the midst of a critical transition from crisis to recovery to turn the page on an era of irresponsibility and to adopt a set of policies, regulations and reforms to meet the needs of the 21st century global economy.
2. When we last gathered in April, we confronted the greatest challenge to the world economy in our generation.
3. Global output was contracting at pace not seen since the 1930s. Trade was plummeting. Jobs were disappearing rapidly. Our people worried that the world was on the edge of a depression.
4. At that time, our countries agreed to do everything necessary to ensure recovery, to repair our financial systems and to maintain the global flow of capital.
5. It worked.
6. Our forceful response helped stop the dangerous, sharp decline in global activity and stabilize financial markets. Industrial output is now rising in nearly all our economies. International trade is starting to recover. Our financial institutions are raising needed capital, financial markets are showing a willingness to invest and lend, and confidence has improved.
7. Today, we reviewed the progress we have made since the London Summit in April. Our national commitments to restore growth resulted in the largest and most coordinated fiscal and monetary stimulus ever undertaken. We acted together to increase dramatically the resources necessary to stop the crisis from spreading around the world. We took steps to fix the broken regulatory system and started to implement sweeping reforms to reduce the risk that financial excesses will again destabilize the global economy.
8. A sense of normalcy should not lead to complacency.
9. The process of recovery and repair remains incomplete. In many countries, unemployment remains unacceptably high. The conditions for a recovery of private demand are not yet fully in place. We cannot rest until

---

(Box 6.4 continued)

(Box 6.4 continued)

the global economy is restored to full health, and hard-working families the world over can find decent jobs.

10. We pledge today to sustain our strong policy response until a durable recovery is secured. We will act to ensure that when growth returns, jobs do too. We will avoid any premature withdrawal of stimulus. At the same time, we will prepare our exit strategies and, when the time is right, withdraw our extraordinary policy support in a cooperative and coordinated way, maintaining our commitment to fiscal responsibility.

11. Even as the work of recovery continues, we pledge to adopt the policies needed to lay the foundation for strong, sustained and balanced growth in the 21st century. We recognize that we have to act forcefully to overcome the legacy of the recent, severe global economic crisis and to help people cope with the consequences of this crisis. We want growth without cycles of boom and bust and markets that foster responsibility not recklessness.

12. Today we agreed:

13. *To launch a framework that lays out the policies and the way we act together to generate strong, sustainable and balanced global growth.* We need a durable recovery that creates the good jobs our people need.

14. We need to shift from public to private sources of demand, establish a pattern of growth across countries that is more sustainable and balanced, and reduce development imbalances. We pledge to avoid destabilizing booms and busts in asset and credit prices and adopt macroeconomic policies, consistent with price stability, that promote adequate and balanced global demand. We will also make decisive progress on structural reforms that foster private demand and strengthen long-run growth potential.

15. Our Framework for Strong, Sustainable and Balanced Growth is a compact that commits us to work together to assess how our policies fit together, to evaluate whether they are collectively consistent with more sustainable and balanced growth, and to act as necessary to meet our common objectives.

16. *To make sure our regulatory system for banks and other financial firms reins in the excesses that led to the crisis.* Where reckless behavior and a lack of responsibility led to crisis, we will not allow a return to banking as usual.

17. We committed to act together to raise capital standards, to implement strong international compensation standards aimed at ending practices that lead to excessive risk-taking, to improve the over-the-counter derivatives market and to create more powerful tools to hold large global firms to account for the risks they take. Standards for large global financial firms should be commensurate with the cost of their failure. For all these reforms, we have set for ourselves strict and precise timetables.

(Box 6.4 continued)

(*Box 6.4 continued*)

18. *To reform the global architecture to meet the needs of the 21st century.* After this crisis, critical players need to be at the table and fully vested in our institutions to allow us to cooperate to lay the foundation for strong, sustainable and balanced growth.

19. We designated the G-20 to be the premier forum for our international economic cooperation. We established the Financial Stability Board (FSB) to include major emerging economies and welcome its efforts to coordinate and monitor progress in strengthening financial regulation.

20. We are committed to a shift in International Monetary Fund (IMF) quota share to dynamic emerging markets and developing countries of at least 5% from over-represented countries to under-represented countries using the current quota formula as the basis to work from. Today we have delivered on our promise to contribute over $500 billion to a renewed and expanded IMF New Arrangements to Borrow (NAB).

21. We stressed the importance of adopting a dynamic formula at the World Bank which primarily reflects countries' evolving economic weight and the World Bank's development mission, and that generates an increase of at least 3% of voting power for developing and transition countries, to the benefit of under-represented countries. While recognizing that over-represented countries will make a contribution, it will be important to protect the voting power of the smallest poor countries. We called on the World Bank to play a leading role in responding to problems whose nature requires globally coordinated action, such as climate change and food security, and agreed that the World Bank and the regional development banks should have sufficient resources to address these challenges and fulfill their mandates.

22. *To take new steps to increase access to food, fuel and finance among the world's poorest while clamping down on illicit outflows.* Steps to reduce the development gap can be a potent driver of global growth.

23. Over four billion people remain undereducated, ill-equipped with capital and technology, and insufficiently integrated into the global economy. We need to work together to make the policy and institutional changes needed to accelerate the convergence of living standards and productivity in developing and emerging economies to the levels of the advanced economies. To start, we call on the World Bank to develop a new trust fund to support the new Food Security Initiative for low-income countries announced last summer. We will increase, on a voluntary basis, funding for programs to bring clean affordable energy to the poorest, such as the Scaling Up Renewable Energy Program.

24. *To phase out and rationalize over the medium term inefficient fossil fuel subsidies while providing targeted support for the poorest.* Inefficient fossil fuel subsidies

(*Box 6.4 continued*)

(Box 6.4 continued)

encourage wasteful consumption, reduce our energy security, impede investment in clean energy sources and undermine efforts to deal with the threat of climate change.

25. We call on our Energy and Finance Ministers to report to us their implementation strategies and timeline for acting to meet this critical commitment at our next meeting.

26. We will promote energy market transparency and market stability as part of our broader effort to avoid excessive volatility.

27. *To maintain our openness and move toward greener, more sustainable growth.*

28. We will fight protectionism. We are committed to bringing the Doha Round to a successful conclusion in 2010.

29. We will spare no effort to reach agreement in Copenhagen through the United Nations Framework Convention on Climate Change (UNFCCC) negotiations.

30. We warmly welcome the report by the Chair of the London Summit commissioned at our last meeting and published today.

31. Finally, we agreed to meet in Canada in June 2010 and in Korea in November 2010. We expect to meet annually thereafter and will meet in France in 2011.

Source Group of Twenty (2009).

What has been the extent of G-20 Stimulus package? The details of fiscal stimulus are given in Table 6.1.

Monetary Policy Measures for Crisis Intervention

The crisis necessitated action on two fronts—sizeable easing in terms of the conventional interest rate instruments as well as new and innovative monetary policy measures. Advanced economy central banks cut policy interest rates to historical lows with most of them reducing their policy rates to the effective zero nominal bound. Several central banks committed to keeping interest rates at very low levels for a period beyond the interval between monetary policy announcements. For example, in April 2009, the Bank of Canada (BoC) committed to keep overnight rates at 0.5 percent, conditional on inflation developments, until the end of the second quarter of 2010 to influence rates at longer maturities. The Federal Reserve Bank (Fed) also committed to maintaining a low policy interest rate (0–0.25 percent) for an extended period. Early in 2009, the

TABLE 6.1
G-20 Countries—Fiscal Expansion

(as % of GDP)

	2009			2010		
	Overall balance	Crisis-related discretionary measures	Other factors	Overall balance	Crisis-related discretionary measures	Other factors
Argentina	-1.8	-1.5	-0.3	-0.4	0.0	-0.4
Australia	-5.8	-2.9	-2.9	-6.8	-2.0	-4.8
Brazil	-1.0	-0.6	-0.4	1.6	-0.6	2.1
Canada	-6.5	-1.9	-4.6	-5.7	-1.7	-4.0
China	-4.8	-3.1	-1.7	-4.8	-2.7	-2.1
France	-5.6	-0.7	-5.0	-5.9	-0.8	-5.0
Germany	-3.7	-1.6	-2.1	-4.2	-2.0	-2.2
India	-6.0	-0.6	-5.4	-5.6	-0.6	-5.0
Indonesia	-1.4	-1.4	0.0	-0.9	-0.6	-0.2
Italy	-4.1	-0.2	-3.9	-4.1	-0.1	-4.0
Japan	-7.4	-2.4	-5.0	-7.5	-1.8	-5.7
Korea	-6.2	-3.6	-2.6	-6.2	-4.7	-1.5
Mexico	-3.5	-1.5	-2.0	-2.3	-1.0	-1.3
Russia	-13.4	-4.1	-9.3	-10.0	-1.3	-8.6

(Table 6.1 continued)

(Table 6.1 continued)

(as % of GDP)

	2009			2010		
	Overall balance	Crisis-related discretionary measures	Other factors	Overall balance	Crisis-related discretionary measures	Other factors
Saudi Arabia	-10.8	-3.3	-7.5	-5.7	-3.5	-2.2
South Africa	-5.6	-3.0	-2.6	-5.9	-2.1	-3.8
Turkey	-4.9	-1.2	-3.7	-3.2	-0.5	-2.7
United Kingdom	-8.9	-1.6	-7.4	-10.6	0.0	-10.6
United States	-6.4	-2.0	-4.4	-6.5	-1.8	-4.7
G-20 Countries (GDP PPP weighted)	-5.9	-2.0	-3.9	-5.7	-1.6	-4.0
Advanced G-20 economies	-6.3	-1.9	-4.4	-6.5	-1.6	-4.8
Emerging G-20 economies	-5.4	-2.2	-3.2	-4.4	-1.6	-2.8

Source IMF (2009b).

pace of reduction of policy interest rates was accelerated as the speed and magnitude of the global economic contraction became clear.

It was soon clear that the crisis was deeper and interest rate reduction alone would not suffice. The transmission channels of monetary policy were already weakened by the outbreak of the subprime crisis and the ensuing stress in money and other financial markets. On top of it all, the failure of Lehman Brothers and intervention of AIG led to the hoarding of liquidity by financial and nonfinancial companies and further constrained private sector balance-sheet monetary policy transmission channels. Consequently, central banks responded by immediately commencing injections of large amounts of domestic and foreign exchange liquidity. Initially these efforts took the form of enhanced access to standing facilities, increase in the number of counterparties, and expanded eligible collateral. Illustratively, the European Central Bank (ECB) provided substantial liquidity at a one-year maturity. Although the primary effect of liquidity easing came from higher levels of bank reserves, the other changes in operational procedures also served to enhance the availability of liquidity and improve confidence. Most central banks in advanced economies, especially those with policy interest rates close to or at zero shifted their focus to "balance sheet policies" or what popularly came to be known as unconventional measures. Changes in the size, composition, and duration of central bank balance sheets took on a leading policy role and evolved and grew as the economic situation worsened.

Broadly, such policies took a few main forms across central banks. Systemic liquidity easing measures were used to generally boost liquidity and alleviate systemically important liquidity shortfalls in key funding markets and for the financial system as a whole. They were implemented by easing access to standard central bank liquidity providing instruments and by increasing the level and lengthening the duration of central bank assets. Second, purchase of long-term public sector securities were principally intended to lower longer-term interest rates and also alleviate stress in longer-term credit markets. They boosted long-term assets of the central bank and were unsterilized so that bank reserves rise as well. Holdings of public securities are large and still growing for a few central banks. The Fed and BoE started purchases of targeted amounts of public sector securities after their policy interest rates hit the lower bound. These purchases were intended to lower long-term interest rates, primarily for the purchased securities, but also were aimed at improving overall credit conditions. Purchases by the Fed of mortgage-backed securities guaranteed by government sponsored agencies are also counted here as public sector securities, even though they are formally claims of the Fed on the private sector. The BoE also emphasized that the effects of the increased bank reserves mirror the purchases of government securities. The BoE expanded the targeted size of asset purchases by £25 billion to £200 billion. Third, purchase of private sector securities were intended to boost credit in key markets for mainly macroeconomic objectives. In practice, these purchases were also not sterilized and thus they contributed to the expansion of bank reserves. Only a few central banks purchased private securities; these holdings are now small. The Fed, ECB, BoE, and BoJ introduced facilities for the direct and indirect purchase of private securities mainly to shore up stressed credit markets. Among them, only the Fed purchased a large amount, mostly via the Commercial Paper Funding Facility (CPFF). The outstanding amount of private securities has decreased to a relatively low level for all these central banks. The BoJ terminated its facility to purchase commercial paper and corporate bonds at end–December 2009 and the Fed recently reaffirmed the scheduled expiration date for the CPFF. Fourth, foreign exchange liquidity provision was undertaken to address shortages in the market. Injections took the form of sales of foreign reserves or foreign exchange swaps or other derivatives. These measures were not primarily aimed at influencing the exchange rate. In addition, a number of currency swap facilities between central banks were established to transfer foreign currency. The Fed established dollar swap arrangements with 14 central banks and the ECB and the Swiss National Bank also supplied liquidity in their currencies.[2] These arrangements increased both sides of central bank balance sheets.

Differences in the magnitude and modalities of liquidity injection across central banks reflected varied market structures and financial stress. The Fed, BoE, and ECB provided the most liquidity in relation to GDP, reflecting the relatively high degrees of stress in their financial systems. The Fed employed the largest array of measures, probably due to the complexity of US financial markets. Other advanced economy central banks provided ample liquidity but on a smaller scale.

Most central banks have rolled back liquidity easing measures in line with improving conditions in key funding markets. The Reserve Bank of Australia (RBA) has pared back bank reserves to well below the levels that prevailed before the crisis. The ECB and the BoC decided to gradually shorten the maturity of fund-supplying operations. The outstanding amount of short-term operations by the Fed and BoE has decreased substantially. In December 2009, the Fed reaffirmed that several liquidity easing facilities would expire on February 2010, as scheduled. In contrast, the BoJ introduced in December 2009 a new fund-supplying operation to encourage a further decline in long-term interest rates in an effort to support the recovery. In the United States and United Kingdom, bank reserves remain very high, but this is due to purchases of long-term securities. Foreign exchange liquidity provision has virtually ceased. The RBA and the Bank of Korea (BoK) have stopped offering dollar-providing operations, though explicit announcements of the termination have not been made. Currency swap arrangements between Fed and other central banks terminated on February 1, 2010. Subsequently, in May 2010, the FOMC announced that it had authorized dollar liquidity swap lines with the Bank of Canada, the BoE, the ECB, the BoJ, and the Swiss National Bank.

Balance sheet policies seemed to have helped improve confidence although their effectiveness is hard to measure. Balance sheet policies also have costs and risks. First, central banks may face pressure in the future to maintain the expanded policy role that they took on during the crisis, compromising central bank independence and monetary policy objectives. Second, balance sheet policies also pose financial risks to central bank balance sheets. These risks, once materialized, may require budgetary support if the losses are large enough to threaten the financial soundness of central banks. Third, balance sheet policies could distort the relative prices of credit instruments. Targeted treatment of specific market instruments could create an unlevel playing field and cause resource misallocation. Fourth, large-scale systemic liquidity provision could crowd out money markets with adverse long-term consequences. The supplanting of money markets by the central bank can, over time, shrink the infrastructure needed to support these markets, as well as lead banks to cut back on their own market-based liquidity management, as was the case in Japan (Table 6.2).

The Role of the International Financial Institutions

The aftershock of the Great Depression of the 1930s and World War II reverberated through human societies so profoundly that it led to fundamental political developments and eventually to the creation of a world

TABLE 6.2
Advanced Economy Central Banks: Crisis Measures

(as of end-December, 2009)

		US	UK	Euro Area§	Japan	Canada‡	Australia	South Korea
Policy Rate	Latest Peak	5.25	5.75	4.25	0.5	4.5	7.25	5.25
	(Last date)	(Sept. 17, 07)	(Dec. 5, 07)	(Oct. 7, 08)	(Oct. 30, 08)	(Dec. 3, 07)	(Sept. 2, 08)	(Oct. 8, 08)
	Latest bottom	0.0–0.25	0.5	1.0	0.1	0.25	3.0	2.0
	(Last date)	(Current)	(Current)	(Current)	(Current)	(Current)	(Oct. 6, 09)	(Current)
	Last Policy Rate	0.0–0.25	0.50	1.00	0.10	0.25	3.75	2.00
	change (Date)	(Dec. 16, 08)	(Mar. 5, 09)	(May 7, 09)	(Dec. 19, 08)	(Apr. 21, 09)	(Dec. 2, 09)	(Jan. 9, 09)
Number of Policy Measures (Latest/Maximum)	Systemic Liquidity Easing Measures	8/9	5/5	6/7	8/9	4/6	0/2	1/3
	Purchase of Private Securities	3/4	2/2	0/1	0/2	–	–	1/1
	Purchase of Public Securities*	2/3	1/1	–	–	–	–	–
	Forex Liquidity Easing	–	1/1	3/5	1/1	–	1/1	3/3
	Forex Swap Arrangements	1/1	1/1	3/3	2/2	1/1	1/1	3/3
	Emergency Liquidity Assistance	2/2	0/3	–	–	–	–	–

Balance Sheet Impact (Latest/Maximum, % of GDP)							
Bank Reserves†	7.1/8.1	9.0/10.2	1.9/3.4	2.3/2.7	0.9/1.8	0.1/0.7	0.2/1.2
Purchase of Private Securities	0.4/2.5	0.1/0.2	0.3/0.3	0.0/0.3	–	–	–
Purchase of Public Securities*	9.2/9.2	13.3/13.3	–	–	–	–	–
Forex Liquidity Easing	–	0.0/5.1	0.1/4.3	0.0/2.4	–	0.0/3.5	0.0/2.3

Source IMF (2010).

Notes * Cumulative changes from end-August 2008.
    † Purchases conducted solely for liquidity provision purposes are included in Liquidity Easing Measures.
    ‡ Bank reserves for Canada include deposits by government.
    § Bank reserves for Euro Area include deposit facility.

economic order based on the Bretton Woods Institutions in the form we know them today. The crisis put these very institutions to the razor's edge and soul-searching on the gaps in the international financial architecture that let the current crisis happen has led to questions about the legitimacy and effectiveness of these institutions. There is a close scrutiny on issues relating to how well the present economic order has served the world in this time of crisis. It is increasingly becoming clearer that a serious comprehensive review of the existing international financial architecture is now inescapable. So far, contagious crises have by and large been associated with the developing world and, accordingly, the international monetary and financial system which has essentially served the interests of developed countries has been regarded as immune to change. This crisis originated in the most developed country in the world and took the most grievous toll on the developed world. Mercantilist capitalism, which powered the hegemony of the developed countries, has proved to be the god that failed. It is said that it is impossible to resist an idea whose time has come. Indeed, this defines the ongoing quest for redesigning the international financial architecture.[3]

Some Limitations of the Global Financial Architecture

Over the second weekend of October 2008 during the annual meetings of the IMF and the World Bank in Washington, when the crisis was in its most virulent stage, the call for coordinated action began to be heard and built into a crescendo. In many fora, representing different segments of the international community, the message of globally coordinated action was reiterated. It was clear that it was not so much the specific actions that were important but that governments across the world should be united in taking up those measures. There could not have been a more powerful endorsement of global interconnectedness. But this would also mean that in recognition of the changing economic realities, organizations like the IMF and the World Bank have to change in terms of their lending practices and size, and more fundamentally, in their attitude, internal governance, and representativeness to be truly meaningful and acceptable in a clearly agnostic world. The world today is very different from 1944 and the IMF and the World Bank are yet to fully reflect those changes.

IMF Surveillance: One of the IMF's core activities is to monitor global, regional, and national economies to assess whether countries' policies are consistent not only with their own interest but also with the interest of the international community. The IMF fulfills this mandate through multilateral, regional, and bilateral surveillance. Multilateral and regional surveillance is provided through the conjunctural analysis in the *WEO*, *Global Financial Stability Report* (*GFSR*), and *Regional Economic Outlooks* (*REOs*).

Article IV consultations, the main instrument of bilateral surveillance is normally held every year with each of the IMF's members. Under Article IV obligations, member countries typically undertake to collaborate with the IMF and with one another to promote the stability of the global monetary and financial system and orderly evolution of exchange rates. In June 2007, the policy framework of surveillance received a major update through the new Decision on Bilateral Surveillance over Members' Policies which clarified:

- that country surveillance should be focused on assessing whether countries' policies promote external stability covering exchange rate, monetary, fiscal, and financial policies, and assessment of risks and vulnerabilities;
- what is and what is not acceptable to the international community in terms of how countries conduct their exchange rate policies; and
- that surveillance should be collaborative, candid, and evenhanded, and take into account countries' specific circumstances.

Notwithstanding the IMF's evolving mandate on surveillance, the origins of the crisis can be traced to the global imbalances and financial excesses that got built up in the first half of this decade which could have been prevented. Instead, were they tacitly incentivized? Did the multilateral watchdog institutions perform the role of surveillance adequately? The inadequacy of the IMF, particularly, in not having focused adequately on financial stability, especially in systemically important countries, over the recent years is now established, even from within the institution. The obsessive focus on exchange rate misalignments underplayed the importance of equally, if not more, critical issues of financial sector stability, the costs and benefits of capital flows and the linkages between the real economy and the financial sector. The limited efficacy of IMF surveillance in developed countries with international financial centers has been starkly exposed.[4] The costs of this failure are being borne by all countries, not just the developed countries themselves where the crisis brewed.

IMF Lending: Since the Eleventh Review of quotas in 1998, there has been no general increase in quotas, and the size of the IMF in terms of total quotas at SDR billion 217.3 (US$343 billion), as on January 4, 2008, appeared grossly inadequate in the context of the magnitude of the impact of the crisis. As a proportion of a number of indicators including global GDP, imports, foreign exchange reserves, and current account transactions, the IMF's resources have fallen quite dramatically over the years. Some projections have indicated that if a major emerging market economy were to have had a crisis similar to the Mexican crisis in 1995 when the IMF provided US$18 billion in support (6.3 percent of GDP), the IMF's resources would have been really stretched or even exhausted. Therefore, even as calls on the IMF's lending in the height of the crisis quickly took the gross amount committed to over SDR 100 billion or nearly half of its lendable resources, the urgent need for an increase in resources was widely recognized. Given that a relatively small number of large players dominate the global capital market and at times of crises they tend to display a pro-cyclical herd like behavior, a sufficiently large IMF as a countervailing power came to be regarded as critical. The potential loss to the global economy in failing to act is much higher than the opportunity costs of a larger IMF.

In parallel, the IMF has to ensure that countries are able and willing to borrow from it at the first signs of a crisis. This would imply that its toolkit of lending instruments would require modifications and, more importantly, the stigma attached to borrowing from it is removed. Accordingly, reforms in lending instruments, terms, maturity, access, and conditionality was keenly felt so that substantial amounts (in multiples of a country's quota) could be lent with rapid triggering and non-stigmatized access.

Regulatory Coordination: The crisis has thrown up the dangers of regulatory arbitrage. Banks are tightly regulated. However, there is a large system of shadow financial sector—comprising investment banks, hedge funds, broker–dealers, private equity, SIVs, and money market funds—which is much more lightly regulated. Because of the arbitrage available, these institutions became relentless in their search for yields with a growing appetite for risk taking and became systemically too important to fail. Issues related to "moral hazard" became significant. Cross border issues also arose, complicating the process of crisis resolution. Clearly, rewriting the rules appeared necessary. Applicability of national resolution packages to international banks whether it is deposit guarantees or bailouts came to occupy center stage in various countries as the fight back against the crisis was mounted. How do we overcome the limitations of national regulation of international transactions? Who looks at cross border regulation? This is at present left to a number of informal groupings and clubs of central banks. Many of these organizations may not have clearly spelt out mandates and often lack legitimacy in view of their limited and restricted membership. Have we come to a stage where we need a global central bank? Is the one organization with the legitimacy due to universal membership and a mandate for global financial stability credible and empowered enough to handle the task of coordinating cross border issues which financial regulators and supervisors face? Or should it remain a global body for fiscal and monetary policy and coordination only? These are important questions that we need to reflect on and answer in the days to come.

Recent IMF Responses[5]

Emerging market and developing countries have faced increasing strains from the global economic downturn. As the crisis became prolonged and prospects of recovery tentative, many of these countries found that their room for policy maneuver had become increasingly constrained. In these circumstances, timely IMF financing—if provided in an appropriate amount and form—can cushion the economic and social costs of external shocks. In some cases, IMF assistance could help prevent crises altogether.

In response to the deepening global economic difficulties, the IMF implemented a series of reforms that strengthened its lending framework. These measures reflect consultations with IMF members and stakeholders, and will enable it to respond more effectively to the evolving challenges of crisis-affected countries. In addition, the IMF is seeking to sharply increase both its non-concessional and concessional lending resources, which would enable it to meet expanded financing requirements in the crisis. Reforms of concessional lending instruments for low-income members are also in train.

Modernizing Conditionality: The IMF aims to ensure that conditions linked to loan disbursements are focused and adequately tailored to the varying strengths of countries' policies and fundamentals. In the past, these loans often had too many conditions that were insufficiently focused on core objectives. This modernization is to be achieved in two key ways. First, the IMF will rely more on preset qualification criteria (ex ante conditionality) where appropriate rather than on traditional (ex post) conditionality as the basis for providing countries access to its resources. This principle is embodied in the new Flexible Credit Line. Second, implementation of structural policies in IMF-supported programs will, from now on, be monitored in the context of program reviews, rather than through the use of structural performance criteria, which will be discontinued in all IMF arrangements, including those with low-income countries. While structural reforms will continue to be integral to IMF-supported programs where needed, their monitoring will be done in a way that reduces stigma, as countries will no longer need formal waivers if they fail to meet a structural reform by a particular date.

Flexible Credit Line (FCL):   The IMF introduced a new credit line for countries with very strong fundamentals, policies, and track records of policy implementation. Access to the FCL credit line will be particularly useful for crisis prevention purposes. FCL arrangements are approved for countries meeting preset qualification criteria. Access under the FCL is determined on a case-by-case basis. Disbursements under the FCL is not phased or conditioned to policy understandings as is the case under a traditional IMF-supported program. This flexible access is justified by the very strong track records of countries that qualify for the FCL, which give confidence that their economic policies will remain strong. The terms of the FCL represent a strengthening of the earlier Short-term Liquidity Facility (SLF), which was discontinued. While the SLF was also designed to cater only to very strong-performing members, several of its design features—including its capped access and short repayment period, as well as the inability to use it on a precautionary basis—limited its usefulness to potential borrowers. The concept of a credit line available for either crisis prevention or resolution and dedicated for only very strong-performing countries, with all its flexible features, is new. The FCL's flexibility includes the following:

- assuring qualified countries of large and upfront access to IMF resources with no ongoing (ex post) conditions;

- renewable credit line, which at the country's discretion could initially be for either a 6-month period, or a 12-month period with a review of eligibility after 6 months;
- longer repayment period (3¼ to 5 years versus maximum rollover period of 9 months in the SLF);
- no hard cap on access to IMF resources, which will be assessed on a case-by-case basis (the SLF had a cap on access of 500 percent of quota); and
- flexibility to draw at any time on the credit line or to treat it as a precautionary instrument (which was not allowed under the SLF).

The preset qualification criteria are at the core of the FCL and serve to signal the IMF's confidence in the qualifying member's policies and ability to take corrective measures when needed. At the heart of the qualification process is an assessment that the member: (*a*) has very strong economic fundamentals and institutional policy frameworks, (*b*) is implementing—and has a sustained track record of implementing—very strong policies, and (*c*) remains committed to maintaining such policies in the future. The relevant criteria for the purposes of assessing qualification for an FCL arrangement include: (*a*) a sustainable external position, (*b*) a capital account position dominated by private flows, (*c*) a track record of steady sovereign access to international capital markets at favorable terms, (*d*) a reserve position that is relatively comfortable when the FCL is requested on a precautionary basis, (*e*) sound public finances, including a sustainable public debt position, (*f*) low and stable inflation, in the context of a sound monetary and exchange rate policy framework, (*g*) the absence of bank solvency problems that pose an immediate threat of a systemic banking crisis, (*h*) effective financial sector supervision, and (*i*) data transparency and integrity. Strong performance against all these criteria is not necessary to secure qualification under the FCL, as compensating factors, including corrective policy measures under way, would be taken into account in the qualification process.

More recently, at end-August 2010, the IMF expanded its lending tools further. As part of the efforts to enhance IMF's crisis-prevention toolkit, the duration and credit available under the existing Flexible Credit Line (FCL) has been increased and a new Precautionary Credit Line (PCL) has been established for members with sound policies who nevertheless may not meet the FCL's high qualification requirements.

In specific terms, the enhancements include three major features. First, the duration of the credit line has been doubled.[6] Second, the implicit cap on access of 1, 000 percent of a member's IMF quota has been removed (with access decisions based on individual country's financing needs). Third, the procedure for approval has been strengthened (by requiring early IMF's Executive Board involvement in assessing the contemplated level of access and the impact of such access on the IMF's liquidity position).

The new PCL is available to a wider group of members than those that qualify for the FCL. In practice, qualification is assessed in five broad areas, namely: (*a*) external position and market access, (*b*) fiscal policy, (*c*) monetary policy, (*d*) financial sector soundness and supervision, and (*e*) data adequacy. While requiring strong performance in most of these areas, the PCL permits access to precautionary resources to members that may still have moderate vulnerabilities in one or two of these dimensions. Features of the PCL include: (*a*) streamlined ex post conditions designed to reduce any economic vulnerabilities and (*b*) frontloaded access with up to 500 percent of quota made available on approval of the arrangement and up to a total of 1,000 percent of quota after 12 months.

Enhanced Stand-By Arrangements (SBA):   Reforms to the SBA—the IMF's workhorse lending instrument for crisis resolution—aim to increase its flexibility and ensure its availability as a crisis prevention instrument for members that may not qualify for the FCL. The new SBA framework will enable high-access on a precautionary basis and provide increased flexibility by allowing frontloading of access and reducing the frequency of reviews and purchases where warranted by the strength of the country's policies and the nature of the balance of payments problem faced by the country.

Doubling Access Limits: Non-concessional loan access limits for countries have been doubled, with the new annual and cumulative access limits for IMF resources being 200 and 600 percent of quota, respectively. These higher limits aim to give confidence to countries that adequate resources would be accessible to them to meet their financing needs. Access above these limits will continue to be provided on a case-by-case basis under Exceptional Access procedures, which have also been clarified and streamlined.

Adapting and Simplifying Cost and Maturity Structure: To create the right incentives for borrowing from the IMF, the cost and maturity structures for high-access and precautionary fund lending have been overhauled. The elimination of the time-based repurchase expectations policy—an administrative mechanism meant to induce early repayments—will effectively lengthen grace periods and simplify the repayment schedules of IMF lending. This administrative mechanism is replaced by the introduction of a new time-based surcharge, which together with streamlined level-based surcharges, will help mitigate credit risks without increasing the cost of borrowing to countries that make timely repayments to the IMF. The new schedule of commitment fees, which increases with the size of precautionary lending, would help mitigate liquidity risks to the IMF without discouraging early access to IMF resources.

Reform of Facilities for Low-income Country Members: In addition to the reform of structural conditionality, which applies also to concessional loan facilities available for low-income countries, the IMF has considered modifications to its concessional lending facilities to strengthen its lending tools for providing short-term and emergency financing to low income countries. The IMF provides two primary types of financial assistance to low-income countries: (*a*) *low*-interest loans under the Poverty Reduction and Growth Facility (PRGF) and the Exogenous Shocks Facility (ESF) and (*b*) debt relief under the Heavily Indebted Poor Countries (HIPC) Initiative and the Multilateral Debt Relief Initiative (MDRI). These resources come from member contributions and the IMF itself, rather than from the quota subscriptions. They are administered under the PRGF ESF, PRGF–HIPC, MDRI–I and MDRI–II Trusts, for which the IMF acts as Trustee. The PRGF ESF Trust was established to provide lending in support of PRGF and ESF arrangements and to subsidize the market rate of interest down to the concessional interest rate of 0.5 percent per annum. Loan resources of about US$26 billion have been committed by 17 contributors to the Trust, while a larger number of IMF member countries have made subsidy contributions. The PRGF–HIPC Trust was established to provide debt relief under the HIPC Initiative and to subsidize PRGF lending. The resources available to the Trust consist of grants and deposits pledged from 93 member countries and contributions from the IMF itself. The bulk of the IMF's contribution comes from off-market gold transactions made during 1999–2000.

In July 2009, the IMF approved far-reaching reforms of the concessional facilities, in which a new Poverty Reduction and Growth Trust (PRGT) replaced the PRGF–ESF Trust. As part of the reform package, it also agreed to provide exceptional interest relief on its concessional loans to all low-income countries, with zero interest payments through end-2011, to help them cope with the crisis. These reforms will become effective when all current lenders and bilateral subsidy contributors to the PRGF–ESF Trust have consented to the reforms. It is expected that these reforms will boost the resources available to low-income countries to US$17 billion through 2014, including about US$8 billion over the next two years. To meet the new financing commitments, additional loan resources of SDR 9 billion (US$14 billion) and new subsidy resources of SDR 1.5 billion (US$2.3 billion, end-2008 net present value terms) will need to be mobilized. It is envisaged that, as in the past, the required additional loan resources will be mobilized through bilateral contributions. Most of the needed subsidy resources will, however, come from the IMF's internal resources—including use of resources linked to gold sales, with additional bilateral contributions of SDR 0.4 billion (US$0.6 billion) being sought to complete the financing package. The MDRI–I and MDRI–II Trusts were established in early 2006 to provide debt relief under the MDRI. Financed from the IMF's own resources of SDR 1.5 billion in the Special Disbursement Account (SDA), the MDRI–I Trust is to provide debt relief to countries (both HIPCs and non-HIPCs) with per capita incomes at or below US$380 a year (on the basis of 2004 gross national income). The MDRI–II Trust is to provide debt relief to HIPCs with per capita incomes above US$380 a year, with financing from bilateral resources of SDR 1.12 billion transferred from the PRGF–ESF Trust. In addition to the above, there is a separate administered account financed by a group of member countries for interest subsidies on IMF emergency assistance to PRGF-eligible countries in post-conflict or natural disaster situations.

Simplifying Lending Toolkit: Some facilities that have not been recently used (Supplemental Reserve Facility and the Compensatory Financing Facility) have been eliminated.

Efforts are under way to further increase IMF resources. Box 6.5 lists out the major initiatives in this direction.

Boosting the IMF's resource: A substantial increase in the IMF's resources is required to give full confidence to countries that it will have sufficient money available should they need to borrow. Japan has already provided the IMF with an additional US$100 billion to bolster the IMF's lendable resources available to address the crisis to about

BOX 6.5
Main Initiatives of the IMF in Response to the Crisis

- **Stepping up crisis lending:** The IMF has enhanced its lending commitments to a record level of US$157 billion.
- **New credit line for well-run emerging market economies:** Disbursements are not phased and there are no conditions to meet once a country has been approved for the IMF's Flexible Credit Line. Colombia, Mexico, and Poland have been provided credits totaling US$78 billion.
- **New rules for terms of IMF lending:** Starting May 1, structural performance criteria have been discontinued for all IMF loans, including for programs with low-income countries.
- **Streamlined loan conditions:** Conditionality is now more tightly focused on core objectives. The number of structural conditions has decreased in many programs, and has been increasingly limited to the most critical measures, in particular urgent public financial management reforms.
- **Creating a Crisis Firewall—Tripling of IMF resources:**

  o The April 2, 2009 G-20 Summit in London supported a dramatic increase in IMF lending resources to help combat the crisis.
  o The G-20 agreed to triple the IMF's lending capacity to US$750 billion and enabling it to inject extra liquidity into the world economy via a US$250 billion allocation of SDRs—the IMF's quasi-currency.
  o An immediate doubling of IMF resources from US$250 billion will come from bilateral pledges, including US$100 billion each from Japan and the European Union, along with other sources.
  o An increase in resources to US$750 billion will be achieved by expanding and modernizing its New Arrangements to Borrow (NAB). Expanding the number of participants from the current 26, enlarging the credit provided to up to US$500 billion (including the roughly US$250 billion of contributions provided bilaterally), and making the NAB more flexible will provide a much stronger backstop.
  o A general allocation of SDRs equivalent to US$250 billion will result in a near 10-fold increase in SDRs. It will represent a significant increase in reserves for many countries, including low-income countries. The allocation will be about 77 percent of quota for each participant.

Source   Authors.

US$350 billion, and the European Union has committed €75 billion. A chronological list of countries that upto April 2010 had pledged to help boost the IMF's lending capacity is given below (Box 6.6).

BOX 6.6
Details of Bilateral Borrowing Arrangements with the IMF

Japan—US$100 billion

- US$100 billion Borrowing Agreement with Japan (February 13, 2009)

European Union—US$178 billion

- Up to €1.3 billion Borrowing Agreement with the Bank of Finland (April 26, 2010)
- Up to €2.47 billion Borrowing Agreement with the Swedish Riksbank (April 7, 2010)
- €1.03 billion Borrowing Agreement with the Czech National Bank (March 31, 2010)
- €120 million Borrowing Agreement with the Central Bank of Malta (February 12, 2010)
- €4.74 billion Borrowing Agreement with the National Bank of Belgium (February 12, 2010)
- €440 million Borrowing Agreement with the Slovak Republic (February 12, 2010)
- €1.06 billion Borrowing Agreement with Banco de Portugal (November 30, 2009)
- €1.95 billion Borrowing Agreement with the Danish Central Bank (November 4, 2009)
- €5.31 billion Borrowing Agreement with De Nederlandsche Bank (October 5, 2009)
- €4 billion Borrowing Agreement with Spain (October 5, 2009)
- €15 billion Borrowing Agreement with Deutsche Bundesbank (September 22, 2009)
- €11 billion Borrowing Agreement with France (September 4, 2009)
- US$15 billion Borrowing Agreement with the United Kingdom (September 1, 2009)
- €120 million Borrowing Agreement with the Central Bank of Malta (February 12, 2010)
- Borrowing up to €4.74 billion with the National Bank of Belgium (February 12, 2010)
- Borrowing up to €440 million with the Slovak Republic (February 12, 2010)

(Box 6.6 continued)

(*Box 6.6 continued*)

Norway—US$4.5 billion

- US$4.5 billion Borrowing Agreement with Norway's Central Bank (July 6, 2009)

Canada—US$10 billion

- US$10 billion Borrowing Agreement with Government of Canada (July 8, 2009)

Switzerland—US$10 billion

- US$10 billion in Financial Support for the IMF (April 8, 2009)

United States—US$100 billion

- US Congressional Approval of IMF-Related Legislation, including US Financial Commitment of up to US$100 billion (June 18, 2009)

Korea—At least US$10 billion

- Korea Finances IMF's Lending Resources (May 4, 2009)

Australia—US$5.7 billion

- Australian Commitments to IMF and Asian Development Bank (May 12, 2009)

Russia—Up to US$10 billion

- Russian Federation's Intention to Purchase the First-ever Notes Issued by the IMF (May 27, 2009)

China—Up to US$50 billion

- US$50 billion Note Purchase Agreement with China (September 2, 2009)

Brazil—Up to US$10 billion

- IMF Signs US$10 billion Note Purchase Agreement with Brazil (January 22, 2010)

India—Up to US$10 billion

- India's Commitment to Buy up to US$10 billion of IMF Notes (September 5, 2009)

Singapore—US$1.5 billion

- Singapore's Commitment of Additional Financial Support for the IMF (September 8, 2009)

Chile—US$1.6 billion

- Chile's Commitment of Additional Financial Support for the IMF (September 24, 2009)

Source Authors.

Reforms in IMF surveillance

As mentioned earlier, in June 2007, the policy framework of surveillance received a major update through the new Decision on Bilateral Surveillance over Members' Policies. In 2009, the IMF moved further in this regard to eliminate the use of labeling in the form of characterizing exchange rate regimes as misaligned, preferring instead to engage in dialogue and persuasion as a confidential adviser rather than as a policeman.

In September 2008, the Executive Board of the IMF reviewed the implementation of bilateral surveillance. Based on this review, the IMF issued a statement of surveillance priorities for the period 2008–11 in October 2008 (economic priorities had been revised prior to the annual meeting of October 2009 to, *inter alia*, enable the IMF to coordinate exit strategies). The economic priorities are to resolve financial market distress; to strengthen the global financial system by upgrading domestic and cross-border regulation and supervision, especially in major financial centers; to facilitate adjustment to sharp changes in commodity prices; and to promote the orderly reduction of global imbalances. Operational priorities cover refining risk assessment tools to provide clear early warnings to members, financial sector surveillance and improved analysis of real-financial linkages, informing bilateral surveillance with multilateral perspectives, and more robust analysis of exchange rates and external stability risks.

A key aspect of these priorities is the integration of macroeconomic and financial sector surveillance. The Financial Sector Assessment Program (FSAP), a joint IMF and World Bank effort introduced in May 1999, seeks to identify the strengths and vulnerabilities of a country's financial system, to determine how key sources of risk are being managed, to ascertain the sector's developmental and technical assistance needs, and to help prioritize policy responses. Reports on Observance of Standards and Codes (ROSCs) are a key component of the FSAP. The FSAP also forms the basis of Financial System Stability Assessments (FSSAs), in which IMF staff addresses issues of relevance to IMF surveillance, including risks to macroeconomic stability stemming from the financial sector and the capacity of the sector to absorb macroeconomic shocks.[7] In the context of the global financial crisis, the International Monetary and Financial Committee (IMFC) reiterated the importance of embedding financial sector surveillance more effectively in Article IV consultations, and integrating its results into the Fund's broader macro-economic surveillance. The financial crisis pushed macro-financial sector issues into center stage in IMF surveillance and program work. On October 6, 2008, the Executive Board emphasized the need for a more effective integration of the IMF's bilateral surveillance with its regional and global analyses alongside a sharpening of its stability assessments and financial market analyses (this objective has been reinforced by significant reforms in the FSAP in October 2009). The joint letter issued by the Managing Director, IMF and the Chairman, FSF on November 13, 2008 delineated institutional mandates and clarified that surveillance of the global financial system is the responsibility of the IMF.

In January and September 2009, the Fund held informal seminars on integrating financial sector issues and assessments under the FSAP into its surveillance. Key issues that were discussed for follow-up work were: the focus and depth of analysis of macro-financial issues in Article IV consultations and scope for improvement, reshaping the FSAP and integrating it more effectively in to bilateral surveillance, and approaches for bridging the gap between multilateral and bilateral surveillance. Accordingly, several important reforms have been undertaken. The option of modular assessments was introduced to allow greater flexibility and to help align the FSAP better with country needs—FSAP modules will be focused on stability or developmental aspects when country circumstances warrant. This approach would facilitate a higher frequency of assessments and a more continuous dialogue. The IMF will continue to refine stress-testing methodologies and improve the analysis of macro-financial linkages with greater emphasis on ensuring data quality, assessing off-balance sheet exposures, calibrating the shocks, and exploring more fully liquidity and cross-border risks. The Bank will enhance analytical tools to benchmark financial sector development and improve the analysis of areas such as competition issues, incentives, and governance, and will incorporate lessons from the crisis for financial sector strengthening, supervision, and regulation. Stability assessments will become more rigorous, standardized, and comparable across countries through the introduction of a Risk Assessment Matrix. Although the FSAP is inherently a bilateral instrument, assessments will focus more squarely on cross-border linkages and incorporate the findings of multilateral analyses, such as the WEO, GFSR, the vulnerability exercise, and the Early Warning Exercise.

More recently, in September 2010, financial stability assessments under the FSAP have been made a regular and mandatory part of the IMF's surveillance for member countries with systemically important financial sectors. A total of 25 countries were identified as having systemically important financial sectors, based on a methodology that combines the size and interconnectedness of each country's financial sector.[8] Each of these 25 countries will have a mandatory financial stability assessment every five years. These mandatory financial stability assessments will comprise three elements: (a) an evaluation of the source, probability, and potential impact of the main risks to macro-financial stability in the near term, (b) an assessment of each countries' financial stability policy framework, involving an evaluation of the effectiveness of financial sector supervision against international standards, and (c) an assessment of the authorities' capacity to manage and resolve a financial crisis in terms of the country's liquidity management framework, financial safety nets, crisis preparedness, and crisis resolution frameworks.

The G-20 Working Group on Enhancing Sound Regulation and Strengthening Transparency has recommended that the FSAP and Article IV consultations should be utilized to monitor that: (a) financial system stability is taken into account in the mandates of all national financial regulatory authorities, (b) within each country, effective mechanisms are in place for domestic financial sector authorities to jointly assess systemic risks across the financial system and to coordinate domestic policy responses, (c) financial sector authorities have suitable macro-prudential tools to address systemic vulnerabilities, (d) information on systemic risk is collected and monitored though a globally coordinated mechanism, (e) national authorities have authority to enforce compliance by rating agencies to changes in practices and procedures for managing conflict of interest, and assuring transparency and quality with appropriate sharing of information between national authorities responsible for the oversight of credit rating agencies, (f) all G-20 members commit to undertake an FSAP and publish its conclusions—national authorities may also periodically undertake a self-assessment of their regulatory frameworks based on internationally agreed methodologies and tools, (g) the FSAP process is expanded to encompass macro-prudential oversight, the scope of regulation, and supervisory oversight of the influence of the structure of compensation schemes at financial institutions on risk taking, (h) the progressive adoption of the Basel II capital framework, which will continue to be improved on an ongoing basis, across the G-20, (*i*) effective enforcement of regulation should be a priority of all financial regulators, and (*j*) national authorities should commit to assist each other in enhancing their capacity to strengthen regulatory frameworks.

The Working Group on Reinforcing International Cooperation and Promoting Integrity in Financial Markets recommended that the IMF, with its focus on surveillance, and the expanded FSF or the Financial Stability Board (FSB), with its focus on standard setting, should strengthen their collaboration, enhancing efforts to better integrate regulatory and supervisory responses into the macro-prudential policy framework and conduct early warning exercises. In line with this objective and drawing on their complementary areas of focus, the IMF and the FSB have recently stepped up their collaboration on developing a framework on early warnings for identifying and mitigating systemic risks and vulnerabilities. A pilot Early Warning Exercise (EWE) was conducted for the IMF Spring meeting of 2009. The Group recommended that the IMF and the FSB report the results of the EWEs to the IMFC and the G-20 (and to publish them in joint reports with appropriate modifications). The Working Group expressed the view that the IMF and the FSB should review the effectiveness of their collaboration and, if needed, submit further proposals to strengthen the processes to the IMFC and the G-20.

The Working Group also recognized that for effective early warnings, data collection needs to be strengthened. The IMF is already seeking to enhance its collaboration with national authorities responsible for financial stability assessments to enhance data availability, including with regard to cross-border exposures. The Working Group therefore recommended that the IMF and the FSB explore gaps and provide appropriate proposals for strengthening data collection before the next meeting of G-20 Finance Ministers and Central Bank Governors drawing on the work of the interagency group.

The Working Group supported the IMF's efforts to strengthen its existing surveillance tools, in particular the FSAP. The Group recommended that all countries should commit to undergo an FSAP and to publish the results. Furthermore, countries with systemically important financial sector activities should undergo an FSAP with regular updates more frequently.

The IMF has set up a new macro-financial unit which will focus on developing an analytical framework for better understanding macro-financial linkages. The spring 2009 issue of the GFSR addressed the ongoing development of the IMF's early warning methodologies. The IMF, together with the World Bank, is reviewing the FSAP with a view to better integrating financial sector analyses and FSAP assessments into surveillance. The FSB's vulnerability exercise will draw on and complement the macro-financial analysis undertaken by the IMF and others.

In early-February 2009, the IMF's Executive Board broadly supported a procedure for regular IMF–FSB EWEs. The EWEs would aim at identifying and prioritizing macro-financial risks and systemic vulnerabilities and provide policymakers with options to mitigate risks and vulnerabilities. Both quantitative and qualitative approaches would be employed. The results of the exercises would be communicated to the Board and the IMFC jointly by the IMF Managing Director and the FSB Chair.

Since July 2009, there has been an increasing recognition that the future role of surveillance will encompass improving analysis of macro-financial linkages, cross-border spillovers and sources of systemic risks. Macro-financial linkages refer to large changes in credit and asset prices that are associated with significant movements in macroeconomic variables over the business cycle—real output, consumption, and investment rise above trend during credit booms and fall below trend in the unwinding phase. Credit and asset price booms are often followed by banking and currency crises. Recessions associated with house price busts and credit crunches are both deeper and longer-lasting than are other recessions. The unemployment rate increases notably more in recessions associated with house price busts. These patterns are useful for surveillance as they can help identify the role of asset prices in determining the severity and duration of recessions in advanced countries. Efforts are also underway to imbue surveillance with regional and multilateral perspectives (Box 6.7).

IMF–Financial Stability Forum (FSF)/Financial Stability Board (FSB) collaboration

As already indicated, IMF–FSB collaboration is an essential element of the G-20 recommendations. It was emphasized that that the IMF should continue to enhance its work on financial stability and macro-financial linkages, consistent with its mandate and strategic priorities, and focusing in areas where it adds most value and complements the work of other institutions. The IMF's value-added could stem both

BOX 6.7
Initiatives Taken for Improving Spillovers in Regional and Multilateral Surveillance

- *Cross-cutting Thematic Staff Papers*: Identifying cross-country relevant themes is the key to bridge multilateral and bilateral surveillance. A first thematic report distilling common themes in the Article IV consultations of five systemic economies (China, the Euro Area, Japan, the United Kingdom, and the United States) was done.
- *Regional Outlooks*: Regional Economic Outlooks have proven to be a useful tool to bridge multilateral and bilateral surveillance, as they are a good outreach vehicle to present stylized facts, assess common trends, and discuss broad policy implications while taking into account country-specific features.
- Implementation of regional assessments—regional stress tests have been undertaken in Central and Eastern Europe.
- Steps are being taken for multilateral and cross-country risk and vulnerability analyses to inform country surveillance work more systematically and help with prioritization.
- Leveraging findings from multilateral exercises such as the Global Financial Stability Report, Vulnerability Exercise for Emerging Economies (VEE), Vulnerability Exercise for Advanced Economies (VEA), and the EWE.
- Thematic reports on topics relevant to a group of countries.
- *Spillover Reports*: Identification of potential systemic vulnerabilities through spillover reports to coincide with the relevant Article IV.

Source Authors.

from in-house technical expertise in core financial sector policy areas, and its capacity to put regulatory and supervisory policy challenges into a broader macro-financial stability context. There is also a need to better integrate the IMF's country-specific surveillance with its regional and global analyses, further sharpen its high-frequency market analyses and stability assessments, and maintain an ongoing dialogue with market participants in order to strengthen its early warning capabilities.

In this context, it is pertinent to turn to the Joint Letter of the FSB Chairman and the IMF Managing Director to the G 20 Ministers and Governors on November 13, 2008. In this letter, while deciding to enhance collaboration, the roles of our respective bodies have been clarified as follows:

(i) Surveillance of the global financial system is the responsibility of the IMF.

(ii) Elaboration of international financial sector supervisory and regulatory policies and standards, and coordination across the various standard setting bodies, is the principal task of the FSB. The IMF participates in this work and provides relevant inputs as a member of the FSF.

(iii) Implementation of policies in the financial sector is the responsibility of national authorities, who are accountable to national legislatures and governments. The IMF assesses authorities' implementation of such policies through FSAPs, Report on Observance of Standards and Codes (ROSCs), and Article IV Consultation Reports.

(iv) The IMF and the FSB will cooperate in conducting early warning exercises. The IMF assesses macro-financial risks and systemic vulnerabilities. The FSB assesses financial system vulnerabilities, drawing on the analyses of its member bodies, including the IMF. Where appropriate, the IMF and FSB may provide joint risk assessments and mitigation reports.

Expanding FSF membership

The FSF was established by the G-7 finance ministers and central bank governors in 1999 to promote international financial stability through enhanced information exchange and international cooperation in financial market supervision and surveillance. The FSF comprised national financial authorities (central banks, supervisory authorities, and finance ministries) from the G-7 countries, Australia, Hong Kong, Netherlands, Singapore, and Switzerland, as well as international financial institutions, international regulatory and supervisory groupings, committees of central bank experts, and the European Central Bank.

The FSF decided at its plenary meeting in London on March 11–12, 2009 to broaden its membership and to invite as new members the G-20 countries that are not currently in the FSF. These are Argentina, Brazil, China, India, Indonesia, Korea, Mexico, Russia, Saudi Arabia, South Africa, and Turkey. In addition, Spain and the European Commission also became FSF members.

The G-20 Working Group on Enhancing Sound Regulation and Strengthening Transparency (WG1) recommended that the expanded FSF, together with the IMF, should create an effective mechanism for key financial authorities in each country to regularly come together around an international table to jointly assess the systemic risks across the global financial system and to coordinate policy responses.

On the other hand, the G-20 Working Group on Reinforcing International Cooperation and Promoting Integrity in Financial Markets (WG2) recommended that the IMF, with its focus on surveillance, and the expanded FSF, with its focus on standard setting, should strengthen their collaboration, enhancing efforts to better integrate regulatory and supervisory responses into the macro-prudential policy framework and conduct early warning exercises. The WG2 provided of a number of specific proposals.

(i)   The WG2 expressed the view that the IMF and the FSF have recently taken important steps to strengthen their collaboration, in particular, by developing procedures to conduct regular joint EWEs.

(ii)   Specifically, WG2 called on the IMF and the FSF to report the results of the EWEs to the IMFC and the G-20 and to publish them in joint reports with appropriate modifications.

(iii) Asset prices are expected to be an input into the IMF/FSF EWEs.

(iv)   The WG2 also recognized that for effective early warnings, data collection needs to be strengthened and recommended that the IMF and the FSF need to explore gaps and provide appropriate proposals for strengthening data collection before the next meeting of G-20 finance ministers and central bank governors drawing on the work of the interagency group.

(v)   The WG2 also recommended that the feasibility of establishing a global credit register based on the experience with national credit registers and how this can be incorporated into EWEs could be explored. Some members disagreed that establishing a global credit register could be achieved and therefore did not see a need to explore the matter further.

On April 2, 2009, the membership of the FSF was expanded and the expanded FSF was re-established as the FSB with a broadened mandate to promote financial stability. The FSB consists of a Chairperson, a Steering Committee, the Plenary with member countries, standard setting bodies (SSBs) and international financial institutions, and a Secretariat. While the Chair would oversee the Steering Committee, the Plenary, and the

Secretariat, the Plenary is the decision making organ of the FSB. The Steering Committee provides operational guidance between plenary meetings to carry forward the directions of the FSB. A full-time Secretary General and an enlarged Secretariat based in Basel support the FSB. Jurisdictions eligible for Plenary membership include the current FSF member jurisdictions plus the rest of the G-20, Spain and the European Commission. Eligibility will be reviewed periodically.

As obligations of membership, member countries and territories commit to pursue the maintenance of financial stability, maintain the openness and transparency of the financial sector, implement international financial standards (including the 12 key International Standard and Codes), and agree to undergo periodic peer reviews, using among other evidence IMF/World Bank public Financial Sector Assessment Program reports. The FSB will elaborate and report on these commitments and the evaluation process.

The Plenary has country or regional representation drawn from authorities responsible for maintaining financial stability. Representation is at the level of central bank governor or immediate deputy, head of the main supervisory/regulatory agency, and deputy finance minister. Plenary members also include the chairs of the main SSBs and central bank committees, and representatives of the IMF, World Bank, the BIS, and the OECD. The FSB plenary will meet two times per year and have calls as needed.

Seat assignments in the FSB Plenary reflect the size of the national economy, financial market activity, and national financial stability arrangements. Delegations with more than one seat have one member seated at the back. Members sitting at the back have the rights of the table. Representation at the table can be changed according to topic. The FSB Chair can extend ad hoc invitations to non-members to attend plenary meetings.

Subsequently, at its inaugural meeting on June 26–27, 2009, the FSB set up the internal structures needed to address its mandate, including a Steering Committee and three Standing Committees: for Assessment of Vulnerabilities, for Supervisory and Regulatory Cooperation, and for Standards Implementation. The FSB also established a Cross-border Crisis Management Working Group, and an Experts Group on non-cooperative jurisdictions. With these structures, the FSB has taken forward its work to advance the London reform agenda:

- The Steering Committee has overseen the progress and coordination of international policy development across the range of the London Summit recommendations and their consistent implementation internationally.
- The Standing Committee on Assessment of Vulnerabilities (SCAV) has set up enhanced processes for identifying and assessing vulnerabilities affecting the global financial system and for proposing the policy responses needed to address them. The SCAV's first assessment was presented to the FSB plenary in September and will be part of the joint IMF–FSB EWE.
- The Standing Committee for Supervisory and Regulatory Cooperation has set out next steps to strengthen the operation of supervisory colleges, including the development of a protocol to improve information exchange and coordination among home and host supervisors. The Committee will be developing policy responses for addressing the problem of "too-big-to-fail" institutions.
- The Cross-border Crisis Management Working Group is formulating and overseeing action to implement the FSB *Principles for Cross-border Cooperation on Crisis Management* endorsed by G-20 leaders at the London Summit. Firm-specific cross-border contingency planning discussions have been scheduled for all the main global financial institutions. The group is setting out the expectations and deliverables for these discussions.
- The Standing Committee for Standards Implementation has begun work to develop a peer review mechanism to strengthen adherence to international prudential and regulatory standards, and to identify and incentivize improved compliance by non-cooperative jurisdiction. Its deliverables are described in detail in this note.
- The FSB's Working Group on Sound Compensation Practices has reconvened and is delivering to the Pittsburgh Summit guidance detailed specific proposals to strengthen implementation of the FSB *Principles for Sound Compensation Practices* endorsed by the London Summit.

The FSB has initiated a number of actions (Box 6.8). It remains to be seen how far they are taken forward in the coming years.

BOX 6.8
Actions Initiated by the Financial
Stability Board

- The shortcomings in the Basel capital framework that generated incentives for off-balance sheet securitization activity have been removed.
- The weaknesses in accounting practices and national standards that generated similar incentives for off-balance sheet activities have been addressed. New standards have been set out that enhance the consolidation of special purpose vehicles and the transparency of banks' relationships with such entities.
- The risks that banks assume in their trading activities have been brought under better control. Substantially higher capital requirements against risks in banks' trading activities have been issued.
- Strong new risk management standards for financial institutions have been issued and are being implemented, covering bank governance, the management of liquidity risk, underwriting and concentration risks, stress testing, valuation practices and exposures to off-balance sheet activities.
- Banks' disclosures of their on- and off-balance sheet risk exposures have been materially improved. New disclosure standards for banks have been issued covering valuation and liquidity risk, securitization and off-balance sheet activities.
- The FSB Principles for Sound Compensation Practices have been integrated into the Basel capital framework, and international guidance is under development to reinforce their implementation.
- Central counterparties have been introduced to clear credit default swaps, reducing the systemic risks from this market. Transparency and standardization in this market have been increased and dealers have reduced their cross exposures through trade compression.
- Stronger oversight regimes for credit rating agencies have been developed. New legislation creating oversight regimes has been approved in Japan and is close to final approval in the EU; in the US, amendments to the existing oversight regime have been proposed or already made.
- Internationally agreed principles for the oversight of hedge funds have been issued, and national and regional legislation has been or is in the process of being introduced to implement them.
- Good practices for due diligence by asset managers when investing in structured finance products have been issued, which will reduce their reliance on credit rating agencies.
- Abusive short selling has been addressed. Internationally agreed principles have been issued to counteract the abusive use of short selling while

(Box 6.8 continued)

(*Box 6.8 continued*)

> maintaining the benefits of short selling for the functioning of the markets, and their implementation will be monitored.
> - Supervisory coordination and cooperation in the oversight of the most important global financial firms have improved. Supervisory colleges have been established for all the large complex financial groups that the FSB has identified as needing colleges.
> - Strengthened arrangements for system-wide oversight have been developed in many jurisdictions, bringing together the relevant authorities to better assess risks to financial stability and identify mitigating actions.
> - Firm-by-firm contingency planning is underway to implement the FSB Principles for Cross-border Cooperation on Crisis Management. Relevant authorities will hold contingency planning meetings for major cross-border banks and assess the barriers to coordinated action that may arise in handling severe stress at these firms.
> - Depositors will be protected in a more consistent way around the world. Core Principles for Effective Deposit Insurance Systems have been developed and an assessment methodology is under preparation.
>
> **Source**   Authors.

Filling the Gaps in Trade Finance

In the aftermath of the global financial crisis and as part of the G-20 response, the United States proposed a coordinated trade financing initiative that would mobilize the resources of G-20 governments, their export credit and bilateral investment agencies, and the multilateral development banks to provide a package of short-term trade financing vehicles to support global trade. The deteriorating global financial market conditions led to a dramatic reduction in the total volume of financing flows provided by banks for all activities, including trade finance. The combination of the higher cost of funds, liquidity premiums, and higher risk resulted in an increase in the price of short-term trade finance by 25–300 basis points or more according to the World Bank and the IMF. According to the World Bank, the trade finance gap was estimated at US$25–200 billion with other estimates even higher. The persistence of a gap of these magnitudes could restrain US$100–800 billion of trade over the next two years, if left unaddressed. As the financed-constrained trade losses of these magnitudes would severely undermine current efforts to stimulate domestic economies to protect and create jobs, and reverse the current decline in global economic activity, a coordinated initiative should seek to support over US$200 billion in trade over the next two years.

The coordinated initiative includes the following types of financing tools: (a) working capital to private businesses, (b) short-term credit facilities provided by export credit agencies (as in the Asian financial crisis), (c) program to buy short-term trade papers of banks that have provided revolving credit to exporters, and (d) institutional support for such financial programs would include provision of trade credit through: (i) export credit agencies, (ii) investment agencies, (iii) emerging market official support (government programs), (iv) World Bank and regional development banks, and (v) IFC guarantees and funding Mechanisms. These initiatives should be restricted to only solvent buyers and banks, and governments/institutions implementing should evaluate and manage the underlying risks.

Under Basel II, one of the determinants of a bank's capital requirements is the residual maturity of its exposures. For the purposes of this calculation, maturities are usually subject to a floor of one year. The Basel text does, however, automatically exempt certain exposures from the one year floor, and gives national supervisors the discretion to extend this exemption to other exposures subject to their being carefully defined. Basel also suggests a list of the types of exposure which might be so exempted including "some short-term self-liquidating trade transactions, import and export letters of credit and similar transactions." It is important to make full use of this flexibility to ensure that the supply of trade finance is not restricted by requiring unnecessarily high capital to be held against its provision. A number of countries, including the UK, have already taken action along these lines, e.g., by exempting specific transactions if they are not part of a banks' ongoing financing requirement. Such transactions include:

(1)   import letters of credit (including standby letters of credit issued for similar purposes) and acceptances under them;

(2)   export letters of credit confirmation and negotiation;

(3)   pre-shipment and post-shipment acceptances and financing;

(4)   export and import loans collateralized by underlying goods, up to a maximum maturity of 180 days; and

(5) performance guarantees, bid bonds, and other guarantees (including standby letters of credit issued for similar purposes) relating to the export and import of goods and services.

The IFC Global Trade Liquidity Pool

Trade is an essential part of the global economic recovery. However, world trade slowed in 2009 at its sharpest rate in more than 30 years. Furthermore, conditions in financial markets led to a dramatic reduction in the supply of affordable trade finance which, if left unchecked, could restrain many hundreds of billions of dollars of global trade over the next two years. Around 90 percent of world merchandise trade involves some form of credit, insurance, or guarantee.

In order to restore the world trade volumes, many of the regional development banks have increased the size of their trade finance facilities. The IFC has also increased its trade finance guarantee program to US$3 billion, a six-fold increase since 2007. These steps are welcome, but are insufficient, particularly given the size of liquidity constraints. The IFC, therefore, proposed the establishment of a Global Trade Liquidity Pool (GTLP), which would provide additional liquidity to banks wishing to extend trade finance, helping to compensate for the collapse in secondary market finance.

The GTLP would be financed by the IFC and donors. The facility would effectively leverage their contributions by drawing in co-financing from leading banks engaged in trade finance. The total increase in liquidity would be 2.5 times the IFC/donor contributions. Support would be targeted at emerging markets and developing countries which have experienced particular problems in raising trade finance. The GTLP would use the IFC's and international banks' networks of local banks to distribute funds and would therefore be expected to reach SMEs as well as larger, more established firms. Partner banks would help run the scheme on a commercial basis, charging a market rate for trade finance. Income and any possible write-offs would be shared between the IFC, donors, and the banks, according to the relative shares in financing. A temporary measure, the finance could be wound up when no longer needed and the capital returned to partners. As the GTLP would use existing infrastructure and expertise, it would be quick to establish and operate.

Major Policy Recommendations: The Agenda for the Future

The crisis has generated intense interest amongst policymakers, multilateral organizations, and academia, spawning a substantial literature on this subject which, at the very least, provides useful pointers on which way to go from here. While it may be impossible to survey exhaustively the full gamut of evolving ideas, we take up five major reports on the crisis for specific citation as being the most influential in shaping the ongoing debate and defining the broad canvas of collective wisdom. Needless to say, the selection of the reports also reflect our eclectic assessment of the likely traction that they will have with policymakers in the period ahead as they strive to prevent the recurrence of such crises.

The Geneva Report

The 2008 annual Geneva Conference organized together with the Center for Economic Policy Research (CEPR) by the International Center for Monetary and Banking Studies made important recommendations for financial market regulation. The Geneva Report on the World Economy entitled "The Fundamental Principles of Financial Regulation" was released on January 27, 2009.[9]

Locating the root cause of the crisis in faulty regulation, not greed or financial innovation, the Report stated that the goal of regulation should be to moderate financial cycles (Box 6.9). It regarded the prevention of crises in the banking system as more important than in the case of other industries because costs to society are invariably enormous. The social cost of systemic financial collapse exceeds the private cost to the individual financial institutions. Effective regulation should provide incentives for financial institutions to internalize these externalities. The main tool is capital adequacy requirements.

The first proposal of the Geneva Report is to make capital requirements countercyclical. Regulators should increase the existing capital adequacy requirements (based on an assessment of inherent risks) by two multiples. The first is related to above-average growth of credit expansion and leverage. Regulators should agree on the degree of bank asset growth and leverage that is consistent with the long-run target for nominal GDP. The multiple on capital charges rises the more credit expansion exceeds this target. The purpose of this capital charge is not to

---

BOX 6.9
Financial Crises and Regulation

Since busts usually follow booms, financial crashes do not occur randomly, but generally follow booms. The role of current market prices in financial behavior has intensified through a number of avenues, some regulatory, some not, but often in the name of sophistication and modernity. These avenues include mark-to-market valuation of assets; regulatory approved market-based measures of risk such as credit default swap spreads in internal credit models or price volatility in market risk models; and the increasing use of credit ratings, which tend to be correlated, directionally at least, with market prices.

Micro-prudential regulation examines the responses of an individual bank to exogenous risks. By construction, it does not incorporate endogenous risk. It also ignores the systemic importance of individual institutions such as size, degree of leverage and interconnectedness with the rest of the system. It is in this context that there is a need to complement micro-prudential regulation with macro-prudential regulation. The purpose of macro-prudential regulation is to act as a countervailing force to the natural decline in measured risks in a boom and the subsequent rise in the ensuing collapse. Macro-prudential regulation has to be as rule-based as possible. Supervisors have plenty of discretion, but their ability to utilize it is limited by the general short-sighted desire to prolong a boom and by bankers pleading for equality of treatment.

Source   Authors.

---

eliminate the economic cycle, something which would be unrealistically ambitious. Rather, the aim is to ensure that banks are putting aside an increasing amount of capital in a boom, when risk measures are suggesting banks can safely leverage or lend more. Some of this capital can then be released when the boom ends and asset prices fall back.

The second multiple on capital charges should be related to the mismatch in the maturity of assets and liabilities. Indeed, one of the significant lessons of the crisis is that the risk of an asset is largely determined by the maturity of its funding. Northern Rock and other casualties of the crash might well have survived with the same assets if the average maturity of their funding had been longer. When regulators make little distinction between how assets are funded, there is a tendency for financial institutions to rely on cheaper, short-term funding, which increases systemic fragility. The Geneva Report proposed to adjust mark-to-market accounting to provide a further incentive to reduce maturity mismatch. This can be done by imposing a capital cost that is inversely related to the maturity of funding of long-term assets.

The vast majority of banks are small so that their failure would not have the kind of repercussions that the demise of Lehman Brothers triggered. It stands to reason that regulation should acknowledge that some banks are systemically important. The Geneva Report accordingly recommended that in each country, the regulators/supervisors should establish a list of systemically important institutions.

All banks, and any other financial institution subject to deposit insurance, would be subject to some (low) minimum capital requirement as a protection for the deposit insurance fund. Systemically important institutions would be subject both to micro-prudential regulation and to macro-prudential regulation related to their contribution to systemic risk. This can be done by adjusting the micro-prudential ratio by a coefficient corresponding to macro-prudential risk.

The Geneva Report does not share the zeal of some for governments to be involved in the decisions of private firms in matter of executive compensation. While not ruling out particular measures, it argues that macro-prudential regulation will push banks to develop incentive packages that are more encouraging of longer-term behavior. Macro- and micro-prudential instruments differ in the professionalism needed. Macro-prudential regulation should be carried out by central banks and micro-prudential regulation by financial services authorities.

How to deal with banks which are present in several countries? Currently, unless local banks are set up as independent subsidiaries, regulation and supervision is carried out in the home country. Yet financial conditions normally differ from country to country. The Geneva Report proposed that each host country should have the right to designate a cross-border subsidiary, or branch, as "systemic." Systemic branches should be required to become subsidiaries. Foreign-owned subsidiaries should be subject to the same capital requirements, and to hold them in domestic assets as domestic banks.

The Group of Thirty Report (Chair: Paul Volker)

In July 2008, the Group of Thirty (G-30) launched a project on financial reform under the leadership of a Steering Committee chaired by Paul A. Volcker (with the late Tommaso Padoa-Schioppa and Arminio Fraga

Neto as Vice Chairmen). They were supported by other G-30 members who participated in an informal working group. The report of the group, entitled "Financial Reform: A Framework for Financial Stability", was published on January 15, 2009.

The report addressed the following questions: (*a*) policy issues related to redefining the scope and boundaries of prudential regulation, (*b*) reforming the structure of prudential regulation, including the role of central banks, the implications for the working of "lender-of-last-resort" facilities and other elements of the official "safety net", and the need for greater international coordination, (*c*) improving governance, risk management, regulatory policies, and accounting practices and standards, and (*d*) improving transparency and financial infrastructure arrangements.

The reform proposals of this report consist of an extensive set of inter-related changes in policies, practices, and market standards. As mentioned in the report, these recommendations can be best viewed in the context of the following four broadly stated core recommendations:

- Gaps and weaknesses in the coverage of prudential regulation and supervision must be eliminated.
- The quality and effectiveness of prudential regulation and supervision must be improved.
- Institutional policies and standards must be strengthened, with particular emphasis on standards for governance, risk management, capital, and liquidity.
- Financial markets and products must be made more transparent, with better-aligned risk and prudential incentives. The infrastructure supporting such markets must be made much more robust and resistant to potential failures of even large financial institutions.

Some of the recommendations of the report are truly far-reaching, including:

- special regulation of systemically important banking institutions;
- a framework for national-level consolidated prudential regulation and supervision over large internationally active insurance companies;
- reorganization of money market funds as "special purpose banks" if they offer transaction features;

- special prudential regulation of "systemically significant" private pools of capital (such as hedge funds and private equity); and
- a special legal regime that would provide regulators with authority to require early warning, prompt corrective actions, and orderly closings of regulated banking organizations, and other systemically significant regulated financial institutions.

The EU Report (Chair: Jacques de Larsosiere)[10]

This report was commissioned in November 2008 by José-Manuel Barroso, President of the European Commission. Submitted in February 2009, this report provides fine analysis of the manifold causes of the financial crisis and set out an approach that would rethink the EU supervisory landscape. The Group headed by Jacques de Larosière, former Managing Director of the IMF, proposed some far-reaching solutions, such as: (a) revising Basel II, (b) broadening supervision to include credit rating agencies, and (c) introducing dynamic provisioning for banks. The Group emphasized that financial sector rules should be adopted in EU-wide regulations rather than in directives that are translated into 27 national laws and suggested dropping most national exemptions to EU financial standards by 2011.

Previous attempts to overhaul EU financial regulation have exposed divisions between countries in favor of a single European regulator and those opposed to the idea. The de Larosière Report stopped short of recommending a single European financial services supervisor, but set out 31 recommendations for closer coordination between national regulatory bodies and some EU-wide regulatory standards. Furthermore, the report proposed a new European Systemic Risk Council to collect information and analyze it to detect sources of systemic risk and financial instability. It would bring together representatives from the central banks and financial regulators of all the EU's 27 member states, under the chairmanship of the European Central Bank. The report also recommended creating a new European System of Financial Supervision to ensure financial stability in the EU and its member states, working closely with national regulators. As part of this, the three existing pan-European committees of banking, insurance and securities regulators would be replaced by three new authorities run by full-time independent professionals. They would coordinate the application of common supervisory standards, ensure strong cooperation with the other supervisors and make it easier for regulators to supervise institutions based in other countries.

On EU-wide issues, the report called for the regulation of credit rating agencies by the new authority responsible for securities supervision. It also sought measures to inhibit the emergence of "parallel banking systems," which hid from regulators the extent of risk-taking in the international financial system. It also recommended that remuneration in financial services should ensure that only performance over the long-term is rewarded.

More generally, the report held that the Basel II banking rules need to be overhauled to gradually increase the amount of capital banks must hold, reduce the tendency of the rules to make downturns worse and introduce stricter rules for off-balance sheet items.

The UK–FSA Review (Chair: Adair Turner)

A Panel chaired by Lord Turner, Chairman of the UK FSA was asked by the Chancellor of the Exchequer to review the events that led to the financial crisis and to recommend reforms. The Review was submitted in March 2009. The Review identified three underlying causes of the crisis: (a) macroeconomic imbalances, (b) financial innovation of little social value, and (c) important deficiencies in key bank capital and liquidity regulations. These were underpinned by an exaggerated faith in rational and self-correcting markets. The Review recommended various ways and means to avert such banking crises in the future.

In the field of capital adequacy, accounting and liquidity, it recommended that the quantity/quality of overall capital in the global banking system should be increased/improved resulting in minimum regulatory requirements significantly above existing Basel rules. The Turner Panel emphasized that the transition to future rules should be carefully phased, given the importance of maintaining bank lending in the current macroeconomic climate. Furthermore, capital required against trading book activities should be increased significantly and a fundamental review of the market risk capital regime (e.g., reliance on value at risk or VAR measures for regulatory purposes) should be launched. It was somewhat critical of Basel II and recommended that regulators should take immediate action to ensure that the implementation of the current Basel II capital regime does not create unnecessary pro-cyclicality.

This can be achieved by using "through the cycle" rather than "point in time" measures of probabilities of default and at the same time, a counter-cyclical capital adequacy regime should be introduced with capital buffers which increase in economic upswings and decrease in recessions. Furthermore, a maximum gross leverage ratio should be introduced as a backstop discipline against excessive growth in absolute balance sheet size. While ensuring that liquidity regulation and supervision should be recognized as of equal importance to capital regulation, more intense and dedicated supervision of individual banks' liquidity positions should be introduced, including the use of stress tests defined by regulators and covering system-wide risks. Finally, it recommended introduction of a "core funding ratio" to ensure sustainable funding of balance sheet growth.

In terms of institutional and geographic coverage of regulation, the Panel, while maintaining that regulatory and supervisory coverage should follow the principle of economic substance and not legal form, categorically recommended expansion of regulatory/informational net over the shadow banking system. To quote:

> Authorities should have the power to gather information on all significant unregulated financial institutions (e.g. hedge funds) to allow assessment of overall system-wide risks. Regulators should have the power to extend prudential regulation of capital and liquidity or impose other restrictions if any institution or group of institutions develops bank-like features that threaten financial stability and/or otherwise become systemically significant. Offshore financial centres should be covered by global agreements on regulatory standards. (FSA 2009)

As far as credit rating agencies are concerned, the Panel preferred that credit rating agencies should be subject to registration and supervision to ensure good governance and management of conflicts of interest and that credit ratings are only applied to securities for which a consistent rating is possible. Rating agencies and regulators should ensure that communication to investors about the appropriate use of ratings makes clear that they are designed to carry inference for credit risk, not liquidity or market risk. Furthermore, the Panel asked for a fundamental review of the use of structured finance ratings in the Basel II framework.

Contrary to the popularly perceived separation of monetary policy and banking supervision in the UK, the Panel recommended that in macro-prudential analysis, both the BoE and the FSA should be extensively and collaboratively involved. Measures such as countercyclical capital and liquidity requirements should be used to offset these risks. Institutions such as the IMF must have the resources and robust independence to conduct high quality macro-prudential analysis and, if necessary, to challenge conventional intellectual wisdom and national policies.

The Panel has also went into the issue of compensation and recommended that "remuneration policies should be designed to avoid incentives for undue risk taking; risk management considerations should be closely integrated into remuneration decisions."

As far as supervision in the UK is concerned, the Panel suggested that the FSA should complete the implementation of its Supervisory Enhancement Program (SEP) which entails a major shift in its supervisory approach with: (a) increase in resources devoted to high impact firms and, in particular, to large complex banks; (b) focus on business models, strategies, risks, and outcomes, rather than primarily on systems and processes; (c) focus on technical skills as well as probity of approved persons; (d) increased analysis of sectors and comparative analysis of firm performance; (e) investment in specialist prudential skills; (f) more intensive information requirements on key risks (e.g., liquidity); and (g) a focus on remuneration policies.

The Panel suggested that new capital and liquidity requirements should be designed to constrain commercial banks' role in risky proprietary trading activities. However, a more formal and complete legal distinction of "narrow banking" from market making activities is not feasible.

In defining issues relating to the global cross-border banks, the Panel put forward the idea that international coordination of bank supervision should be enhanced by: (a) the establishment and effective operation of colleges of supervisors for the largest complex and cross-border financial institutions, and (b) the preemptive development of crisis coordination mechanisms and contingency plans between supervisors, central banks, and finance ministries.

Interestingly, the Panel put forward certain open questions for further debate to which no definitive answers are found so far and which needs further informed public debate. The following list is illustrative:

- Should the UK introduce product regulation of mortgage market LTV or loan-to-income (LTI)?
- Should financial regulators be willing to impose restrictions on the design or use of wholesale market products (e.g., CDS)?

- Does effective macro-prudential policy require the use of tools other than the variation of countercyclical capital and liquidity requirements, e.g., (*a*) through the cycle variation of LTV or LTI ratios, and (*b*) regulation of collateral margins ("haircuts") in derivatives contracts and secured financing transactions?
- Should decisions on, for instance, short selling recognize the dangers of market irrationality as well as market abuse?

The UN Commission (Chair: Joseph Stiglitz)[11]

To review the workings of the global financial systems and to explore ways and means to secure a more sustainable and just global economic order, the Secretary General of the United Nations (UN) convened a Commission of Experts chaired by Professor Joseph Stiglitz and comprised of a number of outstanding economists, policymakers, and practitioners drawn from Japan, Western Europe, Africa, Latin America, South and East Asia.[12] The preliminary recommendations of the Commission, which were released on March 19, 2009, form the basis of the review here.

This Report's stance is reflected in its preamble: "The rapid spread of financial crisis from a small number of developed countries to engulf the global economy provides tangible evidence that the international trade and financial system needs to be profoundly reformed to meet the needs and changed conditions of the 21st century." While maintaining that this inclusive global response will require the participation of the entire international community, it went on to add that "it must encompass more than the G-7 or G-8 or G-20, but the representatives of the entire planet, from the G-192."

While the Commission delved into various aspects of global financial architecture and towards global institutional arrangements for governing the global economy, including putting forward a proposal for a Global Financial Regulatory Authority; a Global Competition Authority, it suggested the following 10 immediate measures:

(i) All developed countries should take strong, coordinated, and effective actions to stimulate their economies.

(ii) Developing countries need additional funding.

(iii) Mobilizing additional development funds by the creation of a new credit facility.

(iv) Developing countries need more policy space.

(v) The lack of coherence between policies governing trade and finance must be rectified.

(vi) Crisis response must avoid protectionism.

(vii) Opening advanced country markets to least developed countries' exports.

(viii) Learning from successful policies to undertake regulatory reforms.

(ix) Coordinating the domestic and global impact of government financial sector support.

(x) Improved coordination of global economic policies.

As far as the agenda for systemic reforms is concerned, the Commission's recommendations included: a new global reserve system, reforms of the governance of the international financial institutions, a Global Economic Coordination Council, better and more balanced surveillance, and reforming central bank policies to promote development. The Commission was candid in its recommendations on financial markets which included, *inter alia*, financial product safety, comprehensive application of financial regulation, regulation of derivatives trading, regulation of credit rating agencies, and host country regulation of foreign subsidiaries.

While the recommendations of the Commission have been termed as the "new recipe for reforming globalization," lack of coherence with the principles for reforming the international financial system as enunciated in the leading international financial institutions like World Bank and IMF as well as Financial Stability Forum (Board), or G-20 declarations makes them somewhat difficult to implement.[13]

Conclusion

The global economy appears to be pulling out of the downturn, led by a strong rebound in Asia. Commodity prices (especially oil) are firming and world trade is picking up. Capital flows in the form of bond issuances and portfolio flows are returning to the emerging markets of Asia and Latin America. The main trigger for the turnaround is strong monetary and fiscal stimulus across advanced and emerging economies. On the other hand, unemployment is rising and projected to stay above 10 percent in the US and western Europe through 2010 and 2011. Consumer spending is still sluggish, investment is anemic, corporate bankruptcies are still high in the advanced economies, and economies across the world continue to face constraints in credit availability due to tightening of lending standards by banks in spite of some improvement in liquidity and financial conditions. By current reckoning, the recovery is sluggish and protracted, jobless, and credit constrained. Output losses on account of the crisis are likely to be relatively permanent.

The main concern is what will happen when the effects of policy stimulus wears off. In this context, concerns are being expressed about the risk of a "double-dip" or "W"-shaped path for the global economy in the months ahead and even of the danger of an extended stagnation or "L"-shaped recession. The key risk to recovery is a premature withdrawal of policy stimulus due to resistance in some countries and lack of headroom (high debt/deficits) in others. The immediate tasks are: (a) follow through on existing commitments of fiscal stimulus and be ready for more if warranted, and (b) repair the monetary transmission to ensure smooth credit flow. There is an unfinished agenda on repairing the financial system—toxic assets, cleaning banks' balance sheets, and capitalization/resolution of failing banks. The perimeter of regulation also has to be expanded not just to unregulated institutions but also to markets, instruments, and havens, while being intensified over systemically important financial centers.

Looking ahead beyond recovery, several medium-term challenges confront policymakers and will have to be resolved so that a strong, sustainable, and balanced growth path for the global economy can be anchored. These are: (a) returning to fiscal sustainability and viable sovereign debt/debt servicing, (b) unwinding central bank balance sheets without destabilizing financial markets while ensuring that excess liquidity does not build inflationary pressures, (c) avoiding trade and financial protectionism, (d) raising productivity, efficiency, employment, and capital use to fight the potential output loss, (e) expanding the perimeter and efficacy of financial sector regulation without stifling innovations and risk-taking, (f) instituting structural reforms to promote flexibility in labor markets and product markets and facilitate increase in investment, and (g) resuming the fight against poverty.

Annex TABLE 6.1A
Current Financial Arrangements under the IMF's General Resources Account
(as of August 19, 2010)

(in millions of SDRs)

Member	Effective date	Expiration date	Amount agreed	Undrawn balance	Total GRA credit, outstanding	Total GRA credit, as % of quota
I. Stand-By Arrangement						
Angola	Nov. 23, 2009	Feb. 22, 2012	859	515	344	120
Antigua and Barbuda	Jun. 7, 2010	Jun. 6, 2013	81	64	17	125
Bosnia	Jul. 8, 2009	Jun. 30, 2012	1,015	710	304	180
Dominican Republic	Nov. 9, 2009	Mar. 8, 2012	1,095	815	510	233
El Salvador	Mar. 17, 2010	Mar. 16, 2013	514	514	–	–
Georgia	Sept. 15, 2008	Jun. 14, 2011	747	170	577	384
Greece	May 9, 2010	May 8, 2013	26,433	21,627	4,806	584
Guatemala	Apr. 22, 2009	Oct. 21, 2010	631	631	–	–
Hungary	Nov. 6, 2008	Oct. 5, 2010	10,538	2,901	7,637	735
Iceland	Nov. 19, 2008	Aug. 31, 2011	1,400	630	770	655
Iraq	Feb. 24, 2010	Feb. 23, 2012	2,377	2,080	297	25
Jamaica	Feb. 4, 2010	May 3, 2012	821	343	478	175
Kosovo	Jul. 21, 2010	Jan. 20, 2012	93	93	–	–
Latvia	Dec. 23, 2008	Dec. 22, 2011	1,522	539	982	775
Maldives	Dec. 4, 2009	Dec. 3, 2012	49	41	8	100
Mongolia	Apr. 1, 2009	Oct. 1, 2010	153	31	123	240
Pakistan	Nov. 24, 2008	Dec. 30, 2010	7,236	2,300	4,936	478

(Annex Table 6.1A continued)

(Annex Table 6.1A continued)

(in millions of SDRs)

Member	Effective date	Expiration date	Amount agreed	Undrawn balance	Total GRA credit, outstanding	Total GRA credit, as % of quota
Romania	May 4, 2009	May 3, 2011	11,443	2,412	9,031	877
Serbia, Republic of	Jan. 16, 2009	Apr. 15, 2011	2,619	1,391	1,228	262
Sri Lanka	Jul. 24, 2009	Jul. 23, 2012	1,654	965	694	168
Ukraine	Jul. 28, 2010	Dec. 27, 2012	10,000	8,750	8,250	601
Total			**81,277**	**47,521**	**40,992**	
II. Flexible Credit Line						
Colombia	May 7, 2010	May 6, 2011	2,322	2,322	–	–
Mexico	Mar. 25, 2010	Mar. 24, 2011	31,528	31,528	–	–
Poland	Jul. 2, 2010	Jul. 1, 2011	13,690	13,690	–	–
Total			**47,540**	**47,540**	–	–
III. Extended Arrangements						
Armenia	Jun. 28, 2010	Jun. 27, 2013	133	116	368	400
Moldova	Jan. 29, 2010	Jan. 28, 2013	185	145	40	32
Seychelles	Dec. 23, 2009	Dec. 22, 2012	20	15	16	185
Total			**338**	**275**	**424**	
IV. Grand Total of 27 SBA, FCL, and EFF			**129,155**	**95,336**	**41,416**	

Source IMF website, www.imf.org

Annex TABLE 6.1B
Current Financial Arrangements under the IMF's Poverty Reduction and Growth Trust
(as of August 19, 2010)

(in millions of SDRs)

Member	Effective date	Expiration date	Amount agreed	Undrawn balance	Total PRGT loans, outstanding	Total PRGT loans, as % of quota
Extended Credit Facility						
Afghanistan	Jun. 26, 2006	Sept. 25, 2010	81	6	75	47
Armenia	Jun. 28, 2010	Jun. 27, 2013	133	115	84	91
Benin	Jun. 14, 2010	Jun. 13, 2013	74	64	35	57
Burkina Faso	Jun. 14, 2010	Jun. 13, 2013	46	39	77	128
Burundi	Jul. 7, 2008	Jul. 6, 2011	46	13	71	92
Central African Rep.	Dec. 22, 2006	Dec. 31, 2010	70	9	50	90
Comoros	Sept. 21, 2009	Sept. 20, 2012	14	8	8	90
Congo, Dem. Rep. of	Dec. 11, 2009	Dec. 10, 2012	346	247	210	39
Congo, Rep. of	Dec. 8, 2008	Dec. 7, 2011	8	5	16	19
Cote d'Ivoire	Mar. 27, 2009	Mar. 26, 2012	374	143	254	78
Djibouti	Sept. 17, 2008	Sept. 16, 2011	13	7	9	55
Gambia, The	Feb. 21, 2007	Feb. 20, 2011	25	5	20	65
Ghana	Jul. 15, 2009	Jul. 14, 2012	387	238	255	69

(Annex Table 6.1B continued)

(*Annex Table 6.1B continued*)

(*in millions of SDRs*)

Member	Effective date	Expiration date	Amount agreed	Undrawn balance	Total PRGT loans, outstanding	Total PRGT loans, as % of quota
Grenada	Apr. 18, 2010	Apr. 17, 2013	9	8	18	151
Guinea	Dec. 21, 2007	Dec. 20, 2010	70	45	33	31
Guinea–Bissau	May 7, 2010	May 6, 2013	22	14	8	59
Haiti	Jul. 21, 2010	Jul. 20, 2013	41	33	8	10
Lesotho	Jun. 2, 2010	Jun. 1, 2013	42	34	20	57
Liberia	Mar. 14, 2008	Mar. 13, 2011	239	9	24	19
Malawi	Feb. 19, 2010	Feb. 18, 2013	52	45	88	127
Mali	May 28, 2008	May 27, 2011	28	4	32	34
Mauritania	Mar. 15, 2010	Mar. 14, 2013	77	66	21	33
Moldova	Jan. 29, 2010	Jan. 28, 2013	185	105	174	142
Nicaragua	Oct. 5, 2007	Oct. 4, 2010	78	24	96	74
Niger	Jun. 2, 2008	Jun. 1, 2011	23	10	39	60
Sao Tome	Mar. 2, 2009	Mar. 1, 2012	3	2	3	43
Sierra Leone	Jul. 1, 2010	Jun. 30, 2013	31	27	70	68
Tajikistan	Apr. 21, 2009	Apr. 20, 2012	104	52	52	60

Togo	Apr. 21, 2008	Apr. 20, 2011	95	23	72	99
Yemen	Jul. 30, 2010	Jul. 29, 2013	244	209	59	24
Zambia	Jun. 4, 2008	Jun. 3, 2011	220	37	238	49
Total			**3,181**	**1,644**	**2,224**	
Exogenous Shocks Facility						
Ethiopia	Aug. 26, 2009	Oct. 25, 2010	154	40	147	110
Maldives	Dec. 4, 2009	Dec. 3, 2011	8	6	2	25
Total			**162**	**46**	**149**	
Stand-By Credit Facility						
Solomon Islands	Feb. 6, 2010	Jan. 12, 2011	12	9	3	30
Grand Total 34 ECF, ESF, and SCF			**3,355**	**1,700**	**2,376**	

Source IMF website, www.imf.org

Notes

1. The International Monetary and Financial Committee of the IMF in its eighteenth meeting held in Washington, DC on October 11, 2008 endorsed their agenda.
2. The US Fed authorized the arrangements between the Federal Reserve and each of the following central banks, viz., the Reserve Bank of Australia, Banco Central do Brasil, the Bank of Canada, Danmarks Nationalbank, the Bank of England, the European Central Bank, the Bank of Japan, the Bank of Korea, Banco de Mexico, the Reserve Bank of New Zealand, Norges Bank, the Monetary Authority of Singapore, Sveriges Riksbank, and the Swiss National Bank.
3. British Prime Minister Gordon Brown (on October 13 and 15, 2008) called for world leaders to come together to remake the Bretton Woods Agreement to tackle a 21st century globalized financial system. He said: (a) "Sometimes it does take a crisis for people to agree that what is obvious and should have been done years ago can no longer be postponed. But we must now create the right new financial architecture for the global age"; (b) "With the same courage and foresight of their founders, we must now reform the international financial system around agreed principles of transparency, integrity, responsibility, good housekeeping, and cooperation across borders"; (c) "Future financial architecture must be global rather than European"; (d) "It is obvious now that we are dealing with global financial markets. Ten, 20 years ago we had national capital markets. What we do not have is anything other than national and regional regulation and supervision."
4. Ironically, the 2007 *Article IV Report* of the IMF Surveillance (on July 11, 2007) for the United States mentioned that: (a) "*Core commercial and investment banks are in a sound financial position and systemic risk appears low*" (p. 14; para 23); (b) "*US financial markets remain highly innovative, supporting capital inflows and long-term growth*" (p. 19; para 30). The subprime crisis emerged in the public domain in August 2007.
5. The discussion is based on IMF's Public Information Notice on "Nonconcessional Lending Facilities and Conditionality" on April 3, 2009, available at www.imf.org.
6. FCL arrangements can now be approved for either one year or two years with an interim review of qualification after one year, whereas they were previously either for six months or one year with an interim review after six months.
7. India's FSAP in 2001 is one of the earliest conducted by the IMF and the World Bank. This has been followed by two self assessments, the most recent one being in 2008.
8. These countries/jurisdictions are: Australia, Austria, Belgium, Brazil, Canada, China, France, Germany, Hong Kong SAR, Italy, Japan, India, Ireland, Luxembourg, Mexico, the Netherlands, Russia, Singapore, South Korea, Spain, Sweden, Switzerland, Turkey, the United Kingdom, and the United States. This group of countries covers almost 90 percent of the global financial system and 80 percent of global economic activity. It includes 15 of the G-20 member countries and a majority of members of the FSB.
9. The report has been prepared by Markus Brunnermeier, Andrew Crockett, Charles Goodhart, Avinash Persaud, and Hyun Shin.
10. The other members were: Leszek Balcerowicz, Otmar Issing, Rainer Masera, Callum Mc Carthy, Lars Nyberg, José Pérez, and Onno Ruding.

11. The Full name of the Commission is: "The Commission of Experts of the President of the UN General Assembly on Reforms of the International Monetary and Financial System".

12. Other members of the commission are: Andrei Bougrov (Russia), Yousef Boutros–Ghali (Egypt), Jean–Paul Fitoussi (France), Charles A.E. Goodhart (UK), Robert Johnson (USA), Jomo Kwame Sundaram (United Nations), Benno Ndulo (Tanzania), José Antonio Ocampo (Colombia), Mr Pedro Páez (Ecuador), Avinash Persaud (Barbados), Yaga Venugopal Reddy (India), Rubens Ricupero (Brazil), Eisuke Sakakibara (Japan), Chukwuma Soludo (Nigeria), Heidemarie Wieczorek–Zeul (Germany), Yu Yongding (China), and Zeti Akhtar Aziz (Malaysia).

13. The recently released UN Secretary General's Report highlighted the following possible impacts of the crisis, viz., (*a*) rapid increases in unemployment, poverty, and hunger; (*b*) deceleration of growth, or severe economic contraction; (*c*) negative effects on trade balances, balance of payments, and foreign reserves; (*d*) dwindling levels of foreign direct investment; (*e*) large and volatile movements in exchange rates; (*f*) growing budget deficits and falling tax revenues; (*g*) drastic reduction of world trade; (*h*) sharp contraction in exports; (*i*) falling prices for primary commodities; (*j*) declining remittances to developing countries; (*k*) sharply reduced revenues from tourism; and (*l*) massive withdrawal of private capital flows, also increasing the funding problem of the private sector in emerging and developing countries.

7
Lessons from the Crisis and the Way Forward

Introduction

Since the onset of the financial crisis, there has been active and intense engagement across the world in assessing the underlying causes of the turmoil and drawing lessons to promote financial stability. There is now a broad agreement that the seeds of the crisis were sown during the preceding years of high growth and low interest rates that bred excessive optimism and risk-taking and spawned a broad range of failures—in market discipline, financial regulation, macroeconomic policies, and global oversight. While there are differences in perception on the relative importance of each, there is clearly a need for remedial actions across a broad front and at many levels, implying an ambitious agenda for policymakers and the need for coordinated actions.

Over the last two years, the debate is evolving onto a much larger canvas as both national authorities and supranational institutions strive to lay a foundation for the way ahead in terms of crafting focused and specific courses of action to prevent the recurrence of such crises, and if they do recur, to mitigate their deleterious consequences. Wide-ranging reforms are being contemplated in all these areas.

Evolving Policy Framework

Macroeconomic Policies

There are several important factors relating to the conduct of macro-economic policies that underlie the mutation of the crisis into its present form. First, the obsessive focus of monetary policy on the inflation objective may have actually led to negligence of the asset price bubble. Low and stable inflation anchored by the credibility earned by monetary policy resulted in lowering returns on investments in the real sectors of the economy and made investing in financial assets more rewarding. This arbitrage opportunity created by monetary policy setting could have been a major force driving the relentless search for yields that led up to the current crisis. Second, it is important to recognize the limits and dangers of monetary policy accommodation. The so-called mild recession in the aftermath of the dotcom crash was essentially due to the role of monetary policy in transferring the bubble to the housing sector and then lax regulation took over. Third, the separation of financial regulation from monetary policy also could have contributed to the crisis. There is a considerable body of empirical evidence indicating that regulation of the financial sector guided by the Basel I minimum capital standards has been inherently prone to increasing the riskiness of balance sheets. In order to meet the capital requirements, banks took to stripping their balance sheets of the most rewarding assets, securitizing them and trading them off-balance sheet, and/or placing them with special purpose vehicles. Fourth, bank-lending needs to be invariably supported by collateral; it is the responsibility of the monetary/regulatory authority to ensure that the collateral is of the highest quality and that functioning markets exist for these assets to enable continuous price discovery.

In the light of the experience with the ongoing financial crisis, the traditional view that monetary policy is too blunt an instrument to deal with asset-price fluctuations is giving way to a broader macro-prudential advocacy for expanding the mandate of monetary policy to explicitly include macro-financial stability, rather than just price stability, without taking away from the central role prudential regulation should play in addressing credit booms. Monetary policy should be assigned the objectives of both price and financial stability with relative weights depending on underlying circumstances. The appropriate approach is a risk-minimization strategy in which all booms are monitored carefully and continuously with a view to intervening in the interest of macro-financial stability, if warranted. Credit/GDP ratios should be monitored in conjunction with the composition of credit, leverage indicators such as credit–deposit ratios, and exposures to sensitive sectors.

It has been argued that fiscal policy did not play a direct role in the run-up to the crisis. This view is, however, open to serious question.

In many countries, budget deficits had not been reduced sufficiently during the boom years when revenues were high, and consequently, the available fiscal space to fight the crisis was limited. Further, in several countries, the structure of taxation promoted leverage and debt financing—a bias that increases the vulnerability of the private sector to shocks. In this sense, fiscal policy had a major role to play in the crisis by being accommodative and masking the incubation of the causal factors. The existence of large fiscal deficits in some advanced economies also facilitated a flight to safety when risk aversion set in and this was reflected in sizeable capital outflows from a host of emerging countries which were at the periphery of the crisis and got hit by knock-on effects as the contagion spread.

Fiscal buffers should be established in boom times. One possible approach is to estimate trend levels of tax buoyancy so that when tax buoyancy rises above trend in good times, it provides a trigger for calibrated cutbacks on pre-decided elements of discretionary public expenditure. This would help to build up fiscal headroom, which, as the current crisis has shown, is vital in the event of a downturn. Tax distortions and other fiscal incentives that could have played a role in asset price volatility warrant closer scrutiny.

Discussion on the role of global imbalances in the buildup of systemic risk has also turned contentious. Polarities have tended to be focused upon: excessive consumption in some countries and excess saving in others, misalignment in exchange rates, and surges of capital flows, often volatile. Although it is widely held that financial integration has helped transmit these risks, the lesson that is drawn is not that capital flows should be sharply curtailed. Rather, there is a felt need to revisit macroeconomic and structural policy responses to large imbalances, stressing consideration of financial and real spillovers, and to examine the scope for prudential measures to reduce systemic risk associated with capital flows. In a globalized world, the counterpart of large fiscal and current account imbalances is inevitably reflected in movements of capital and tolerance to the buildup of macro imbalances in national interest tends to be obfuscated in political economy and blame games.

Financial Regulation and Supervision

The current financial crisis has its roots in the failure of market discipline in systemically important advanced countries. As misaligned incentives led to excessive leverage and risk taking, new and complex financial instruments that were poorly understood emerged—these culminated to liquidity mismanagement and, ultimately, to increased systemic risk. Regulation and supervision failed to stem this excessive risk-taking, in part because of inadequate assessments of interlinkages between regulated and non-regulated institutions and markets. When the crisis ensued, policy responses were hampered by fragmented regulatory structures, inadequate disclosures of risks, and weaknesses in crisis management and bank resolution frameworks, especially in dealing with cross border stress.

Against this backdrop, a range of reform priorities are under active consideration. First, the perimeter of regulation should be expanded to include a wider range of institutions and markets, and be underpinned by more effective cross-functional regulation and cooperation. Second, existing regulatory and institutional practices should be re-examined with a view to reducing pro-cyclicality. Third, liquidity management practices and regulatory policies must also change to ensure that financial institutions maintain larger liquidity buffers. Fourth, strengthened public disclosure practices for systemically important financial institutions and markets should be a priority. Policymakers need to take the lead in translating disclosures into effective assessments of institutional and systemic risk, and incorporating this information into early warning frameworks and the formulation of macro-prudential policies. Fifth, cross-border and cross-functional regulation and cooperation should be improved and promote level playing fields across markets. Finally, national liquidity frameworks need to be strengthened and at the international level, enhanced mechanisms for providing cross-border liquidity are vital.

The dilemmas for regulators are, however, manifold: How to be comprehensive? What is the preferred mode of regulation—a single regulator for all financial intuitions or multiple regulators for different institutions? What should the role of central banks be in the regulation of financial institutions? Indeed, stability in its broadest connotation is the reason why monetary authorities exist. It is in this context that it has been argued that monetary policy and financial regulation/supervision should be unified—or reunited where they have been divorced—under the aegis of a single authority. This would require a blending of pure monetary instruments such as interest rates, reserve requirements, and open market operations with regulatory tools such as capital, provisioning, risk weighting, exposure limits and the like in varying proportions depending on the assessment of macroeconomic, and financial conditions. Were then efforts in select countries to separate regulatory and the monetary authorities misplaced? Furthermore, these lessons suggest the need for re-evaluating the appropriateness of Basel II norms. In particular, supervisory oversight and due diligence cannot be substituted by imposition of capital based norms and exclusive reliance on them.

Looking ahead, history will judge the responses of central banks to assuage seizures of liquidity that gripped financial markets as they froze in a crisis of confidence. Issues relating to the asset quality in the central bank balance sheets, the increased use of "quasi-fiscal" instruments and mechanisms being contemplated to transfer these assets to fiscal authorities so as to prevent central bank losses and consequent fiscal costs will have to interface with the potential impact on the health of public finances and the ultimate burden, perhaps unjustly, on the tax payer. It is perhaps necessary to draw up contingency plans to deal with these challenges of the future, including the threat of liquidity traps and deflation/future inflation, and volatility in capital flows.

Global Architecture and the IMF[1]

The crisis has once again highlighted the gaps in the global financial architecture. First of all is the costly failure in delivering adequate warnings prior to the crisis, especially in what is currently regarded as the core. Even where risks were identified, too often they were expressed vaguely or were too muted to gain traction with policymakers. In this regard, the IMF should have been more effective in identifying, communicating, and promoting coordinated responses to systemic risks to the global economy. Second, this underscores the urgent need to intensify and strengthen surveillance. The tacit presumption that risks lie mainly in less mature markets should give way to surveillance of all types of systemic risk, in advanced and emerging market countries alike. Sharpening the FSAP and more generally strengthening financial sector analysis in the context of bilateral surveillance are immediate remedial steps that need to be taken. Third, greater attention should also be paid to large cross-border flows in surveillance activities in a framework of well-defined rules or collaboration agreements among financial regulators on resolution and burden sharing. There needs to be a renewed supervisory focus on globally active and systemically important financial institutions and markets; developing compatible bank resolution and information-sharing frameworks; and agreeing on minimum supervisory practices for the oversight of cross border firms. Fourth, another fault line in the global architecture has been inadequate liquidity support and financing and insurance facilities to help countries weather the turbulence in global capital markets. It is in this context that efforts are underway to augment the IMF's lending capacity and in general to enhance the resources of international financial institutions (IFIs) substantially. Reforms of IMF lending instruments, conditionality, surcharges and commitment fees, and IMF governance are each important issues in their own right in this regard.

The recognition of these gaps should lead to even-handed surveillance by the IMF, given its near universal membership. We look forward to the concrete steps that should be taken to make such surveillance more effective without adding to the obligations of developing countries that have for long been treated as the usual suspects. It is also important to recognize that the networks that exist outside of the IMF, including the G-20 and the FSB, play a useful and complementary role. Global financial stability is perhaps too important and significant to be left exclusively to one organization. The existence of other networks adds to creative tension and helps to optimize outcomes, sometimes by reminding the IMF of its own shortcomings. The IMF needs to be at the center of any global response to a crisis; but in order to play this role, it also needs to be substantially reformed.

The first and most important reform will undoubtedly be a significant and meaningful quota and voice reform beyond the 2010 agreement. As is well known, quotas play multiple roles in the IMF. A substantial quota increase with appropriate rebalancing on an accelerated calendar by the end of 2014 has to be an essential part of the crisis response. Such a reform should address issues of adequacy of resources and of enhanced access for many countries. It should also lead to significantly enhancing the stake in the IMF of those dynamic emerging market countries and regions of the world which have the potential of sustaining the global growth momentum. Second, an important element of the representation reform in the IMF is the need to move to a truly open choice for IMF management. Unwritten rules which reserve the position for certain regions or countries are anachronistic and need to be changed, unambiguously and demonstrably. Third, there is the issue of a higher level policy engagement of ministers and policymakers with a decision-making role in the affairs of the IMF.

This raises the question as to what the decision-making rules would be for such a policy group—would it be voting on the basis of the present voting shares in the Executive Board or would it be a consensus based body? If it is to be consensus based decision-making, the International Monetary and Financial Committee (IMFC) as it exists should suffice, with some changes to the formalistic structure of meetings. On the other hand, if decisions are to be vote based, then such a "political mechanism" should be put in place only after meaningful quota and voice reforms are first effected.

In sum, these lessons provide much food for serious and constructive reflection. Close collaboration among all stakeholders and intense dialogue will be crucial for developing a clear perspective on the next steps. Greater clarity on the road map and time frame for implementing the identified solutions will involve intensified multilateral coordination backed by concerted affirmative actions by all.

Some Debates Raised by the Crisis

The crisis has challenged many of our fundamental beliefs about economic resilience and financial market stability. Ruling orthodoxies and mainstreams appear to have fallen by the wayside and a fundamental revision of the relationship between the state and markets and the manner of dealing with market failure seems to be underway. Against this backdrop of heightened uncertainty, it is worthwhile to visit some of the important debates that have been thrown up in the context of the current crisis. Some of these debates have already been addressed in the preceding section in the context of drawing lessons. Yet, in the interest of expository comprehensiveness, and given the summarizing objective in this final chapter, it is worthwhile to reiterate them. Sifting through the key questions that are being posed with a view to identifying the right ones may eventually help to gather the lessons that can be drawn from the recent experience.

Did Globalization Cause the Crisis?

In the years preceding the crisis, global growth and world trade was the highest in recorded history but roughly consistent with potential since inflation was low and stable in most countries. Interest rates were low, partly reflecting accommodative monetary policy. Did these benign conditions feed the buildup of systemic risk? Did high growth, low inflation, low interest rates, and excessive optimism prompt a search for yield and underestimation of risks until it was too late? Is it that opening up has made national economies exposed to adverse happenings in distant corners of the globe?

Is There Any Case for Promoting Financial Integration?

What accounts for the decoupling of the emerging market economies between August 2007 and September 2008 and what caused the swift re-coupling thereafter? How should these countries guard against the collapse of trade and financial flows and a shock of the scale and pervasiveness as the current one? If the impact of the downturn is more deleterious, advanced countries could have to contend with feedback effects and this underlines the critical need for a more multilateral effort. As the recent experience has shown, when financial crises are transmitted from advanced economies and generate synchronous recessions, prudent macroeconomic policies or stable macroeconomic fundamentals, or even international reserves offer no protection. In any case, the buildup of reserves has been less impressive than the growth of trade volumes—one of the conduits of transmission of the crisis. Under these conditions, advocacy for financial integration as essential to the world economy is difficult to endorse. Higher capital account openness is clearly associated with higher stress. To quote Prof. Bhagwati:

> When we penetrate the fog of implausible assertions that surrounds the case for free capital mobility, we realize that the idea and the ideology of free trade and its benefits … in effect, been hijacked by the proponents of capital mobility. They have been used to bamboozle us into celebrating the new world of trillions of dollars moving about daily in a borderless world, creating gigantic economic gains, rewarding virtue and punishing profligacy. The pretty face presented to us is, in fact, a mask that hides the warts and wrinkles underneath. (Bhagwati 1988)

What Is the Role of Global Imbalances in the Crisis?

There has been considerable debate on the role of global imbalances and how to secure a soft unwinding, given systemic risk and potential policy implications. The main worry has been that investors might change their mind, and that large capital inflows into the United States might suddenly reverse to yield disorderly adjustment, including in the value of the dollar. In the event, the crisis took a different form. Leverage turned out to be the crucial factor, and the dollar has strengthened. Nevertheless, global imbalances played a role in the buildup of systemic risk. They contributed to low interest rates and to large capital inflows into US and European banks and then contributed to a search for yield, higher leverage, and the creation of riskier assets. Thus, the crisis raises two issues. The first is the need to revisit when and how to react to large imbalances through macroeconomic and structural policies that affect saving and investment. As elsewhere, an attitude of benign neglect has proven to be a mistake. The second is the potential role for regulatory measures to reduce systemic risk by limiting or shaping capital inflows, e.g., through constraints on the foreign exchange exposure of domestic institutions and other borrowers. Although global macroeconomic conditions might not be at the origin of the crisis, they might have contributed to it.

Apart from these general issues, a number of policy debates have been raised in the current context of the global financial crisis.

How Can Global Surveillance Be Improved?

A key issue concerns the strength and focus of warnings prior to the crisis. It is now believed that, in general, the warnings were too scattered and unspecific to attract even domestic—let alone collective—policy reaction. Although the IMF was hardly alone in this, surveillance significantly underestimated the combined risk across sectors, and the importance of financial sector feedback and spillovers. The IMF warned about global imbalances but missed the key connection to the looming dangers in the shadow banking system. If so, what should be the shape of future surveillance? Is it possible to develop early warning systems by bringing together the expertise scattered across institutions (e.g., the IMF, the FSB, and the BIS) or is it better to focus each institution on a specific set of issues? For instance, the focus should be on better integrating financial sector issues into the *World Economic Outlook* and IMF's bilateral *Article IV Reports* and sharpening FSAPs.[2] How to make surveillance even-handed? The tacit presumption that risks lie mainly in less mature markets should give way to surveillance of all sources of systemic risk, in advanced and emerging market countries alike. What happens to the IMF's traditional mandate relating to exchange rates and external stability, in general?

Is the Responsibility for Financial Stability National or Does Multilateralism Have a Chance?

It is generally believed that the machinery and commitment for coordinated actions has proved to be inadequate. For example, the disorderly unwinding of global imbalances was acknowledged as a major systemic risk for many years. Yet, as noted earlier, collective action proved elusive. Even after the onset of the crisis, the initial policy response was far from collaborative, let alone coordinated. Countries rushed to protect their own financial systems at the risk of causing runs elsewhere; liquidity provision initially focused on home markets, even though the need was no less in other money centers; and the lack of pre-agreed burden sharing mechanisms meant that countries were quick to ring-fence assets in their jurisdictions when cross-border entities showed signs of failing. While the need for cooperation is now finally recognized, there is still no agreed central locus of debate. Do these factors underscore the need for a central body to assume leadership for responses to systemic risks in the global economy? The IMF has not been effective in this role, reflecting its rigid power structures and formalistic ways that shifted the policy debate to smaller and more flexible groups like the various Gs and the FSB. The latter are not, however, without their own problems of legitimacy and capacity for follow up, but their relevance to policy coordination is undeniable. If the IMF is to be at the center of global policy debate and action, it will need to address its underlying deficits in ownership and efficiency primarily by rebalancing quota shares.

How Far Is Financial Innovation Responsible for the Crisis?

An obvious candidate in the blame game is financial innovation. A question that often arises is: how far have these new financial products been welfare augmenting? We have already noted that Warren Buffet has termed the financial derivatives in general and collateralized debt obligations in particular as "weapons of mass destruction." While the precise purpose of many of the financial innovations is risk mitigation, these newer instruments could not reduce systemic risks. Furthermore, in a number of cases, the aim of a particular financial innovation is to evade the impact/purview of a financial regulation. It then becomes altogether a matter of judgment whether the constraining regulation or the consequent financial innovation is the responsible factor. In this current crisis, while the so-called toxic assets were innovated to mitigate the risk associated with lending to subprime borrowers, after the bundling of subprime contracts, the product started looking remarkably safe so much so that the investing entity became completely unaware of the underlying risks. A typical example is that of a Russian doll wherein dolls of smaller size are planted under each bigger doll so that the summed mass of the constituent dolls would be a multiple of the final visible big-sized doll. The key question, thus, is: how do we decide about the extent of welfare improving capacity of a particular financial innovation?

Do We Need the Separation of Commercial and Investment Banking?

Since investment banks, their failure and highly exposed balance sheets have been the focus of the crisis, a question often raised is: do we need a separation of the commercial bank from investment banking? In the US context, is the *Gramm–Leach–Bliley Act of 1999*, which repealed part of the *Glass–Steagall Act of 1933*, prohibiting any one institution from acting as both an investment bank and a commercial bank (or as both a bank and an insurer) responsible for the crisis? Paul A. Volcker, the former chairman of the US Fed, is reported to have favored a two-tier financial system, whereby commercial banks would continue to take bank deposits and offer loans and would be highly regulated, while securities firms would have the freedom to take on more risk and conduct trading, relatively free of regulation. The recent discussion on the Volcker rule in the US brings this issue to the fore.

How Big Should Financial Institutions Be?

In terms of the neoclassical paradigm, free entry and exit are features of a competitive economy. Apart from the natural monopolies, the size of a firm will be determined by institutional, technological, and transactions costs-related factors. However, when a firm is too big to fail, there are welfare implications of its exit strategy. The question then arises: should there be regulations governing firm size, limiting the extent of its diversification? This question has become increasingly relevant in the context of the rescue strategy of a number of financial conglomerates in the US. Or, is it not the size but the extent of complexity and inter-connectedness that matters for designing rescue packages?

Are All Risks Fiscal?

Traditional public finance theories make the distinction between public and private goods in terms of externalities and non-rival consumption. Consequently, it is assumed that the private costs of a firm failure will be borne by its shareholders. However, the recent financial crisis has shown the limitation of this approach. After all, when the private firm is of systemic importance, the government has to step in to counter its failure. Does this mean that, in the event of a large-scale financial crisis, irrespective of the ownership of the firm, all risks turn out to be fiscal? Is the sovereign the ultimate risk bearer exposed to all systemic risks? Does socialization of all such private losses raise issues relating to inter-generational equity and modes of financing of such losses?

Do We Need to Reform the Compensation Structure?

Compensation structure in a private firm is expected to be determined by the employees' bargaining skill intertwined with firm-specific and industry-specific features. Regulatory regimes as well as government have little role in it, except perhaps to put in place some norms like minimum wage legislation. Nevertheless, the issue of compensation structure in the financial industry has come to the fore during the financial crisis. Questions are raised as to whether the existing compensation structure in the financial services industry created some perverse incentive for the employees for excessive risk taking. National authorities in a number of countries are proposing far-reaching reforms in compensation structure in the financial sector. The question is: how far do we go? Will wage regulation affect the efficiency and productivity of the industry? And the dilemma is: without reforms in the compensation structure, are we developing a pool of human resources in the financial sector which makes it inherently risky?

To summarize, we live in a world of heightened uncertainty; we are confronted with increasingly unknown unknowns. The jury is still out on the causes of the crisis. There are no clear answers to these debates now and when the crisis is over, the world may not be the same again. Hopefully, the lessons of this crisis when they are gathered will put us on guard and help to fortify us to prepare for the future.

Shape of Things to Come—Some Crystal Ball Gazing[3]

How do we see the future in the aftermath of the current global crisis? At the time of writing this book, the global economy is transiting through a zone of heightened uncertainty that is obscuring a clear view of the shape of things to come. Yet there is an underlying coagulation, however mysterious and unpredictable. Human nature intrinsically seeks mean reversion and, therefore, picking whatever information that lead indicators throw up, we venture to etch the possible contours of the "new normal."

The Post-crisis Scenario across the Globe

The recovery from the crisis has turned out to be stronger than widely expected, with the global economy estimated to have grown by 5 percent in 2010, led by Asia. Industrial production and trade provided the impetus for the growth rebound, boosting both consumer and business confidence. Although lead indicators relating to private consumption, housing, employment, and the dramatic deterioration in financial markets in response to the sovereign debt crisis in Europe suggest some moderation in 2010 and 2011, the prospects of moderate but steady recovery remain bright at the current juncture. Nevertheless, it is fair to note that downside risks have risen sharply amidst renewed financial turbulence. Fiscal sustainability has become a major issue in the case of Greece and other vulnerable southern Euro Area economies, and this has cast a cloud over the outlook (Box 7.1). More generally, fiscal viability issues in advanced economies have emerged as the main concern facing the immediate prospects for the world economy. Concern over sovereign risk spilled over to banking sectors in Europe since May 2010,

---

BOX 7.1
Averting the Greek Tragedy of 2010

The global economic crisis has taken a severe toll on the fortunes of Greece. Over the years, Greece turned into a highly indebted nation as public sector spending grew and revenue fell substantially. At the end of 2009, the general public deficit reached 13.6 percent of GDP and public debt had increased to 115 percent of GDP. As the global crisis hit, financing costs for Greece rose rapidly, adding to the already high debt burden. The dramatic worsening of the budget deficit in 2009 revealed much more than fiscal stress faced by an economy in recession—years of declining competitiveness with wages outpacing productivity growth, structural rigidities, and a deteriorating business environment, but camouflaged by high fiscal and external deficits.

These adverse developments approached a flashpoint as soaring financing costs threatened to lead into a snowball of rating downgrades, extreme risk aversion, and markets shutting out access. In the face of a searing upsurge of social and political tensions, Greek authorities decided to undertake a painful process of large and front-loaded adjustment. Accordingly, in May 2010, they approached the IMF with a request for a three-year Stand-By Arrangement under the exceptional access policy and the emergency financing mechanism for €30 billion with an initial purchase of €5.5 billion. The Eurozone prepared to commit €80 billion with a first disbursement of €14.5 billion. It is an extraordinary international support effort for what needs to be an extraordinary Greek adjustment effort. The major elements on the IMF program, which is in coordination with the European Commission and the European Central Bank, are as follows:

- Fiscal policy adjustment is frontloaded with measures of 7.5 percent of GDP in 2010, 4 percent of GDP in 2011, and 2 percent of GDP in 2012 and 2013, each.
- The fiscal deficit is targeted to drop below 3 percent of GDP by 2014, and the debt-ratio would peak at 149 percent of GDP in 2013.
- The program includes provisions to shield low-income households from the brunt of the adjustment effort; including exempting those living on the minimum from the reductions in wages and pensions, and social expenditures will provide the safety net for the most vulnerable.
- A Financial Stability Fund has been established to ensure adequate capitalization of the banking system. Liquidity pressures are addressed, including with ECB support.
- Coordination with the European Commission (EC) and the ECB on program implementation and financing is regarded as crucial to the success of the program.

(*Box 7.1 continued*)

(Box 7.1 continued)

> After the first drawal under the Stand-By Arrangement, the IMF's Executive Board determined that Greece has successfully met performance criteria under the first review of the program and approved a second disbursement of SDR 2.2 billion in September 2010. Nevertheless, there are substantial risks to the Greek economy. The adjustment needs are un-precedented and fatigue could set in. Any unforeseen shock could weigh on the economy and the banking system even if the fiscal program is on track. Greece needs to persevere with its strategy to ensure continued inter-national support.
>
> **Source** IMF (2010d).

aggravating funding and liquidity risks, and prompting a flight to safety while forcing a sell-off in other markets. Inevitably, these developments have fed uncertainty about policy responses and raised questions about sustainability of the strength of the global recovery. As risk aversion became pronounced and widespread, assets in other regions, including emerging markets, also experienced substantial sell-offs in currency, equity, and commodity markets. Once again, it is the trade and financial channels that are regarded as the conduits of contagion and evaporation of confidence that was witnessed at the height of the global financial crisis. Risks of volatility of capital flows to some emerging market economies have resurfaced.

So far, there is limited evidence of negative spillovers to real activity at a global level. Moreover, some comfort is provided by the institution of the European Stabilization Mechanism in May 2010, which initially shocked and awed markets in demonstrating the resolve to preserve financial stability and implement policies to rebuild confidence, sup-ported by the positive effects of euro depreciation (Box 7.2). Contagion to other regions is limited so far and the disruption in capital flows to emerging and developing economies could be transient by current judgment. According to the IMF, global output is expected to expand by 4.45 percent on average during 2010–11, with advanced economies growing by 2.5 percent in this period (Table 7.1). While the US economy is expected to average growth of about 3.1 percent, this may be offset by somewhat weaker growth of 1.1 percent in the Euro Area and the UK. Japan, on the other hand, could shrug off the decade of lost growth and post an expansion of 2.1 percent on average during 2010 and 2011. Challenging the recovery in all these economies are high levels of public

BOX 7.2
The European Support Package

Faced with rapidly rising turbulence in Euro Area financial markets stemming from concerns about the longer-term sustainability of sovereign debt positions, the European Community, the IMF, and the ECB announced a package of support measures in May 2010. These measures came on top of already agreed bilateral three-year loans to Greece worth €110 billion. There are two broad elements in the support package—additional financial support backed jointly by Euro Area member governments and the IMF for liquidity loans to governments at risk, and new actions by the ECB to help ensure financial stability in the Euro Area.

The European Community and the IMF announced the creation of a new European stabilization mechanism, capable of providing up to €500 billion of financial assistance over a three-year period, with up to €250 billion of matching funding from the IMF. These funds, plus the loans for Greece, are equivalent to close to 9.5 percent of Euro Area GDP. The interest rate charged on the new funds appears likely to be similar to that charged on the bilateral loans to Greece, at around 5 percent. The new stabilization mechanism has two parts:

- The establishment of a new SPV, able to make loans to Euro Area states in need of assistance of up to €440 billion, subject to strong conditionality. These loans are to be guaranteed by Euro Area member states (in proportion to their voting rights at the ECB). The SPV is due to last for three years and will raise funding on the markets, backed by government credit guarantees (€660 billion is just over 7.3 percent of Euro Area GDP). It will likely take some time to put this measure, and the modalities under which it will operate, fully into place. In particular, technical work needs to be undertaken by the European Commission to set up the SPV, and the loan guarantees will need legislative approval by member states.
- A financial stabilization mechanism providing loans or credit lines of up to €60 billion, operated by the European Commission and available to help all EU member states in financial need. Funding for this facility is raised in the markets by the European Commission, using the EU budget as collateral, as with the existing medium-term balance-of-payments facility for non-Euro Area member states, which has already been used to help Latvia, Hungary, and Romania in the past two years. The additional €60 billion funding is backed by all EU member states and is available subject to strong conditionality, and in the context of joint EU/IMF support.

(Box 7.2 continued)

(*Box 7.2 continued*)

> The ECB announced that it would:
>
> - Begin to purchase private and government debt securities on the secondary markets (i.e., not directly from member governments), in those segments which are "dysfunctional." This would not amount to quantitative easing, as actions would be taken to sterilize all such purchases, preventing any direct impact on the monetary base.
> - Re-activate measures to supply unlimited three- and six-month liquidity to banks. The three-month liquidity is to be provided using a fixed rate procedure, whereas the rate for the six-month liquidity operation will be fixed *ex post* at the average minimum bid rate of the main refinancing operations over the life (the six-month interval) of the operation.
> - In addition to these measures, a range of bilateral currency swap arrangements with the US Federal Reserve was also announced, including with the ECB. This raises the availability of US dollar denominated funding for European financial institutions. All in all, the three-year government loans and guarantees, together with the significant steps taken by the ECB, should solve current liquidity problems in the markets. They cover the likely funding needs of the most-exposed governments and should enable the financial institutions most exposed to the sovereign liabilities of those countries (and therefore most exposed to the possible risk of default) to obtain the near-term funding they require on adequate terms.
>
> **Source**   OECD (2010).

debt, unemployment, and constrained bank lending. Output growth in emerging and developing economies is expected to average 6.2 percent, but with considerable diversity—Asia and Latin America continuing to lead. With commodity prices buoyed by safe haven effects, growth prospects remain favorable for many developing countries in sub-Saharan Africa as well as for commodity producers in all regions. Nimble policy responses and stronger economic frameworks are helping many emerging economies to expand internal demand and attract capital flows. The ongoing rebound in global trade is also supporting the recovery.

Prices of many commodities fell during the financial market shocks in May and early June of 2010, although they seem to have recovered some ground more recently, as concern about the real spillovers of the financial turbulence has eased. At the same time, waning appetite for risk has prompted gold prices to settle higher. The IMF's baseline petroleum price projection was revised down in July 2010 to US$75.3

TABLE 7.1
Global Growth and Inflation

	2009	2010	2011 (Projections)
World Output	**-0.5**	**5.0**	**4.4**
Advanced Economies	**-3.4**	**3.0**	**2.4**
United States	-2.6	2.8	2.8
Euro Area	-4.1	1.7	1.6
Emerging and Developing Economies	**2.7**	**7.3**	**6.5**
Russia	-7.8	4.0	4.8
China	9.2	10.3	9.6
India	6.8	10.4	8.2
Brazil	-0.6	7.5	4.5

(Table 7.1 continued)

(*Table 7.1 continued*)

	2009	2010	2011 (*Projections*)
World Trade Volume (Goods and services)	**−10.9**	**12.4**	**7.4**
Imports			
Advanced Economies	−12.6	11.2	5.8
Emerging and Developing Economies	−8.3	13.5	10.2
Exports			
Advanced Economies	−12.2	12.0	6.8
Emerging and Developing Economies	−7.5	14.5	8.8
Commodity Prices (US dollar)			
Oil	−36.3	27.9	35.6
Nonfuel	−15.8	26.3	25.1
Consumer Prices			
Advanced Economies	0.1	1.6	2.2
Emerging and Developing Economies	5.2	6.2	6.9

Source World Economic Outlook, IMF, April 2011, Washington D.C.

a barrel for 2010 and US$77.5 a barrel for 2011 (from US$80 and US$83, respectively, in April 2010).[4] Inflation pressures are expected to remain subdued in advanced economies with risks of deflation receding. In contrast, emerging and developing economies are facing heightened inflation pressures with several of them forced to chart a swifter than expected withdrawal of monetary accommodation. For the group as a whole, inflation is expected to edge up to from 6.2 percent in 2010 to 6.9 percent in 2011.

In the near term, the main risk is an escalation of financial stress due to sovereign risk in advanced economies. This could lead to additional increases in funding costs, weaker bank balance sheets, and tighter lending conditions for all economies, apart from erosion of confidence and eventually substantially lower global demand. In this downside scenario, world growth in 2011 could fall to 3 percent from the 4.5 percent assumed earlier. In addition, growth prospects could suffer from an overly severe or poorly planned fiscal consolidation. The risks to growth in advanced economies also complicate macroeconomic management in some of the larger, fast-growing economies in emerging Asia and Latin America. The IMF also projects that the growth of world trade volumes could decelerate from 12.4 percent in 2010 to a little over 7 percent in 2011, and this presents an additional demand shock to the outlook for the global economy in the near-term. A number of vulnerability indicators indicate that many advanced economies have significant weaknesses, exposing their economies and financial systems to heightened downside risks (Table 7.2).

In a historical perspective, it may be noted that the prolonged period of low inflation and high growth in the advanced economies with intermittent crises creating at worst blips that were essentially short term in nature appears to be over. The boon of "Greenspan's Put," whereby any crisis could be averted by the US Fed incrementally lowering the federal funds rate would no longer be available. Thus, the post-crisis scenario across the globe is going to be more vulnerable to high intensity shocks. This vulnerability may get accentuated by the fact that notions of decoupling have turned out to be largely unfounded for the emerging world.

To extend these trends further, a bipolar world could emerge wherein the emerging economies could experience high growth and above-normal inflation while a number of advanced countries could have low growth and low inflation. Needless to say that such a scenario is difficult

TABLE 7.2
Sovereign Market and Vulnerability Indicators

	Fiscal and Debt Fundamentals			Financing Needs	External Funding	Banking System Linkage		
	Gross General Govt Debt	Net General Govt Debt	Primary Balance	Gross Govt Debt Maturing (Second Half 2010–11)	General Govt Debt Held Abroad	(% of 2010 GDP)	(% of Depository Institutions Assets)	BIS reporting banks' cross-border claims on public sector
Australia	22.8	5.4	-4.7	8.8	7.2	2.2	1.2	2.6
Austria	70.1	60.0	-2.9	14.7	58.0	16.0	4.3	13.7
Belgium	100.3	91.3	-1.3	45.9	60.7	21.8	6.2	20.4
Canada	81.2	32.5	-5.0	31.7	14.0	n.a.	n.a.	3.4
Czech Republic	39.4	n.a.	-2.8	19.9	10.3	14.8	12.8	4.5
Denmark	51.2	3.1	-5.1	20.4	16.4	14.8	3.3	6.7
Finland	49.9	-41.5	-5.4	21.4	40.6	5.2	1.9	9.6
France	84.4	74.7	-5.8	40.1	52.2	19.1	4.5	9.8
Germany	75.9	58.9	-2.4	22.0	39.1	21.9	7.1	10.7
Greece	130.2	109.5	-2.4	31.4	94.2	20.6	9.0	30.0
Ireland	85.7	53.5	-14.5	25.4	54.4	14.5	1.4	11.6
Italy	118.7	99.2	-0.9	43.0	56.3	31.9	12.4	18.0
Japan	226.6	121.2	-8.3	105.4	11.7	74.9	23.7	1.3
Korea	32.1	n.a.	n.a.	22.0	3.2	6.9	4.8	4.1

Netherlands	66.6	46.3	−4.5	37.3	44.7	12.8	3.3	8.4
New Zealand	32.0	3.3	n.a.	18.2	13.0	5.8	3.1	2.8
Norway	53.8	−149.5	8.4	−12.0	19.8	n.a.	n.a.	7.0
Portugal	85.1	80.7	−4.3	34.4	62.5	16.3	4.9	24.1
Slovak Republic	41.8	n.a.	−6.8	18.1	12.8	20.6	23.6	5.8
Slovenia	34.5	n.a.	−4.5	9.8	24.5	8.9	6.1	6.9
Spain	63.7	54.3	−7.5	31.0	31.6	22.4	6.7	8.1
Sweden	41.4	−12.7	−3.1	12.8	17.3	6.5	2.2	4.8
United Kingdom	76.7	70.1	−7.6	26.5	18.9	6.2	1.3	2.9
United States	93.0	66.1	−9.5	47.6	26.6	7.8	5.4	3.0

Source IMF, *Global Financial Stability Report*, various issues, Washington D.C.

to sustain and the possibility of a double-dip cannot be ruled out in such an eventuality. While we do not foresee a doomsday scenario—our gut-sense about the post-crisis scenario across the globe in the near future is one of "cautious pessimism."

Economic Forecasting under Siege

Whatever be the shape of things to come in the global economy, ways and methods of making economic forecasts are facing a serious credibility question and systematic projection methodologies that can provide meaningful guidance on the future are perhaps going to be more perilous than ever before. The American film-maker Woody Allen is credited to have said, "Forecasting is difficult particularly for the future." In the aftermath of the crisis, a question repeatedly asked is: why did the economists and forecasters fail to foresee the crisis?

The Queen of England raised this question when she visited the London School of Economics in November 2008. The British Academy convened a forum on June 17, 2009 to debate this question, with contributions from a range of experts from business, the city of London, its regulators, academia, and government. The deliberations of the forum concluded that

> ...the failure to foresee the timing, extent and severity of the crisis and to head it off, while it had many causes, was principally a failure of the collective imagination of many bright people, both in this country and internationally, to understand the risks to the system as a whole. (Besely et al. 2009)

In a recent highly critical paper, eight American and European economists argue that academic economists were too disconnected from the real world to see the crisis forming. In their view:

> The economics profession appears to have been unaware of the long build-up to the current worldwide financial crisis and to have significantly underestimated its dimensions once it started to unfold ... This lack of understanding is due to a misallocation of research efforts in economics. We trace the deeper roots of this failure to the profession's insistence on constructing models that, by design, disregard the key elements driving outcomes in real world markets. (Colander et al. 2009)

The paper, generally referred to as the *Dahlem Report*, condemns a growing reliance over the past three decades on mathematical models, a major feature of which is the assumption that markets and economies are inherently stable. This view often disregards influences of bounded rationality, animal spirits, imperfect information, and non-atomistic size of the agents. More importantly, these models often tend to ignore differences in the way various economic players make decisions, revise their forecasting methods, and are influenced by social factors. The *Dahlem Report* further argues that by relying so heavily on the view of humans as rational, economists ignore evidence of irrational behavior that is well documented in other disciplines like psychology and sociology. Even if an individual does act rationally, it could be wrong to assume that large groups of people will react to given conditions as an individual would.

Furthermore, it has been argued that economists underestimated the risks of new types of derivatives, which are financial instruments whose value fluctuates, often to extremes, according to the changing values of underlying securities. Traditional derivatives such as stock options and commodity futures are well understood; but exotic derivatives devised in recent years, including securities built upon pools of mortgages, turned out to be poorly understood, the authors say.

A conference on the theme of "The Economic Crisis and the Crisis in Economics" in King's College, Cambridge, UK, April 8–11, 2010 delved into the causes of economists' inability to detect the formation of the crisis. In reality, however, while the "mainstream models" did not work well, there were many strands of economic analysis, developed over the past quarter century, that could provide insight into what happened as well as alternative policy advice to prevent a recurrence. There are many assumptions of the standard economic models which are unrealistic, like those related to representative agent, competition, rational expectations, ignoring the distinctions between risks and uncertainty, labor market rigidity, corporate governance, and those related to capital markets (Stiglitz 2010a). Specifically, attention was not paid to the fact that markets are not, in general, efficient, even when all market participants have rational expectations, and also all markets are not competitive. Besides, whenever risk markets are incomplete and information is imperfect, pecuniary externalities matter and are pervasive. In terms of modeling challenges of the profession, tasks like incorporating heterogeneous agents, formalizing bankruptcy and default, understanding individual behavior towards risks, and externalities are going to come up in the days to come. After all,

> ...bad models lead to bad policy: central banks, for instance, focused on the small economic inefficiencies arising from inflation, to the exclusion of the far, far greater inefficiencies arising from dysfunctional financial markets and asset price bubbles. After all, their models said that financial markets were always efficient. Remarkably, standard macroeconomic models did not even incorporate adequate analyses of banks. (Stiglitz 2010b)

Soul searching was on by other participants in this conference as well. Illustratively, Dominique Strauss-Kahn, then Managing Director of the IMF, pointed out in this conference that after the crisis, "our confidence in markets, institutions, and the *status quo* turned out to be complacency; we learnt how fallible, fragile, and interconnected we are." Y.V. Reddy, former Governor of the Reserve Bank of India, flagged various dimensions of globalization of finance and globalization of regulation and added that these could be considered as part of a process of rebalancing between (*a*) financial sector regulation, monetary policy, and fiscal policy by formally recognizing the inter-dependencies at the national level; (*b*) between the governments within supra national, but sub-global levels such as in Asia and the Euro Area; and (*c*) strengthening the global financial architecture.[5]

A key issue, thus, remains how far was the current crisis predictable? Is it what is called "a black swan" event which can hardly be predicted? There are, however, some people who do not think so (Box 7.3).

A generic issue in this context is the efficacy of forecasting methods. While we all hope that the future would be a bit like the past, possibilities of an extreme event cannot be ruled out. Furthermore, the role of the philosophy of the forecasters cannot be underestimated. Illustratively, in a lighter vein it has been pointed out that the predicted value from the series of three numbers 1, 2, 3 could be 4 if one believes in a linear trend, could be 3 if one believes that yesterday is the best predictor of today, could be 2 if one believes in "mean reversion tendencies," and could be 1 if one believes in the philosophy that "all that goes up must come down." It is pertinent to refer to the famous forecasting experiment of the renowned statistician Spyors Makridakis who, after forecasting a large number of time series variables, arrived at two broad conclusions. First, complex models capable of explaining the past often fail to

---

BOX 7.3
Some People Who Saw the Crisis Coming

Ron Paul, US Representative in his testimony on September 10, 2003, before US House Financial Services Committee, said:

> Ironically, by transferring the risk of a widespread mortgage default, the government increases the likelihood of a painful crash in the housing market. This is because the special privileges granted to Fannie and Freddie have distorted the housing market by allowing them to attract capital they could not attract under pure market conditions. (Paul 2003)

Nururiel Roubini, Professor of Economics at the New York University (who is nicknamed as "Dr Doom"), is reported to have told an audience of IMF staff in September 2006 that there was a more than 50 percent risk of a US recession the following year and added that over the past several years, US consumers had gone on a spending binge, with many using their home equity as an "ATM" (Loungani 2009).

Raghuram Rajan, Professor of Finance at the Chicago University, in a paper presented at a conference organized by the Federal Reserve Bank of Kansas in 2005 (while he was the Chief Economist at the IMF) pointed towards a possibility that financial development could have made the world riskier and went on say that "we should be prepared for the low probability but highly costly downturn" (Rajan 2005). Rajan in his recent book *Fault Lines* described his experience of presenting that paper to the audience of central bankers and economists in Kansas City Fed as one of "an early Christian who had wandered into a convention of half-starved lions" (Rajan 2010).

William White, Adviser at the Bank for International Settlement (BIS), warned against a possible crisis as early as 2006 and remarked: "One hopes that it will not require a disorderly unwinding of current excesses to prove convincingly that we have indeed been on a dangerous path" (White 2006).

Source   Compiled by authors.

---

predict extreme events. Second, instead of rule of thumb and any purely judgment-based forecasting, simple models often do better (Makridakis, Hogarth, and Gaba 2009).

How do we see the future? Has the crisis made us wiser in terms of our capability to predict the possibility of a crisis occurring? This issue has been discussed intensively in the policy circles in recent years. A major effort that is underway in this context is the joint IMF–FSB early warning exercise (Box 7.4).

BOX 7.4
Early Warning Exercise (EWE) of the IMF and the FSB

The joint IMF–FSB EWE aims at improving analysis of the linkages between the financial sector and the real economy, assessments of fiscal risks as well as cross-border spillovers and sources of systemic risk. In concrete terms, instead of making any attempt to predict the crisis, the EWE tries to identify existing vulnerabilities and looks for possible triggers that could precipitate a crisis. It also recommends risk-mitigating actions and suggests contingency plans.

The EWE is part of the IMF's efforts to strengthen surveillance. It is conducted on a semi-annual basis, in close coordination with the *World Economic Outlook* and the *Global Financial Stability Report*, the IMF's flagship publications on global surveillance, and draws on other IMF analytical and policy work, including the *Fiscal Monitor*. The IMF's regular country, regional, and global surveillance activities are used to follow up on EWE findings and policy recommendations.

While the methodology of the EWE is yet to be firmed up, it combines the use of analytical tools with the wider qualitative view of potential risks from discussions with stakeholders. Macro-financial vulnerability is sought to be tracked through various formal models. These include crisis risk models, house price models, bank contagion models, equity price models, crisis duration models, and financing gaps. Fiscal risks are sought to be assessed through various market indicators of sovereign risks, near-term rollover financing risks, and fiscal vulnerability indicators. Such macro analysis is complemented by market-based tools, contingent claims analysis, capital market contagion, and regime switching models.

Source   IMF (2009b).

Maintaining Macroeconomic Stability

As we move hesitantly towards a more durable recovery, maintenance of macro-financial stability assumes paramount importance as such phases of transition tend to be particularly vulnerable to shocks. As the recovery strengthens and gets entrenched, rebuilding global resilience in the context of future crises by fortifying shock absorbers as well as by dampening shock transmitters and amplifiers will take priority. A review of the crisis experience enables us to draw four basic lessons in this regard: (*a*) putting in place a framework of macro stability in terms of sound fiscal and monetary policies, (*b*) ensuring financial stability so as to contain systemic risks, (*c*) building adequate self insurance, and (*d*) setting up a functional and more representative global financial architecture that can improve global resilience.

Monetary and fiscal policy

Carefully designed and targeted fiscal and monetary policy programs to meet growth aspirations, human development, and sustainability objectives need to go hand in hand with efforts to generate demand and protect vulnerable groups. In the current context, we are inclined to believe that a premature exit from monetary and fiscal policy support could pose a grave risk to a firm recovery. At the same time, addressing policy fragilities is a top priority.

As regards monetary policy, there appears to be relatively broad consensus on the way forward. In advanced countries where inflationary pressures are subdued and considerable slack exists in the economy, monetary policy can remain accommodative for some more time, and this is seen as the main stimulative force anchoring the recovery. Tensions do exist relating to the size of the central bank balance sheets bloated by the impact of unconventional anti-crisis measures and, consequently, by credit and market risks. Greater coordination with fiscal policy is certainly a consideration here—as fiscal accounts strengthen, there should be scope for some of these assets to be transferred to the fisc, especially those that cannot be sold off in the market. This is important from the point of view of preserving the independence of central banks. For most emerging and developing countries, the path for monetary policy is rather straightforward—withdrawal of monetary accommodation to normalize the policy stance with a view to dealing with rising inflationary pressures and readying for orthodox tightening should inflation tensions aggravate. Liquidity management will, however, remain an abiding concern, reflecting the traumatic experience with the crisis. In this context, there is an important source of tension—accommodative monetary policy in advanced economies is operating as a push factor, posing challenges of dealing with capital flows and consequent liquidity effects in the emerging economies. This is an important area for improving cross-border policy coordination.

In the context of fiscal policy, coordination issues are more daunting. Accordingly, it is worthwhile to assign greater focus to those issues in the following paragraphs. In many advanced and some emerging and developing economies where the economic slowdown and stimulus measures have pushed debts and deficits to very high levels, there is a

pressing need to design and communicate credible medium-term fiscal
consolidation strategies. Such strategies should include clear time frames
to bring down gross debt-to-GDP ratios to more prudent levels as well
as concrete measures to raise potential output over the medium-term.
With fiscal deficits rising to 9 percent of GDP and debt/GDP ratios set
to exceed 100 percent of GDP by 2014 in advanced economies, room for
policy maneuver has either been exhausted or is very limited. Heightened
concerns about sovereign risks are dampening investor confidence and
threatening financial stability—the immediate concern is about Europe
where it could turn into a full-blown crisis. Bank exposures to real estate
and household indebtedness continue to pose downside risks, mainly in
the United States and Europe. There are, thus, regional and economy-
specific considerations which need to be taken into account in the intense
debate that is underway on stimulus versus austerity (Box 7.5).

BOX 7.5
The Path of Fiscal Consolidation
and the Ongoing Debate

Against the backdrop of the fiscal crisis in Europe and new signs that the
recovery may be encountering headwinds, a number of leading economists
and economic commentators engaged in an animated exchange in the
Financial Times in July–August 2010. It is interesting to traverse the range of
diverse opinions.

Martin Wolf (July 18, 2010): Why the battle is joined over tightening

At the anti-deficit extreme are those who argue fiscal deficits have no
impact on activity since they lead to offsetting behaviour by private
people.... [On the other hand] the "cutters" argue that such huge fiscal
deficits—never seen in peacetime in big developed countries, notably the
US—threaten long-term fiscal credibility and depress private confidence
and spending.... The "postponers" agree there must be decisive slowing
of the growth of long-term spending.... But on one thing everybody
agrees: this debate matters.

Brad DeLong (July 19, 2010): It is far too soon to end expansion

Here we have the crux: Greece, Ireland, Spain, Portugal and Italy need to
be austere. But Germany, Britain, America and Japan do not. With their
debts valued by the market at heights I had never thought to see in my
lifetime, the best thing they can do to relieve the global depression is to
engage in co-ordinated global expansion. Expansionary fiscal, monetary
and banking policy are all called for on a titanic scale.

(Box 7.5 continued)

(Box 7.5 continued)

Lawrence Summers (July 18, 2010): America's sensible stance on recovery

We will see clearly in the years ahead that pushing growth and reducing deficits are complementary, not competing, objectives.

Jean-Claude Trichet (July 22, 2010): Stimulate no more—it is now time for all to tighten

With hindsight, we see how unfortunate was the oversimplified message of fiscal stimulus given to all industrial economies under the motto: "stimulate", "activate", "spend"! A large number fortunately had room for manoeuvre; others had little room; and some had no room at all and should have already started to consolidate.

Martin Feldstein (July 22, 2010): A double dip is a price worth paying

Critics of the European countries' decisions to front-load their deficit reductions miss the importance of seizing the current moment of crisis to take politically difficult budget actions.... [G]radual adjustment strategy cannot work politically in countries where voters are sceptical about government promises of future deficit reductions. Immediate action is necessary to make future deficit cuts credible.

Montek Singh Ahluwalia (July 22, 2010): Message from Delhi: do not cut too soon

Political polarisation in industrialised countries has fuelled a resurgence of fiscal conservatism. On the other side, with growth weakening as the effect of stimulus wears off and with high unemployment, there are calls for more stimulus. Academics on each side are lambasting the opposing arguments as voodoo economics.

Andy Xie (July 22, 2010): More stimulus will not stop Asia's rise

[M]ain players in today's globalisation are not countries, but multinational companies. These large businesses now allocate investment and production across the world, taking cost and regulation levels into account. Because companies can now move their investments across borders, government spending to boost demand in one country now leaks across borders into others. This leakage dramatically decreases the effectiveness of any Keynesian stimulus.

(Box 7.5 continued)

(*Box 7.5 continued*)

Kenneth Rogoff (July 20, 2010): No need for a panicked fiscal surge

Aggressive fiscal stimulus in the run-up to the financial crisis was reasonable as part of an all-out battle to avoid slipping into a depression. The risk of a second Great Depression was palpable, the huge cost of insurance arguably worth it. Today, the panic has abated, and a more sober cost–benefit analysis is required.

Olivier Blanchard and Carlo Cottarelli (August 11, 2010): The great false choice, stimulus, or austerity

The debate on the need for further fiscal stimulus or quicker retrenchment has become too ideological, and too extreme. Underneath it, however, there is more agreement on the basics than may be apparent at first blush.... Today's debt problems, therefore, result not from how fiscal policy was managed during the crisis, but rather from how it was mismanaged before the crisis.

Source   *Financial Times*, various issues during July–August 2010.

We set out below some of the critical issues in the context of the Euro Area and the US where the dilemma is arguably the sharpest.

Euro Area

A consideration of the Euro Area merits special attention. While monetary policy is unified in the Euro Area, provision of fiscal stimuli, including financial sector stabilization, remains a national responsibility. The lack of a "fiscal euro zone" has, in our view, hampered an effective response to the economic downturn. Experience has shown that fiscal rules—the stability and growth pact which puts a cap on budget deficits and public debt—falls short on delivery. In the pre-crisis years, the emphasis on the costs to others of fiscal indiscipline meant that countries were careful to behave no worse than their peers, rather than trying to be prudent on their own behalf. Thus, public finances tended to add to, not subtract from, demand pressures. The costs of fiscal laxity were low—borrowing costs for high- and low-debt countries were similar. When the crisis struck, the lack of unified fiscal policy appears to have worked against a swift response and undermined confidence in the euro, driving up the US dollar's lure as a safe haven. National interests continue to prevent cross-border coordination—instinctive preference for thrift in some countries, peer pressure in others, and fears of leakages overall.

Amplifying the fiscal consolidation risk to growth is the simultaneous move by several Euro Area countries to consolidate, which is bound to have international spillovers that could result in retarding global demand. In our view, this is a time for coordination and sequencing, not synchronization. Countries with less pressing need to win market confidence and, with policy space available, need to maintain fiscal stimulus for a longer period so as to provide a window to market-beleaguered countries to undertake consolidation. Unfortunately, there seems to be a preference gaining ground among fiscally strong members to consolidate more aggressively so as to exert peer pressure! The net fiscal impulse of the Euro Area should be positive in 2011, given its systemic importance in the global economy and the commensurate responsibility to anchor the global recovery.

The sovereign debt crisis has highlighted the need for the Euro Area to strengthen significantly its institutional and operational architecture to dissipate doubts about the long-term viability of its monetary union. Fiscal discipline and its surveillance is a minimum and needs to be taken as far as possible in the direction of a *de facto* fiscal union. At the same time, ensuring the quality of fiscal adjustment assumes importance. The difficult task facing the Euro Area is to "strike the right balance" between the short-term demands of stabilizing aggregate demand and the long-term need for sustainability. The recent experience shows that in this regard, undifferentiated numerical rules are far from optimal either because they are abandoned due to political demands or they produce highly pro-cyclical policy during downturns. The Eurozone's Stability and Growth Pact illustrates the limitations of numerical constraints.

Effectiveness requires an element of independent judgment or constrained discretion which can be provided by independent fiscal policy councils (FPCs), as the limited country experience has shown. An FPC composed of independent persons chosen for competence in fiscal policy and budgetary planning with its mandate in the form of a debt target and a horizon and its instrument as the budget balance can focus on recommending publicly the most desirable budget balance path. It will have to prove its mettle, establish credibility, and demonstrate the quality of proposals. An FPC is likely to be unpalatable to politicians because it is perceived as a threat by those interest groups that lie at the root of a deficit bias. Yet, it can effectively act as a pro-discipline pressure group, offering a responsible government an argument to turn down pressure from interest groups.

The United States

The fiscal stimulus in the US has provided confidence in a period marked by the confluence of extremely adverse forces acting in concert. While there will inevitably be a deterioration in the fiscal imbalance which will sharply push up public debt—support to the financial sector may be largely deficit neutral but will add to public indebtedness and contingent liabilities—and pose constraints for medium-term issues such as health care, this must be weighed against the opportunity costs of the absence of the fiscal effort. If economic and financial conditions do not improve as the fiscal stimulus wanes out through 2010, more will need to be done. So far, the response of financial markets to the erosion in the fiscal position in the US has been muted. A premature withdrawal of the stimulus risks adverse reactions from markets and from consumer and business confidence. The recovery could be faster if the boost from the second stimulus is larger and aimed into the crisis year—according to the OECD, the fiscal multiplier in the US is about 0.6 currently. Such plans could be set in coordination with a transparent, credible, and aggressive commitment to debt/deficit consolidation once the recovery is on track and the financial system returns to normal functioning. We agree that very substantial fiscal consolidation will be required and early announcement of plans could anchor medium-term expectations. Changes could be legislated now that would begin later and be phased in—a gradual increase in eligibility ages for Social Security and Medicare, gradual increases in energy taxes, and gradual elimination of some programs. Such steps might improve confidence by reducing uncertainty about huge budget deficits or fears of a bigger government.

The US seems to have handled the fiscal policy exit well, especially by the provision for the "placeholder" to cushion the impact of withdrawing the 2009 stimulus as well as the flexibility to deal with the size of front-loading. The US commitment to reduce the federal deficit from 10.6 percent in 2010 to 5.1 percent by 2013 is indeed ambitious, especially as the expiry of the fiscal stimulus appears to be the most important risk to growth. Independent estimates place the potential loss at about 2 percentage points of GDP growth, which is more than half of the trend growth rate.

Main Policy Challenges including Exit Strategies

The key issue in deciding the pace of fiscal retrenchment is the speed of crowding in private spending. A reduction in private balances in a weak economy may in fact warrant an increase in cyclical fiscal spending which could become structural if growth does not become self-sustaining. The first step in any sound fiscal strategy is to promote the recovery. As this is achieved, strong steps can be taken to bring down the deficit to sustainable levels and a stronger economy can bear that burden. Premature fiscal stabilization can potentially derail the global economy. Boosting growth and reducing deficits should be seen as mutually reinforcing, not competing objectives. Strengthening growth now will lay the ground for reducing the deficits in the medium-term. The key policy task ahead is to ensure a smooth transition of demand from government to the private sector and from economies with excessive external deficits to those with excessive surpluses. The challenge for some emerging economies is to absorb rising capital inflows and nurture domestic demand without triggering a new boom–bust cycle. While the timing of exit depends on individual country circumstances, international policy coordination is critical to minimizing negative spillovers and sustaining strong, balanced growth. In many advanced and some emerging and developing economies with debt/deficits at very high levels, there is a pressing need to design and communicate credible medium-term fiscal consolidation strategies and embark on them by 2011—clear time frames to bring down gross debt-to-GDP ratios to more prudent levels, return to rule-based fiscal policy, and entitlement reforms contributing to long-term fiscal sustainability.

Ensuring Financial Stability

As far as ensuring financial stability is concerned, the G-20 summit of June 26–27, 2010 in Toronto rightly emphasized four pillars, viz., (a) strong regulatory framework, (b) effective supervision, (c) resolution and addressing systemic institutions, and (d) international assessment and peer review.

The crisis has revealed a number of weaknesses of the existing global architecture of financial supervision as epitomized in Basel II (Dewatripont, Rochet, and Tirole 2010). First, there is confusion about the objectives of prudential regulation and banking supervision. Second, the predictive power of quantitative models has been highly exaggerated under Basel II. It is in this context that the Basel Committee on Banking Supervision (BCBS) made some progress towards a new global regime for bank capital and liquidity as enunciated in terms of what is known as Basel III (Box 7.6). The amount of capital is expected to be significantly higher and the quality of capital will be significantly improved when the new reforms are fully implemented. More and improved capital should enable banks to withstand significant stresses. It is expected that all systemically important countries in general, and G-20 members in particular, will adopt the new standards which will be phased in over a timeframe consistent with sustained recovery and limiting market disruption.

BOX 7.6
BASEL III: Main Elements

1. **Definition of capital:** Major changes have been proposed with respect to treatment of minority interest, investments in other financial institutions, allowing IFRS treatment (where different from national GAAP), treatment of significant investments in the common shares of unconsolidated financial institutions and deferred tax assets from timing differences.

2. **Counterparty credit risk:** Modification is made to address hedging, risk capturing, effective maturity and double counting, and banks' mark-to-market and collateral exposures to a central counterparty.

3. **Leverage ratio:** A simple, transparent, non-risk based measure of leverage ratio is being developed as a credible supplementary measure to the risk based requirements. As far as transition to the leverage ratio is concerned, it was agreed to divide the transition period into the following phases: (*a*) the supervisory monitoring period commences January 1, 2011 and (*b*) the parallel run period commences January 1, 2013 and runs until January 1, 2017.

4. **Regulatory buffers, provisions, and cyclicality:**

   (a) *Regulatory buffers:* A countercyclical buffer proposal was issued. The capital conservation buffer should be available to absorb banking sector losses conditional on a plausible severe stressed financial and economic environment.

   (b) *Mitigating cyclicality of the minimum:* Possible approaches to address any excess cyclicality of the minimum requirement are being explored.

(Box 7.6 continued)

(*Box 7.6 continued*)

> (c) *Forward looking provisioning:* While capital focuses on unexpected losses, a concrete proposal to operationalize the expected loss approach to provisioning is being developed.
>
> 5. **Systemic banks, contingent capital, and a capital surcharge:** In addition to the reforms to the trading book, securitization, counterparty credit risk, and exposures to other financials, there are number of proposals to help address systemic risk. Illustratively, a proposal based on a requirement that the contractual terms of capital instruments is going to allow the banks at the option of the regulatory authority to be written-off or converted to common shares in the event that a bank is unable to support itself.
>
> 6. **Global liquidity standard**
>
>   (a) *Liquidity coverage ratio (LCR):* Revisions to the definition of qualifying liquid assets are being proposed. The goal is to achieve a calibration and definition that penalizes imprudent liquidity profiles. Treatment of retail and SME deposits, deposits from domestic sovereigns, central banks, and public sector entities (PSEs), secured funding, and undrawn commitments are being reviewed.
>
>   (b) *Net stable funding ratio (NSFR):* The NSFR is thought to be introduced as a longer term structural complement to the LCR.
>
> **Source** BIS (2010).

Effective supervision is another important pillar that needs to be reconstructed for ensuring global financial stability. The FSB, in consultation with the IMF, is working on proposals to strengthen oversight and supervision. In specific terms, the mandate, capacity and resourcing of supervisors (including early intervention) are elements being examined by FSB.

Resolution and addressing systemic institutions is another important pillar. In order to reduce moral hazard risks, there is a need to have a policy framework, including effective resolution tools. A number of G-20 countries have announced or made pledges towards financial sector support. Net of amounts recovered, the fiscal cost of direct support has averaged 2.8 percent of GDP for advanced G-20 countries, as of June 2010. In those most affected, however, unrecovered costs are of the order of 4–6 percent of GDP. Furthermore, largely reflecting the effect of the crisis, government debt in advanced G-20 countries is projected to rise by almost 40 percentage points of GDP during 2008–15. In this context, it is widely perceived that the financial sector should make a fair and substantial contribution towards paying for any burdens associated with government interventions to repair the financial system and reduce risks from the financial system. Proposals on financial sector taxation are being mooted in this connection (Box 7.7).

BOX 7.7
Financial Sector Taxation—Recent Proposals

The G-20 tasked the IMF to look into issues relating to a fair and substantial contribution by the financial sector. After analyzing various options, the IMF in June 2010 submitted a report to G-20 in its Toronto summit. proposing two forms of contribution from the financial sector:

- **Financial Stability Contribution (FSC):** This is linked to a credible and effective resolution mechanism. The main component of the FSC would be a levy to pay for the fiscal cost of any future government support to the sector. This could either accumulate in a fund to facilitate the resolution of weak institutions or be paid into general revenue. The FSC would be paid by all financial institutions, initially levied at a flat rate but refined thereafter to reflect individual institutions' riskiness and contributions to systemic risk. Attributes such as size, interconnectedness, and substitutability could play important roles in this connection.
- **Financial Activities Tax (FAT):** Any further contribution from the financial sector that is desired should be raised by a FAT, levied on the sum of the profits and remuneration of financial institutions, and paid to general revenue.

A number of countries have adopted different versions of such taxation proposals. Financial Crisis Responsibility Fee in the US, Bank Levy in Germany, Temporary Bank Payroll Tax in the UK, Temporary Bonus Tax in France, Permanent Tax on Bonuses and Stock Options in Italy, Systemic Dissolution Fund in the US, Financial Stability Fund in Sweden, and Bank Resolution Funds and Levy in the EU are all illustrations of country-specific attempts of contribution by the financial sector. How much of these measures are temporary in nature? Only time will tell.

Source   IMF (2010a).

Finally, the G-20 has flagged the importance of transparent international assessment and peer review as means towards global risk mitigation.

While strengthening commitment to the IMF/World Bank FSAP and pledging to support robust and transparent peer review through the FSB, international efforts are on relating to non-cooperative jurisdictions based on comprehensive and transparent assessment with respect to tax havens, money laundering, and terrorist financing.

Social Safety Nets

Conceptually, social safety nets (SSN) may be defined as non-contributory transfer programs specifically targeted at the poor and those sections of population which are vulnerable to poverty and shocks. In practice, SSNs take various forms such as: (*a*) cash and in-kind transfers, (*b*) price subsidies, (*c*) social services fee waivers, (*d*) supplemental feeding and nutrition programs, (*e*) public works, (*f*) adapted social security arrangements, and (*g*) microfinance. The choice of instruments varies amongst countries and depends on factors like existing social protection systems, availability of information on the poor and vulnerable, administrative capacity, and budget constraints.

The issue of SSN is important both nationally and globally. Insofar as the national dimension is concerned, two issues need to be noted. First, during the period of crisis, social expenditures are often curtailed. Second, there are early indications that the current recovery could be jobless at least in select countries. Besides, once the stimulus measures are withdrawn, there are possibilities that in select countries, particularly with limited fiscal space, there could be cutbacks in social expenditure. Globally, the crisis has had already led to sharp downturns in welfare. Unlike in the past when international aid has been able to offset partially the effects of crises that began in the developing world, donors may be less willing or able to increase aid in this crisis because of its origin in the advanced countries. All these make the institution of social safety nets of paramount importance.

While the crisis emanated in the developed world, its impact permeated to both poor countries and vulnerable sections of people in advanced economies bringing the issue of SSN to the limelight. Illustratively, the G-20 Leaders' Summit in Pittsburg (September 24–25, 2009) specifically pledged to undertake "structural reforms to increase our potential growth rates" as well as to "improve social safety nets" and added, "We have a responsibility to invest in people by providing education, job training, decent work conditions, health care and social safety net support, and to fight poverty, discrimination, and all forms of social exclusion." The G-20 Toronto Summit (June 26–27, 2010) declaration added "strengthening social safety nets" as a specific pillar of the common agreement along with other more macro and market oriented goals like enhancing corporate governance reform, financial market development, infrastructure spending, and increasing exchange rate flexibility in some emerging markets. Besides, since the early 1990s, the IMF has increasingly sought to incorporate the budgetary cost of social safety nets into adjustment programs and in recent IMF programs, social safety nets have been emphasized (Box 7.8). In recent periods, the idea of a global financial safety net is being talked about within the framework of existing multilateral financial institutions. It could help in rebalancing the global economy and it could also act as an anchor mechanism that would provide liquidity to those countries during times of external crises.

BOX 7.8
Social Safety Net and Select Recent IMF Programs

1. **Armenia:** Social spending under the program rose from 5.7 percent of GDP in 2008 to 7.6 percent of GDP in 2009 towards protecting and better targeting.

2. **Hungary:** The fiscal strategy aims at protecting the poor and low-income earners from the impact of the global crisis. Measures include preserving the purchasing power of low-income civil servants despite the nominal freeze of the public sector wage bill, replacing a universal housing subsidy by a targeted scheme to help the needy have access to adequate housing, and canceling increases in disability pensions while increasing benefits for the poorest disabled.

3. **Iceland:** The fiscal consolidation planned for 2010–2012 aims to ensure a gradual and orderly return to sustainable levels of borrowing while preserving Iceland's Nordic welfare state model. To this end, the 2010 budget has maintained key social spending programs, and even added new programs to deal with specific issues (e.g., youth unemployment and overly indebted households).

4. **Latvia:** The IMF has been working with the national authorities as well as with the European Commission and the World Bank to refine cost-cutting measures to make sure they can deliver the necessary adjustment without putting the most vulnerable groups at a disadvantage.

(Box 7.8 continued)

(*Box 7.8 continued*)

> Measures include guaranteed minimum income payments, covering health co-payments for the most vulnerable, increasing funds for housing support, protecting schooling for five and six-year-olds, and promoting job creation through active labor market policies.
>
> 5. **Romania:** The IMF-supported program provides room for additional spending of 0.05 percent of GDP in 2009 and 0.1 percent of GDP in 2010 to alleviate the immediate impact of the crisis on the most vulnerable households. Overall social assistance has increased by 1.9 percent of GDP in 2009 and by 0.2 percent of GDP in 2010.
>
> 6. **Senegal:** The IMF-supported program has helped to improve the budgetary situation and protect social spending. With support from development partners, the authorities are introducing targeted cash transfers to protect young vulnerable children of poor families on a pilot basis.
>
> 7. **Ukraine:** The IMF program included a substantial increase in social spending during the recession, as well as the following measures: protection of the poor against gas prices increases through the lifeline tariff and housing and utility allowance, protection of the unemployed through the unemployment insurance system, and expansion of two well-targeted social safety programs identified by the World Bank.
>
> **Source**   IMF (2010b).

What are the broad lessons? Countries' experiences seem to suggest a number of interesting trends (Foxley 2010). First, a more open and democratic economy tends to place a higher emphasis on SSN. Second, good macroeconomic policies pay by allowing countries to implement countercyclical social policies. Third, there is a necessity to undertake reforms within the existing institutional framework of SSN. Finally, new social policies must also provide better incentives for entrepreneurship and innovation to expand job creation.

Revisiting Growth Strategies

Policymakers are faced with a key challenge—redesigning growth strategies so as to ensure balance and sustainability. In many advanced and a number of emerging economies, they need to rebalance demand away from the public and toward the private sector, while consolidating public finances and repairing the financial sector. In a number of emerging and developing economies, policymakers need to increasingly tap domestic sources for growth, as demand from other economies will likely remain weaker than before the crisis. These rebalancing acts are not without problems. Many advanced economies continue to struggle to repair and reform their financial sectors, which is essential for sustained growth of private demand. Moreover, pressures remain for trade and financial protectionism. Concurrently, a concern in various emerging economies is that surging capital inflows may cause new boom–bust cycles. Some economies are resisting exchange rate appreciation that could support stronger domestic demand and reduce excessive current account surpluses out of concern that appreciation could destabilize their economies.

Multi-speed recoveries imply that policies will necessarily be tied to individual country circumstances, with the exit from supportive measures dependent on a self-sustaining recovery taking hold. But there are spillovers when the timing of policy actions varies, and economies should take these into account in setting policies. Spillovers related to fiscal policies are particularly relevant in the major advanced economies: domestic tightening has a negative impact on exports of other economies, and large deficits and the lack of well-specified medium-term fiscal consolidation strategies have a negative impact on the interest rates and risk premiums of fiscally challenged economies. In addition, resistance to capital inflows or exchange rate appreciation in some large emerging economies could undermine trade patterns or financial conditions for other emerging or advanced economies. Furthermore, some observers caution that exceptionally low interest rates in advanced economies could spur capital outflows, with potentially destabilizing effects for the recipient emerging economies.

The G-20 Framework for Strong, Sustainable, and Balanced Growth provides a forum to discuss and help achieve the required coordination of national policies. On a request from the G-20, the IMF has analyzed alternative policy scenarios to achieve strong, sustainable, and balanced growth based on G-20 frameworks submitted for the Mutual Assessment Process (MAP). After establishing a baseline scenario on the basis of G-20 submissions and key economic and financial developments thereafter, two alternative scenarios were developed—an upside and a downside case—to explore the potential benefits of further G-20 policy action to help deliver on their shared objectives of strong, sustainable, and balanced growth (Box 7.9).

BOX 7.9
Growth Prospects under the G-20 Mutual Assessment Process

Collaborative policy actions would credibly strengthen outcomes and address key weaknesses in G-20 policy frameworks. Specifically:

- Global growth would be appreciably stronger—world output could be higher by over US$1.5 trillion.
- An estimated 8 million more jobs could be created in advanced economies, over 21 million in emerging Asia and rest of the world, and global employment would rise by around 30 million jobs, lifting an estimated 33 million people out of poverty.
- Global growth would also be more balanced and thus more sustainable under collective action—stronger domestic demand in surplus countries is matched with deficit economies rebuilding saving on the back of stronger external demand.
- Driven by strong, credible, and "growth friendly" consolidation, public finances would be returned onto a sustainable trajectory in G-20 advanced economies with monetary policy accommodation maintained for a more extended period.
- To avoid a global "demand deficit" and slower growth, key structural reforms to boost internal demand in emerging economies with large external surpluses would help in supporting global growth.
- Exchange rate adjustment is shown to be an integral component of global rebalancing.
- Overall, global imbalances (sum of absolute current account positions) narrow by one quarter or three-fourth percentage points of global GDP.

Key policy actions for broader G-20 groups of countries with similar circumstances:

- Credible fiscal consolidation should be a top priority in advanced deficit economies.
- To reduce regulatory uncertainty, advanced economies should also accelerate financial repair and reform.
- Product and labor market reforms are important in advanced surplus economies, to repair possibly lower supply potential and reduce persistently high unemployment.
- In emerging surplus economies, policy should aim at enhancing social safety nets, reforming corporate governance, and developing financial markets, supported by greater exchange rate flexibility to facilitate a rebalancing of demand towards domestic sources.

(Box 7.9 continued)

(*Box 7.9 continued*)

- Greater infrastructure spending in emerging surplus economies, including in major oil exporters, could further address supply bottlenecks in many of these fast-growing economies.
- In emerging deficit economies, policies should focus on simplifying product market regulation, improving infrastructure, and increasing efficiency of the formal sector to strengthen growth and employment.

Source   IMF (2010c).

Conclusion: Post-crisis—A Flatter World?

Looking ahead, it is clear that the world will not be the same when it emerges from the crisis. Repair will be difficult and drawn out, full recovery will be slow and macroeconomic policies will have to be reshaped and reset.

Given the not-so-bright gloomy medium-term outlook, anchoring financial stability in the future will be reoriented around a stronger recognition of market failure and a larger and more legitimate role for public intervention than before. Legislative, legal, and institutional changes will be inevitable to force this outcome and to foster more durable solutions for resolution and restructuring that encompass not only financial institutions but also corporate and even households. Monetary policy will need to expand the frontiers of its mandate to a more encompassing objective of stability that involves markets, institutions, and instruments in price/financial stability. As the crisis recedes, the key challenge will be to calibrate the withdrawal of the monetary stimulus and this may redefine the instruments and conduct of monetary policy itself. The role of fiscal policy and fiscal frameworks, more generally, is likely to go through deep introspection and review. The effectiveness of fiscal policy in dealing with recessions will certainly be a key consideration. Over the medium-term, however, it is likely that restoration of fiscal sustainability will be the overriding concern. Governments have realized that while crises test rules, they also provide the push to reform taxes and expenditures as well as fiscal management, especially when the structure of their economies and populations are undergoing deep-seated change.

What about the future of free-market capitalism which suddenly looks as outdated as socialism? The dominant ideological deity that overthrew the mixed economy Keynesian model of the 1950–1970s has failed and the world is changing again. At the least, the US will lose some supremacy and the authority of China will rise and the new capitalism will have an Asia-Pacific, Latin American flavor—more orderly, more pragmatic, and more flexible—without diminishing, however, US innovation and ability to raise capital or London's financial haute couture. Europe's economy and financial systems are set for substantial refurbishing and rebalancing. Countries previously viewed as recipients of charity may become the new powerhouses. Continents of war and disease could turn into continents of opportunity.

Most emerging economies will return to amassing foreign ex-change reserves and limiting current account deficits/external debt as a risk-minimization strategy. Consequently, global imbalances will con-tinue to prevail. There will be even bigger upheavals in the manner in which markets function or financial sectors are restructured or policy-makers conduct regulation, tending possibly towards de-globalization.

Governments would be increasingly willing to protect companies from active shareholders. Attitudes to compensation are already changing. The search for security will strengthen political control over markets—a shift away from global to national. Undoubtedly, the main features of capitalism—private property, regulation, and democratic politics—will survive as even this crisis has not prompted a serious alternative vision of society. But financial regulation will not be the same again. If governments must save the financial system from collapse, they must in return demand rights to constrain institutions' behavior and align their risks with society's interests. The current mismatch of globalized finance and national governance is unsustainable—either governance must become more globalized or finance less globalized. It is not that the crisis reflects entirely the failure of markets but instead a failure to create proper markets. It is not the bankruptcy of the social system but the intellectual and moral failure of those who were in charge of it (embodied not least by Mr Greenspan). The downside is that govern-ments are looking more strained in their finances than before to be able to deliver on this augmented role that they envisage. Efforts to con-solidate public finances will therefore dominate the medium-term.

The future is not that capitalism will cease to exist; it will escape from intensive care but with a more human face. Rather, it will be modified to a system in which animal spirits will be watched and possibly tamed. Eventually globalization will cease to be a dirty word. The consensus continues to be that the future of capitalism lies in the preservation of globalization. There are inevitably costs of globalization but they are outweighed by the benefits. The economic cycle is endemic and inescapable and so will it be in the future, but a downturn associated with a financial crisis is devastating and will have to be avoided at all costs.

On the reform of the financial system, countries will not wait for the global solution to arrive, late as usual. Authorities in each country will act preemptively to put their houses in order. Perhaps they will return to the separation of commercial banking from other types of activities that are now conducted under the umbrella of banking. How should investment banking be regulated remains a contentious issue. Or should it be left to the discipline of the marketplace? There is also a view that there is no need to go back to *Glass–Steagall*; instead regulation should simply focus on large institutions with, say, over US$500 million of assets (Fink 2009). Effective antitrust and competition policies and better corporate governance rules need to be put into the mix. Regulators can be expected to look more closely than before at financial products to determine what is safe for human consumption, for whom, and in what dosage (Stiglitz 2010b). Also quick advances in systemic regulation can be anticipated. Here a global view is important so as to eschew regulatory arbitrage.

Keeping financial markets global while making them safe requires tighter, better cooperation among countries—not only on financial regulation, but also on global macroeconomic and monetary policy. Cooperation is particularly pressing for financial policies because of the major spillovers that domestic actions can have on other countries; however, it is equally relevant in other areas as well. The specific design of policies would appropriately vary from country to country, but policymakers should avoid policies—such as the favoring of domestic over foreign lending—that could lead to distortions. More generally, trade and financial protectionist pressures should be resisted. The stark collapse in world trade in the crisis only heightens the importance of a rapid completion of trade negotiations to help open up markets and revitalize global growth prospects on an enduring basis.

The G-20 processes have set the pace of reform in the global architecture that will hold together this renewed effort towards cooperation. The IMF has emerged as the biggest winner and will likely shape the global consensus in the years to come. The IMF visualizes itself as part of the process without claiming leadership. Its main role lies in its surveillance but it also has a broader role in addressing systemic risks. An immediate priority is its resources—enlarging and expanding quota resources, rebalancing New Arrangements to Borrow (NAB), and making it operationally more flexible; bilateral loan agreements; general allocation of SDRs and equitable distribution among IMF members; and strengthening of concessional lending capacity to cover the medium-term financing needs of low-income country members. Reforms of the lending framework have been initiated—higher access; short-term and emergency financing; and proper targeting of lending, particularly to low-income countries. Monitoring and policy advice, as stated earlier, will remain the primary thrust area of the IMF but with a focus on helping countries weather the crisis and restore stability as well as to set out the path to global recovery. Building a more robust global architecture holds the key to global financial stability. The IMF will be expected to contribute by providing effective, candid, independent, and evenhanded surveillance; early warnings of systemic threats; monitoring of systemically important countries with global implications; integrating financial sector assessment into bilateral surveillance; and greater transparency involving not just improvement in quality of analysis, but also candor and traction in terms of policy follow up. Reforming the IMF's governance is critical not just for its legitimacy, but also to enable it to be a more effective leader in responding to unexpected global contingencies. Immediately this involves implementing as soon as possible the April 2008 and December 2010 agreements on quota and voice and the new income model, completing the next quota review by January 2014, and the whole gamut of governance reforms.

It has been remarked that some crises spread hysteria, some clear the mind and focus attention. This crisis has done both. The world has moved from panic to paralysis to do what it takes. Everyone has had time to think and take stock of the lessons. Perhaps, we have learned at a great cost the need to manage the global economy better. Or perhaps not. When the crisis is behind us, history will judge whether or not global cooperation in dealing with financial distress, in coordinating fiscal efforts, in resisting protectionism and competitive depreciation, in generating official financial support for countries in distress due to factors not of their making, and in developing early warnings, multilateral insurance, and bailouts played its part in preventing future shocks or, if not, in minimizing its deleterious consequences so that humanity can look forward to a healthier, safer, and more inclusive global economy of tomorrow.

Notes

1. As this crisis brought the IMF to the forefront of crisis management, we choose not to delve into issues relating to the World Bank and other Regional Development Banks.
2. The initial efforts are on in this direction at the IMF.
3. We are indebted to an anonymous referee for encouraging us to exercise our minds on many of these issues.
4. In the face of the surge in commodity prices that overtook these projections, the IMF, revised its 2011 petroleum price outlook to US$107 a barrel in April 2011.
5. It is interesting to quote what a commentator reported in this context:

   Take the case of Dr Yaga Reddy, the former Governor of the Bank of India, who addressed the meeting. India had no financial crisis. Its high rate of economic growth continued unabated. Why? Because Reddy, over the objections of western bankers, International Monetary Fund kibitzing, and kindred local banking pressures, simply did not allow the Indian banking system to engage in Wall Street-style speculation. (Kuttner 2010)

Annexure I
Causes of the Financial Crisis

Cause (1)	Argument (2)	Counter Argument (3)
I. Macro Factors		
1 Global Imbalances	Global financial flows have been characterized in recent years by an unsustainable pattern: some countries (China, Japan, and Germany) run large surpluses every year, while others (like the US and UK) run deficits. The US external deficits have been mirrored by internal deficits in the household and government sectors. US borrowing cannot continue indefinitely—the resulting stress underlies current financial disruptions.	*None of the adjustments that would reverse the fundamental imbalances has yet occurred—there has not been adequate adjustment in the dollar's exchange value, and US deficits persist.*
2 Excessive Leverage	In the post-2000 period of low interest rates and abundant capital, fixed income yields were low. To compensate, many investors used borrowed funds to boost the return on their capital. Excessive leverage magnified the impact of the housing downturn, and deleveraging caused the inter-bank credit market to tighten.	*Leverage is only a symptom of the underlying problem: mispricing of risk and a credit bubble.*

(Annexure I continued)

(*Annexure I continued*)

II. US Housing Market

Cause (1)	Argument (2)	Counter Argument (3)
3 Imprudent Mortgage Lending	Against a backdrop of abundant credit, low interest rates, and rising house prices, lending standards were relaxed so that many people were able to buy houses they could not afford. When prices began to fall and loans started going bad, there was a severe shock to the financial system.	*Imprudent lending certainly played a role, but sub-prime loans were a relatively small part of the overall US mortgage market and of total credit market debt outstanding.*
4 Housing Bubble	With its easy money policies, the Federal Reserve allowed housing prices to rise to unsustainable levels. The crisis was triggered by the bursting of the bubble.	*It is difficult to identify a bubble until it bursts, and US Fed actions to suppress the bubble may have done more damage to the economy than waiting and responding to the effects of the bubble bursting.*
5 Government-Mandated Sub-prime Lending	Federal mandates to help low-income borrowers (e.g., the *Community Reinvestment Act* [CRA] and Fannie Mae and Freddie Mac's affordable housing goals) forced banks to engage in imprudent mortgage lending.	*The sub-prime mortgage boom was fueled by non-bank lenders (not subject to CRA) and securitized by private investment banks rather than the GSEs.*

6	Lack of Transparency and Accountability in Mortgage Finance	Throughout the housing finance value chain, many participants contributed to the creation of bad mortgages and the selling of bad securities, apparently feeling secure that they would not be held accountable for their actions. A lender could sell exotic mortgages to home-owners, apparently without fear of repercussions if those mortgages failed. Similarly, a trader could sell toxic securities to investors, apparently without fear of personal responsibility if those contracts failed.	*Many contractual arrangements did provide recourse against sellers or issuers of bad mortgages or related securities. Many non-bank mortgage lenders failed because they were forced to take back loans that defaulted, and many lawsuits have been filed against MBS issuers and others.*

III. Regulatory Failure

7	Deregulatory Legislation	Laws such as the *Gramm–Leach–Bliley Act* (GLB Act) and the *Commodity Futures Modernization Act* (CFMA) permitted financial institutions to engage in unregulated risky transactions on a vast scale. The laws were driven by an excessive faith in the robustness of market discipline or self-regulation.	*GLB Act and CFMA did not permit the creation of unregulated markets and activities; they simply codified existing market practices.*
8	Failure of Risk Management Systems	Some firms separated analysis of market risk and credit risk. This division did not work for complex structured products, where those risks were indistinguishable.	*Senior management's responsibility has always been to bridge this kind of gap in risk assessment.*

(Annexure I continued)

Cause (1)	Argument (2)	Counter Argument (3)
9 Relaxed Regulation of Leverage	The US security market regulator (The Securities Exchange Commission) liberalized its net capital rule in 2004, allowing investment bank holding companies to attain very high leverage ratios. Its Consolidated Supervised Entities program, which applied to the largest investment banks, was voluntary and ineffective.	*The net capital rule applied only to the regulated broker/dealer unit; the SEC never had statutory authority to limit leverage at the holding company level.*
10 Fragmented Regulation	US financial regulation is dispersed among many agencies, each with responsibility for a particular class of financial institution. As a result, no agency is well-positioned to monitor emerging system-wide problems.	*Countries with unified regulatory structures, such as Japan and the UK, have not avoided the crisis.*
11 No Systemic Risk Regulator	No regulator had comprehensive jurisdiction over all systemically important financial institutions. While the US Fed had the role of systemic risk regulator by default, it lacked authority to oversee investment banks, hedge funds, or non-bank derivatives dealers.	*Some question whether the problem was lack of authority or failure to use existing regulatory powers effectively.*

| 12 | Shadow Banking System | Risky financial activities once confined to regulated banks migrated outside the explicit government safety net provided by deposit insurance and safety and soundness regulation. Mortgage lending, in particular, moved out of banks into unregulated institutions. This unsupervised risk-taking amounted to a financial house of cards. | *Regulated banks have not really fared much better than investment banks, hedge funds, OTC derivatives dealers, or private equity firms.* |
| 13 | Off-Balance Sheet Finance | Many banks established off-the-books special purpose entities to engage in risky speculative investments. This allowed banks to make more loans during the expansion, but also created contingent liabilities that, with the onset of the crisis, reduced market confidence in the banks' creditworthiness. At the same time, they had allowed banks to hold less capital against potential losses. Investors had little ability to understand banks' true financial positions. | *Beginning in the 1990s, off-balance sheet finance emerged as a legitimate way to manage risk.* |

(Annexure I continued)

Cause (1)	Argument (2)	Counter Argument (3)
IV. Financial Innovation and Structured Products		
14 Financial Innovation	New instruments in structured finance developed so rapidly that market infrastructure and systems were not prepared when those instruments came under stress.	*In a global marketplace, innovation will continue to occur and national regulators' attempts to restrain it will only put their countries' markets at a competitive disadvantage.*
15 Securitization	Securitization fostered the "originate-to-distribute" model which reduced lenders' incentives to be prudent, especially in the face of vast investor demand for sub-prime loans packaged as AAA bonds. Ownership of mortgage-backed securities was widely dispersed, causing repercussions throughout the global system when sub-prime loans went bad in 2007.	*Mortgage loans that were not securitized, but kept on the originating lender's books, have also done poorly.*
16 Complexity	The complexity of certain financial instruments at the heart of the crisis had three effects: (i) investors were unable to make independent judgments on the merits of investments, (ii) risks of market transactions were obscured, and (iii) regulators were baffled.	*Standard economic theory assumes that investors act rationally in their own self-interest, which implies that they should only take risks they understand.*

17 Credit Default Swaps (CDS)	An interesting paradox arose—as credit derivative instruments, developed initially for risk management, continued to grow and become more sophisticated with the help of financial engineering. In becoming a medium for speculative transactions, credit derivatives increased, rather than alleviated, risk.	*Speculation in derivatives generally makes prices of the underlying commodities more stable. Why would this relationship sometimes break down?*
18 Over-the-Counter Derivatives	Since OTC derivatives (including credit swaps) are largely unregulated, limited information about risk exposures is available to regulators and market participants.	*The largest OTC markets—interest rate and currency swaps—appear to have held up fairly well.*
V. Others		
19 Rating Agencies	The credit rating agencies gave AAA ratings to numerous issues of sub-prime mortgage-backed securities, many of which were subsequently downgraded to junk status. Critics cite poor economic models, conflicts of interest, and lack of effective regulation as reasons for the rating agencies' failure.	*All market participants underestimated risk, not just the rating agencies.*

(Annexure I continued)

(Annexure I continued)

Cause (1)	Argument (2)	Counter Argument (3)
20 Mark-to-market Accounting	Accounting standards require institutions to report the fair (or current market) value of securities they hold. Critics of the rule argue that this forces banks to recognize losses based on "fire sale" prices that prevail in distressed markets—prices believed to be below long-term fundamental values. Those losses undermine market confidence and exacerbate banking system problems.	*Many view uncertainty regarding financial institutions' true condition as key to the crisis. If accounting standards—however imperfect—are relaxed, fears that published balance sheets are unreliable will grow.*
21 Short-term Incentives	Since traders and managers at many financial institutions receive a large part of their compensation in the form of an annual bonus, they lack incentives to avoid risky strategies liable to fail spectacularly every 5 or 10 years.	*Shareholders already have incentives and authority to monitor corporate compensation structures and levels.*

Source Adapted from Jickling (2009).

Annexure II
The Global Financial Crisis: A Chronology of Major Events (2007–July 2010)[1]

2010

- **July 27:** Global banking regulators reached an agreement to tighten capital requirements and impose new worldwide liquidity and leverage standards at the BIS (the so-called Basel III standards), but softened some of their proposals and delayed others to at least 2018.
- **July 21:** President Obama signed the *Dodd–Frank Act*, bringing to a close a year-long effort to overhaul the US financial system and its regulators.
- **July 15:** Goldman Sachs agreed to pay a US$550 million fine to settle US regulators' accusations that it misled investors in a mortgage-backed security—a move that ends the highest profile regulatory case since the crisis.
- **May 18:** Germany, in an attack on the financial speculation, announced a ban on naked short selling of shares in the top 10 German financial institutions, euro government bonds, and on related transactions in credit default swaps (CDS).
- **May 17:** The European Central Bank bought €16.5 billion of euro-zone government bonds as part of an international rescue plan, amid widespread investor concern that the intervention is not sufficient to stabilize debt markets.
- **May 9:** The IMF unanimously approved its part of the rescue loans to Greece, and provided €5.5 billion immediately.
- **May 6:** The Greek Parliament voted in favor of various reforms and cuts in an attempt to cut the deficit and stabilize the country both financially and socially. Some of the proposals included public sector pay being frozen until 2014, VAT increase from 19 percent to 23 percent, an increase in the retirement age from 61 to 63, and taxes on fuel, alcohol, and tobacco to rise by 10 percent. These measures are also required to ensure that Greece receives the €110 billion rescue package agreed by the IMF and the EU member states.

- **April 27:** Standard & Poor's downgraded Greece's debt ratings below investment grade to junk bond status.
- **April 16:** The US SEC filed suit against Goldman Sachs, claiming the bank created and sold a synthetic CDO that was secretly intended to fail.
- **January 13:** The first public hearings of the US Congressional Financial Crisis Inquiry Commission took place.

2009

- **December 16:** S&P cuts Greece's rating to BBB+ from A–.
- **November 20:** The Netherlands announced plans to provide ABN Amro and Fortis Bank Nederland with a further €4.4 billion in capital to keep their merger on track. FBN and the Dutch assets of ABN were nationalized a year ago when Fortis, their former owner, collapsed.
- **November 10:** A US Senate committee proposed a major overhaul of the US regulatory system that would cut the powers of the Federal Reserve and create a single banking regulator. The draft legislation creates an agency to oversee systemic risk, which could call for banks to be broken up and impose more stringent capital requirements.
- **November 8:** Gordon Brown's proposed plan for a transactions tax met wide criticism. The so-called "Tobin Tax" had been designed to include insurance levies and funds to finance future bailouts. The US, Canada, Russia, the IMF, and the European Central Bank opposed the proposal.
- **November 5:** The Bank of England announced that a further £25 billion will be injected into the economy, bringing the total amount expended under the quantitative easing program to £200 billion.
- **November 3:** The UK Treasury announced that a further £33.5 billion would be injected into Royal Bank of Scotland in order to ensure that the bank survives the current crisis, bringing the total government investment in the institution up to 84 percent.
- **October 21:** The governor of the Bank of England called for banks to be split into utility companies for their deposit taking and payments systems and risky ventures, a view sharply at odds with the Treasury, the Financial Services Authority and the G-20 proposals.
- **September 25:** The G-20 leaders agreed to support new global standards on remuneration practices produced by the Financial Stability Board (FSB).
- **September 7:** The Basel Committee of central bank governors provisionally agreed on a set of rules based on the principles taken away from the G-20 meeting in London earlier in the month. Key proposals included increases in the size of capital reserves that banks are required to hold, together with much stricter guidelines on the quality of the reserves themselves and a cap on bank borrowings of 25 times the size of assets.

- **September 3:** Alistair Darling, the UK's Chancellor of the Exchequer, warned Germany and France against ending their economic stimulus packages before recovery has been consolidated.
- **August 27:** Lord Turner, chairman of the UK's Financial Services Authority (FSA), suggested that the FSA might regulate the City by way of a so-called "Tobin tax." This would amount to a tax on financial transactions, thereby reducing banks' profits and, thus, the money available to them to allocate as bonuses. President Nicolas Sarkozy also unveiled notable regulatory innovations in announcing a range of measures relating to bankers' pay and bonuses in France. Following the recommendations announced at the most recent G-20 summit, the new regulatory regime will include a prohibition on guaranteed bonuses and a mechanism by which payment will be spread over the years following the period to which the bonus relates.
- **August 12:** In the UK, the FSA published its new remuneration code, which would come into force on January 1, 2010.
- **August 6:** The Bank of England Monetary Policy committee voted to increase its quantitative easing program by an additional £50 billion to a total of £175 billion. The increase was coupled with an announcement that the recession was deeper than first expected, but that the decline appeared to be slowing.
- **June 25:** AIG agreed to give the Federal Reserve Bank of New York stakes in two of its life assurance units (American International Assurance Company, or the AIA, its Asian insurance arm, and American Life Insurance Company, or the Alico) in order to cut the debt it owes to the bank by US$25 billion. AIG will put its equity in AIA and Alico into special purpose vehicles and then give preferred shares of US$16 billion and US$9 billion, respectively, to the Federal Reserve Bank of New York.
- **June 18:** The Swiss National Bank (SNB) called for rules allowing drastic action on the nation's domestic banks if their problems threatened the entire economy and for renewed measures to fight recession and fend off deflation. The SNB also recommended splitting off parts of Switzerland's top two banks, UBS and Credit Suisse, or limiting their size if needed.
- **June 17:** The US government announced a major reform of banking regulation to prevent future financial crises. The reforms require big banks to put more money aside against future losses to curb excessive risk taking and the creation of a special agency to protect the interests of US consumers and regulate the provision of mortgages and credit cards. The US Federal Reserve will also be given the authority to monitor major financial institutions.
- **June 3:** Latvia became the first EU country to face a sovereign debt crisis after failing to sell a single bill at a treasury auction worth US$100 million, prompting fears of a fresh storm in Eastern Europe as capital flight tested currency pegs.

- **May 20:** The US Treasury indicated that a pool of institutions would be allowed to start repaying funds lent under the Troubled Asset Relief Program (TARP). Those institutions whose stress tests indicate they will not need to raise new capital in case of further economic turbulence will be included in the pool.
- **May 7:** The Bank of England announced that it will keep interest rates at the historically low level of 0.5 percent and that it will pump an additional £50 billion into the UK economy via the existing quantitative easing program. The US regulators ordered 10 of the nation's largest banks must raise US$75 billion in equity following the completion of stress tests. The European Central Bank announced that it will cut interest rates to a record low of 1 percent.
- **April 30:** The Federal Reserve left interest rates unchanged and stated that the US economy is demonstrating signs of improvement. The Bank for International Settlements revealed that global cross-border lending by banks shrank by almost US$5 trillion on the nine months to the end of December 2008, the sharpest fall ever recorded. The EU Commission's proposals for new hedge fund rules were released.
- **April 10:** Germany revealed plans for its first nationalization of a bank in the post war era. Hypo Real Estate offered investors €1.39 per share.
- **April 7:** Japan planned US$100 billion fiscal stimulus to fight its recession.
- **April 2:** At the G-20 London Summit, leaders of the world's largest economies agreed to tackle the global financial crisis with measures worth of US$1.1 trillion including US$750 billion more for the IMF, US$250 billion to boost global trade, and US$100 billion for multilateral development banks. They also agreed on establishing a new Financial Stability Board to work with the IMF to ensure cooperation across borders; closer regulation of banks, hedge funds, and credit rating agencies, and a crackdown on tax havens. They could only agree on additional stimulus measures through the IMF and multilateral development bank lending and not through country stimulus packages. The leaders reiterated their commitment to resist protectionism and promote global trade and investment.
- **March 30:** The central banks of China and Argentina reached an agreement for a 70 billion yuan/US$10 billion currency swap for three years, the sixth such swap China concluded with emerging economies including South Korea, Hong Kong, Indonesia, Belarus, and Malaysia.
- **March 24:** The Executive Board of the IMF approved a major overhaul of the IMF's lending framework, including the creation of a new Flexible Credit Line (FCL). The changes to the IMF's lending framework include (a) modernizing IMF conditionality for all borrowers; (b) introducing a new Flexible Credit Line; (c) enhancing the flexibility of the Fund's traditional Stand-By Arrangement; (d) doubling normal access limits for

non-concessional resources; (e) simplifying cost and maturity structures; and (f) eliminating certain seldom-used facilities.

- **March 23:** The US Treasury released the details of its Public Private Partnership Investment Program to address the challenge of legacy toxic assets (mortgages and securities backed by loans) being carried by the financial system. The Treasury and the Federal Deposit Insurance Corporation, with funding from the TARP and private capital, are to purchase eligible assets worth about US$500 billion with the potential to expand the program to US$1 trillion.

- **March 20:** The European Union announced additional support for the IMF's lending capacity in the form of a loan to the IMF totaling €75 billion, about US$100 billion.

- **March 19:** The US Federal Reserve announced a plan to purchase longer-term Treasury securities not just to influence the spread between private interest rates and Treasuries (through its mortgage-backed securities purchases, for example), but also to pull down the entire spectrum of interest rates by driving down the rate on benchmark Treasuries. Key points of yesterday's Fed announcement include:

  - The federal funds rate, with a current target range of 0.0 percent–0.25 percent, is likely to remain exceptionally low for "an extended period;"
  - The Fed will purchase:

    - up to an additional US$750 billion of agency mortgage-backed securities, for a total of US$1.25 trillion, and
    - up to an additional US$100 billion of agency debt for a total of up to US$200 billion.

  - It followed the central banks of the United Kingdom and Japan by announcing its intention to purchase longer-term Treasury securities (up to US$300 billion worth) over the next six months.
  - It launched its Term Asset-Backed Securities Loan Facility (TALF) program to support credit for households and small businesses, and may expand that program to other lending.

- **March 18:** The Federal Reserve announced that it would buy approximately US$1.2 trillion in government bonds and mortgage-related securities in order to lower borrowing costs for home mortgages and other types of loans.

- **March 14:** The G-20 Finance Ministers and Central Bank Governors met in preparation for the April 2 Leaders' London Summit. They agreed to take measures to restore global growth and to strengthen the financial system. They also committed themselves to help emerging and developing economies cope with the reversal in capital flows and agreed on the need to increase resources for the IMF.

- **March 10:** Finance Minister Najib Razak announced a large Malaysian fiscal stimulus package amounting 9.0 percent of GDP.
- **February 24:** US President Barack Obama used his first address to a joint session of Congress to outline how the economic recovery can work. He outlined the rationale behind the economic stimulus and the financial sector rescue plans, conceding costs and risks, but warned of the greater danger of inaction.
- **February 23:** The Chilean Finance Ministry announced that the Central Bank of Chile will conduct US dollar auctions in March 2009 to finance a US$3 billion stimulus plan announced by President Michelle Bachelet in January.
- **February 20:** Several Netherlands' local and provincial councils announced that they are planning to launch local stimulus packages to combat the country's economic crisis.
- **February 18:** The German government agreed on a revised bank bailout plan as the first version, from October 2008, costing €480 billion/US$603.7 billion, had not delivered appropriate results.
- **February 17:** US President Obama signed a US$787 billion economic stimulus bill, including US$575 billion in government spending and US$212 billion in tax cuts.
- **February 17:** US automakers General Motors Corp. and Chrysler LLC submitted recovery plans to the US government requesting US$21.6 billion more in loans to enable their recovery.
- **February 14:** Finance ministers and central bank governors of the Group of Seven (G-7) industrialized nations met in Rome to discuss the financial crisis and economic slowdown. In order to prevent a resurgence of protectionism, the G-7 members pledged to do all they could to combat recession without distorting free trade.
- **February 12:** The Irish government reported a €7 billion (US$9 billion) bank rescue plan for two of the country's largest banks, the Allied Irish Bank and the Bank of Ireland. Each bank will receive €3.5 billion in recapitalization funds. The Swiss government presented a second economic stimulus plan worth 700 million Swiss francs (US$603 million). Australian legislature rejected fiscal stimulus package of US$28 billion as Australian unemployment climbed to two-year high. The Bank of Korea's Monetary Policy Board cut its benchmark seven-day repurchase rate by 50 basis points to a new record low of 2.00 percent, marking the sixth cut since October.
- **February 5:** The Bank of England's Monetary Policy Committee reduced its key interest rate by 50 basis points from 1.50 percent to 1.00 percent. Interest rates reached at their lowest level since the Bank of England was founded in 1694.
- **January 28:** Canada announced a US$32 billion stimulus package that included infrastructure spending and tax cuts. The US House of

Representatives passed the American Recovery and Reinvestment Act of 2009. The cost of the bill was estimated at US$819 billion.

- **January 26:** Australia announced a US$2.6 billion stimulus package.
- **January 21:** The Philippines announced a US$633 million increase to bring its stimulus program to US$6.9 billion.
- **January 15:** The US Senate voted to release the second half of the Treasury's TARP to stabilize the US financial system, granting President-elect Barack Obama authority to spend US$350 billion to revive credit markets and help homeowners avoid foreclosure. The Treasury Department announced it would fund a rescue of Bank of America which guarantees US$118 billion in troubled assets.
- **January 6:** Chile announced a US$4 billion stimulus package.

2008

- **December 23:** Poland's Monetary Policy Council reduced its main policy rate by 75 basis points to 5.00 percent.
- **December 23:** Japanese Cabinet approved record fiscal plan for FY2009. The ¥88.5 trillion (US$980.6 billion) fiscal package for FY2009, which begins April 1, 2009, marks a 6.6 percent increase in spending from initial targets.
- **December 23:** China lowered interest rates for the fifth time in four months. Benchmark one-year lending and deposit rates were both lowered by 27 basis points to 5.31 percent and 2.25 percent, respectively. These rates were lowered by 108 basis points, their biggest margin in 11 years a month ago.
- **December 19:** President Bush announced an automotive rescue plan for General Motors Corp. and Chrysler LLC that will make US$13.4 billion in federal loans available almost immediately.
- **December 18:** Turkey reduced rates for the second consecutive month.
- **December 18:** The Norwegian Central Bank cut its main policy interest rate by 175 basis points to 3.0 percent, the third decrease since October.
- **December 17:** US housing starts plummeted 18.9 percent in November, to a seasonally adjusted annual rate of 625,000 units. This was a record monthly low.
- **December 16:** The US Federal Open Market Committee (FOMC) voted unanimously to lower its target for the federal funds rate more than 75 basis points, to a range of 0.0 percent to 0.25 percent. Long-term bond yields dropped from 2.50 percent to 2.35 percent.
- **December 11:** 27 EU governments' leaders approved a €200 billion (US$269 billion) economic stimulus package. The cost is approximately 1.5 percent of the EU's total GDP. Taiwan's central bank cut its leading

discount rate by three quarters of a percentage point to 2.0 percent, marking the biggest reduction since 1982. It was also the fifth rate cut in two-and-a-half months. The central Bank of Korea reduced the seven-day repurchase rate by one percentage point to a record low of 3.00 percent. Interest rates have been reduced by 225 basis points in two months— 100 basis points in October and 125 basis points in November.

- **November 24:** The UK announced a fiscal stimulus package valued at £20 billion (US$30.2 billion) aimed at limiting the length and depth of the apparent UK recession. The package included a temporary reduction of value-added tax from 17.5 percent to 15.0 percent. The Central Bank of Iceland's currency swap arrangement with Sweden, Norway, and Denmark was extended through December 2009. On the same date, S&P reduced its long-term Iceland sovereign credit rating from BBB to BBB-, while maintaining its short-term Iceland sovereign currency rating at A-3. The US Treasury, Federal Reserve, and Federal Deposit Insurance Corp. said that they will protect Citigroup against certain potential losses and would invest an additional US$20 billion (on top of the previous US$25 billion) in the company.

- **November 15:** At a G-20 summit in Washington, the G-20 leaders agreed to continue to take steps to stabilize the global financial system and improve the international regulatory framework.

- **November 15:** Japan announced that it would make US$100 billion from its foreign exchange reserves available to the IMF for loans to emerging market economies. This was in addition to US$2 billion that Japan is to invest in the World Bank to help recapitalize banks in smaller, emerging market economies.

- **November 14:** The President's Working Group on Financial Markets (Treasury, Securities and Exchange Commission, Federal Reserve, and the Commodity Futures Trading Commission) announced a series of initiatives to strengthen oversight and the infrastructure of the over-the-counter derivatives market. This included the development of credit default swap central counterparties—clearing houses between parties that own debt instruments and others willing to insure against defaults.

- **November 12:** US Treasury Secretary Paulson announced a change in priorities for the US$700 billion TARP approved by Congress in early October. Paulson's new plan also would provide support for the asset-backed commercial paper market, particularly securitized auto loans, credit card debt, and student loans. Between August and November 2007 asset-backed commercial paper outstanding contracted by nearly US$400 billion. Paulson rejected suggestions that TARP funds be made available to the US auto industry. The Central Bank of Russia raised key interest rates by 1 percent. Swiss Economics Minister announced the Swiss government would inject 341 million Swiss Francs/US$286.6 million for economic stimulus.

- **November 10:** The US government announced further aid to AIG, whose September US$85 billion loan was reduced to US$60 billion; the government bought US$40 billion of preferred AIG shares, and US$52.5 billion of AIG mortgage securities. The US support of AIG increased from September's US$85 billion to US$150 billion.
- **November 9:** G-20 meeting of finance ministers and central bank governors in Sao Paulo, Brazil concluded with a communiqué calling for increased role of emerging economies in reform of Bretton Woods financial institutions, including the World Bank and the IMF. China announced a 4 trillion Yuan/US$587 billion domestic stimulus package primarily aimed at infrastructure, housing, agriculture, health care, and social welfare spending. This program represents 16 percent of China's 2007 GDP.
- **November 6:** The IMF announced the following in its updated *World Economic Outlook*: (*a*) "global activity is slowing quickly," and (*b*) "prospects for global growth have deteriorated over the past month." The IMF projected global GDP growth for 2009 at 2.2 percent, three-fourths of a percentage point lower than projections announced in October, 2008. The European Central Bank, ECB, reduced its key interest rate from 3.75 percent to 3.25 percent. The Danish Central Bank lowered its key lending rate from 5.5 percent to 5 percent. The Czech National Bank reduced its interest rate from 3.5 percent to 2.75 percent. In South Korea, the Bank of Korea reduced its key interest rate from 4.25 percent to 4 percent. During October the Bank of Korea reduced its rate from 5.25 percent to 4.25 percent.
- **November 4:** Australia lowered its overnight cash rate by 75 basis points to 5.25 percent, the lowest since March 2005. Furthermore, Chilean President Michelle Bachelet announced a US$1.15 billion stimulus package to boost the housing market and channel credit into small and medium businesses.
- **November 3:** Russian Prime Minister Vladimir Putin reported measures to support the real economy. The measures included temporary preferences for domestic producers for state procurement contracts, subsidizing interest rates for loans intended to modernize production; and tariff protection for a number of industries such as automobiles and agriculture. The new policy aimed to support exporters.
- **October 31:** Three of the six Gulf Cooperation Council (GOC) countries, Bahrain, Kuwait, and Saudi Arabian central banks reduced interest rates to follow the actions of the US Federal Reserve and other central banks.
- **October 29:** The US Federal Reserve lowered its target for the federal funds rate 50 basis points to 1 percent. It also approved a 50 basis point decrease in the discount rate to 1.25 percent. The Federal Reserve also announced establishment of temporary reciprocal currency arrangements, or swap lines, with the central banks of Brazil, Mexico, Korea, Singapore,

and New Zealand. The IMF approved the creation of a Short-term Liquidity Facility, established to support countries with strong policies which face temporary liquidity problems.

- **October 27:** Iceland's Kaupthing Bank became the first European borrower to default on yen denominated bonds issued in Japan (samurai bonds).
- **October 23:** US President Bush called for the G-20 leaders to meet on November 15 in Washington DC to deal with the global financial crisis.
- **October 20:** The Netherlands agreed to inject €10 billion (US$13.4 billion) into ING Group NV, a global banking and insurance company.
- **October 20:** Sweden proposed a financial stability plan, which includes a 1.5 trillion Swedish kronor (US$206 billion) bank guarantee, to combat the impact of the crisis.
- **October 19:** South Korea announced that it would guarantee up to US$100 billion in foreign debt held by its banks and pumped US$30 billion more into its banking sector.
- **October 18:** President Bush, President Nicolas Sarkozy of France, and the president of the European Commission issued a joint statement saying they agreed to "reach out to other world leaders" to propose an international summit meeting to be held soon after the US presidential election, with the possibility of more gatherings after that.
- **October 17:** The Swiss government said it would take a 9 percent stake (US$5.36 billion) in UBS, one of the country's leading banks, and set up a US$60 billion fund to absorb the bank's troubled assets. UBS had already written off US$40 billion of its US$80 billion in "toxic American securities."
- **October 15:** The G-8 leaders (Canada, France, Germany, Italy, Japan, Russia, the United Kingdom, the United States, and the European Commission) stated that they were united in their commitment to resolve the current crisis, strengthen financial institutions, restore confidence in the financial system, and provide a sound economic footing for citizens and businesses. They stated that changes to the regulatory and institutional regimes for the world's financial sectors are needed and that they look forward to a leaders' meeting with key countries at an appropriate time in the near future to adopt an agenda for reforms to meet the challenges of the 21st century.
- **October 14:** In coordination with European monetary authorities, the US Treasury, the US Federal Reserve, and the US Federal Deposit Insurance Corporation (FDIC) announced a plan to invest up to US$250 billion in preferred securities of nine major US banks (including Citigroup, Bank of America, Wells Fargo, Goldman Sachs, and JPMorgan Chase). The FDIC also agreed to temporarily guarantee the senior debt and deposits in non-interest bearing deposit transaction accounts (used mainly by businesses for daily operations).

- **October 13:** The UK Government provided US$60 billion and took a 60 percent stake in the Royal Bank of Scotland.
- **October 12–13:** Several European countries (Germany, France, Italy, Austria, Netherlands, Portugal, Spain, and Norway) announced rescue plans for their countries worth as much as US$2.7 trillion. The plans were largely consistent with a UK model that included concerted action, recapitalization, state ownership, government debt guarantees (the largest component of the plans), and improved regulations.
- **October 8:** In a coordinated effort, the US Federal Reserve, the European Central Bank, the Bank of England, and the central banks of Canada and Sweden all reduced primary lending rates by a half percentage point. Switzerland also cut its benchmark rate, while the Bank of Japan endorsed the moves without changing its rates. The Chinese central bank also reduced its key interest rate and lowered bank reserve requirements. The Federal Reserve's benchmark short-term rate stood at 1.5 percent and the European Central Bank's at 3.75 percent.
- **October 5:** The German government moved to guarantee all private savings accounts and arranged a bailout for Hypo Real Estate, a German lender. A week earlier, Fortis, a large banking and insurance company based in Belgium but active across much of Europe, had received €11.2 billion (US$ 8.2 billion) from the governments of the Netherlands, Belgium, and Luxembourg. On October 3, the Dutch government seized its Dutch operations and on October 5, the Belgian government helped to arrange for BNP-Paribas, the French bank, to take over what was left of the company.
- **October 3:** The US President signed the bill titled the *Emergency Economic Stabilization Act* of 2008, sometimes referred to as the Troubled Assets Relief Program (TARP). The new bill's title included its purpose: "A bill to provide authority for the Federal Government to purchase and insure certain types of troubled assets for the purposes of providing stability to and preventing disruption in the economy and financial system and protecting taxpayers ..." US-based Wells Fargo Bank announced a takeover of Wachovia Corp, the fourth largest US bank. (Previously, Citibank had agreed to take over Wachovia.) Britain's Financial Services Authority said it had raised the amount guaranteed in savings accounts to £50,000 (US$88,390) from £35,000. Greece also stated that it would guarantee savings accounts regardless of the amount.
- **October 1:** US Senate amended the Financial Institutions Rescue Bill.
- **September 30:** Iceland's government took a 75 percent share of Glitnir, Iceland's third largest bank, by injecting €600 million into the bank. The following week, it took control of Landsbanki and soon after placed Iceland's largest bank, Kaupthing, into receivership as well.
- **September 26:** Washington Mutual became the largest thrift failure with US$307 billion in assets. JPMorgan Chase agreed to pay US$1.9 billion

for the banking operations but did not take ownership of the holding company.

- **September 22:** Ireland increased the statutory limit for the deposit guarantee scheme for banks and building societies from €20,000 to €100,000 per depositor per institution.
- **September 21:** The Federal Reserve approved the transformation of Goldman Sachs and Morgan Stanley into bank holding companies from investment banks in order to increase oversight and allow them to access the Federal Reserve's discount (loan) window.
- **September 18:** The US Treasury Secretary Paulson announced a US$700 billion economic stabilization proposal that would allow the government to buy toxic assets from the nation's biggest banks, a move aimed at shoring up balance sheets and restoring confidence within the financial system. An amended bill to accomplish this was passed by Congress on October 3.
- **September 16:** In a US$85 billion deal (later increased to US$123 billion), the US Federal Reserve came to the assistance of American International Group, AIG, an insurance giant on the verge of failure because of its exposure to exotic securities known as credit default swaps.
- **September 15:** Lehman Brothers' bankruptcy at US$639 billion became the largest in the history of the United States.
- **September 14:** Bank of America said it will buy Merrill Lynch for US$50 billion.
- **September 7:** US Treasury announced that it was taking over Fannie Mae and Freddie Mac, two government-sponsored enterprises that bought securitized mortgage debt.
- **July 12:** The US FDIC took control of the US$32 billion IndyMac Bank in what regulators called the second largest bank failure in US history.
- **May 4:** Finance ministers of 13 Asian nations agreed to set up a foreign exchange pool of at least US$80 billion to be used in the event of another regional financial crisis. China, Japan, and South Korea would provide 80 percent of the funds with the rest coming from the 10 members of ASEAN.
- **March 24:** The US Federal Reserve staved off a Bear Stearns bankruptcy by assuming US$30 billion in liabilities and engineering a sale of Bear Sterns to JPMorgan Chase for a price that was less than the worth of Bear's Manhattan office building.
- **March 16:** Bear Stearns got acquired for US$2 a share by JPMorgan Chase in a fire sale avoiding bankruptcy. The deal was backed by the Federal Reserve providing up to US$30 billion to cover possible Bear Stearns losses.
- **February 17:** The British government decided to "temporarily" nationalize the struggling housing lender, Northern Rock. A previous government loan of US$47 billion had proven ineffective in helping the company to recover.

- **January 11:** Swiss banking giant UBS reported more than US$18 billion in write-downs due to exposure to US real estate market. Bank of America acquired Countrywide Financial, the largest mortgage lender in the United States.

2007

- **December 6:** US President announced a plan to voluntarily and temporarily freeze the mortgages of a limited number of mortgage debtors holding adjustable rate mortgages.
- **November 1:** The US Federal Reserve injected US$41 billion into the money supply for banks to borrow at a low rate.
- **October 31:** The US Federal Reserve lowered the federal funds rate by 25 basis points to 4.5 percent.
- **October 15–17:** A consortium of US banks backed by the US government announced a "super fund" of US$100 billion to purchase mortgage-backed securities.
- **October 10:** Hope Now Alliance was created by the US Government and private industry to help some subprime borrowers.
- **September 30:** Affected by the spiraling mortgage and credit crises, Internet banking pioneer NetBank goes bankrupt, and the Swiss bank UBS announced that it lost US$690 million in the third quarter.
- **September 18:** The US Fed lowered interest rates by 50 basis points in an attempt to limit damage to the economy from the housing and credit crises.
- **August 31:** US President announced a limited bailout of US homeowners unable to pay the rising costs of their debts. Ameriquest, once the largest subprime lender in the US, went out of business.
- **August 17:** Federal Reserve lowered the discount rate by 50 basis points to 5.75 percent from 6.25 percent.
- **August 16:** Countrywide Financial Corporation, the biggest US mortgage lender, narrowly avoided bankruptcy by taking out an emergency loan of US$11 billion from a group of banks.
- **August 6:** American Home Mortgage filed for Chapter 11 bankruptcy.
- **June 7:** Bear Stearns informed investors in two of its funds, the High-Grade Structured Credit Strategies Enhanced Leverage Fund and the High-Grade Structured Credit Fund, the that it was halting redemptions.
- **April 2:** New Century Financial, largest US subprime lender, filed for chapter 11 bankruptcy.
- **February–March:** Subprime industry collapsed with more than 25 subprime lenders declared bankruptcy, announcing significant losses or putting themselves up for sale.

- **February 5:** Mortgage Lenders Network USA Inc., the country's fifteenth largest subprime lender with US$3.3 billion in loans funded in 3rd quarter 2006, filed for Chapter 11 bankruptcy.
- **January 3:** Ownit Mortgage Solutions, which owed Merrill Lynch around US$93 million, filed for Chapter 11 bankruptcy.

Note

1. This section draws heavily on the following sources: (*a*) CRS Report for the US Congress, titled "The Global Financial Crisis: Analysis and Policy Implications" (Dick K. Nanto, Coordinator, April 3, 2009); (*b*) The *Global Financial Stability Report*, IMF (various issues); (*c*) Quarterly Review on "International Banking and Financial Market Developments," BIS (various issues); and (*d*) *Norton Rose Group—Global Financial Crisis Chronology.*

References

(All URLs have been accessed during 2009 and 2010)

Acharya, Shankar. 2008. "Global Crisis and India," speech at the Annual General Meeting of the Indian Merchants' Chamber, May 11, Mumbai.

Agarwal, Sumit and Calvin T. Ho. 2007. "Comparing the Prime and Subprime Mortgage Markets," Chicago Fed Letter, August, No. 241.

Ahluwalia, Montek Singh. 2009. Interview. *The Hindu*. Available at http://www. hinduonnet.com/nic/montek.htm

Ashcraft, Adam B. and Til Schuermann. 2008. "Understanding the Securitization of Subprime Mortgage Credit," Federal Reserve Bank of New York Staff Reports, Staff Report No. 318, New York, USA.

Aziz, Jahangir, Ila Patnaik, and Ajay Shah. 2008. "The Current Liquidity Crunch in India: Diagnosis and Policy Response," NIFFP Working Paper, New Delhi, India.

Bahena, Amanda. 2008. "What Role Did Credit Rating Agencies (CRAs) Play in the Financial Crisis?" University of Iowa Center for International Finance and Development Mimeo, Iowa, USA.

Bank for International Settlements (BIS) 2010. "The Group of Governors and Heads of Supervision Reach Broad Agreement on Basel Committee Capital and Liquidity Reform Package," press release of July 26. Available at http://bis.org/press/p100726. htm.

Berger, Allen N. and Christa H.S. Bouwman. 2008. "Financial Crises and Bank Liquidity Creation," University of Pennsylvania Wharton Working Paper No. 08–37, Pennsylvania, USA.

Berger, Allen N. and Gregory F. Udell. 2004. "The Institutional Memory Hypothesis and the Procyclicality of Bank Lending Behavior," *Journal of Financial Intermediation*, 13 (4): 458–95.

Bernanke, Ben S. 2008. "Stabilizing the Financial Markets and the Economy," speech at the Economic Club of New York, New York on October 15, 2008. Available at http://www.federalreserve.gov/newsevents/speech/bernanke20081015a.htm.

Bernanke, Ben. 2009. "The Crisis and the Policy Response," The Stamp Lecture, London School of Economics, London, delivered on January 13, 2009. Available at http://www. federalreserve.gov/

Besley, Tim et al. 2009. "Letter to the Queen of England from the British Academy." Available at media.ft.com/cms.

Bhagwati, Jagdish. 1988. "The Capital Myth: The Difference between Trade in Widgets and Dollars," *Foreign Affairs*, 77 (3): 7–12.

Bhutta, Neil and Glenn B. Canner. 2009. "Did the CRA Cause the Mortgage Market Meltdown?" *Community Dividend*, Federal Reserve Bank of Minneapolis, March.

Blanchard, Olivier. 2009. "The Crisis: Basic Mechanisms, and Appropriate Policies," IMF Working Paper, IMF WP/09/80, Washington D.C, USA.

Blanchard, Olivier and Gian Maria Milesi-Ferretti (2009): "Global Imbalances: in Midstream?" IMF Staff Position Note, SPN/09/29, Washington D.C.

Blanchard, Olivier J. and John A. Simon (2001): "The Long and Large Decline in U.S. Output Volatility," MIT Dept. of Economics Working Paper No. 01–29, Cambridge, Massachusetts, USA.

Brunnermeier, Markus, Andrew Crocket, Charles Goodhart, Avinash D. Persaud, and Hyun Shin. 2009. "The Fundamental Principles of Financial Regulation," *Geneva Reports on the World Economy No. 11*, Geneva: International Center for Monetary and Banking Studies.

Buffet, Warren. 2002. "Chairman's Letter," Berkshire Hathaway Inc., Annual Report. Available at www.berkshirehathaway.com/2002ar/2002ar.pdf.

Colander, David, Hans Follmer, Armin Haas, Michael Goldberg, Katarina Juselius, Alan Kirman, Thomas Lux, and Brigitte Sloth. 2009. "The Financial Crisis and the Systemic Failure of Academic Economists," Kiel Institute for the World Economy, Working Paper No. 1489, Kiel, Germany.

Dell'Ariccia, Giovanni and Robert Marquez. 2006. "Lending Booms and Lending Standards," *Journal of Finance*, 61 (October): 2511–546.

Dewatripont, Mathias, Jean-Charles Rochet, and Jean Tirole. 2010. *Balancing the Banks: Global Lessons from the Financial Crisis*. Princeton: Princeton University Press.

DiLorenzo, Thomas J. 2008. "How Crackpot Egalitarianism Caused the Sub-Prime Mortgage Crisis." Available at http://www.lewrockwell.com/dilorenzo/dilorenzo154.html.

Dunaway, Steven. 2009. "Global Imbalances and the Financial Crisis." Council on Foreign Relations, Council Special Report No. 44, March 2009.

Eichengreen, Barry and Kevin H. O'Rourke. 2009. "A Tale of Two Depressions," Analysis in Vox website, June 4, 2009. Available at http://www.voxeu.org.

Espenilla, Nestor A. 2009. "Regulatory Factors that Contributed to the Global Financial Crisis," *Asia-Pacific Social Science Review*, 9 (1): 35–40.

Financial Services Authority (FSA) UK. 2009. *The Turner Review: A Regulatory Response to the Global Banking Crisis*. London: FSA.

Fink, Ronald. 2009. "Restoring Glass-Steagall Just Part of the Puzzle", Online Blog CFO zone. Available at http://www.cfozone.com.

Foxley, Alejandro. 2010. *Sustaining Social Safety Nets*. Washington D.C.: Carnegie Endowment for International Peace.

Geithner, Timothy. 2009. "Remarks" on "Introducing the Financial Stability Plan," February 10, 2009. Available at http://www.ustreas.gov/press/releases/tg18.htm.

Glaeser, Edward L., Joseph Gyourko, and Albert Saiz. 2008. "Housing Supply and Housing Bubbles," Harvard Institute of Economic Research, Discussion Paper No. 2158, Harvard University, Cambridge, Massachusetts, USA.

Greenspan, Alan. 2004. Testimony on government-sponsored enterprises, before the Committee on Banking, Housing, and Urban Affairs, US Senate, February 24, 2004. Available at http://www.federalreserve.gov/boarddocs/testimony/.

Group of Thirty. 2009. *Financial Reform: A Framework for Financial Stability*. Available at www.group30.org/pubs/reformreport.pdf.

Group of Twenty. 2009. "Leaders' Statement, the Pittsburgh Summit, 25 September 2009." Available at http://www.g20.org/pub_communiques.aspx.

Incisive Media Investments. 2005. *The ABC of Structured Products*. Available at http://db.riskwaters.com/data/asiarisk/pdf/abc/abc.pdf.

International Monetary Fund. 2009a. "Factsheet on IMF-FSB Early Warning Exercise." Available at http://www.imf.org/external/np/exr/facts/ewe.htm.

———. 2009b. "Initial Lessons of the Crisis," prepared by Research, Monetary, and Capital Markets, and Strategy, Policy, and Review Departments. February 6.

———. 2010a. "A Fair and Substantial Contribution by the Financial Sector: Final Report for the G-20," June 2010. Available at www.imf.org/external/np/g20/pdf/062710b.pdf

———. 2010b. "Factsheet on 'The IMF's Role in Helping Protect the Most Vulnerable in the Global Crisis,'" April 16. Available at http://www.imf.org/external/np/exr/facts/protect.htm

———. 2010c. "G-20 Mutual Assessment Process—Alternative Policy Scenarios: A Report by the IMF Staff," June 2010. Available at http://www.imf.org/external/np/g20/pdf/062710a.pdf

———. 2010d. "Greece: Staff Report on Request for Stand-By Arrangement." May 2010, IMF Country Report No. 10/110.

———. 2010e. "United States: 2010 Article IV Consultation—Staff Report; Staff Statement; and Public Information Notice on the Executive Board Discussion." July 2010, IMF Country Report No. 10/249.

Jickling, Mark. 2009. "Causes of the Financial Crisis," US Congressional Research Service Report R40173, Washington D.C., USA.

Jickling, Mark and Edward V. Murphy. 2009. "Who Regulates Whom? An Overview of U.S. Financial Supervision." Congressional Research Services, No. R 40249. Available at assets.opencrs.com/rpts/R40249_20091214.pdf

Jobst, Andreas A. 2006. "What Is Structured Finance?" *The Securitization Conduit*, 8 (2005/2006).

Kiyotaki, Nobuhiro and John Moore. 1997. "Credit Cycles," *Journal of Political Economy*, 105 (2): 211–48.

Knight, Malcolm D. 2008. "Some Reflections on the Future of the Originate-to-distribute Model in the Context of the Current Financial Turmoil," speech by the general manager of the BIS, at the Euro 50 group roundtable, The Future of the Originate and Distribute Model, London, April 21, 2008. Available at http://www.bis.org

Kolb, Robert W. 2010. "Incentives in the Financial Crisis of Our Time." Available at http://www.robertwkolb.com/

Kroszner, Randall S. 2008. "The Community Reinvestment Act and the Recent Mortgage Crisis," speech at the Confronting Concentrated Poverty Policy Forum, Board of Governors of the Federal Reserve System, Washington D.C., December 3.

Krugman, Paul. 2008. "Fannie, Freddie and You," *New York Times*, July 14. Available at www.nytimes.com/2008/07/14/.../14krugman.html

Kuttner, Robert. 2010. "Ask Dr Reddy." *The Huffington Post*, April 11. Available at http://www.huffingtonpost.com/robert-kuttner

Loungani, Prakash. 2009. "Seeing Crises Clearly: Interview of Nouriel Roubini," *Finance and Development*, IMF, March, 46 (1).

Makridakis, Spyros, Robin Hogarth, and Anil Gaba. 2009. *Dance with Chance: Making Luck Work for You*. New York: Oneworld.

Mohan, Rakesh. 2009. "Global Financial Crisis: Causes, Impact, Policy Responses and Lessons," speech at the India at London Business School on April 23, 2009. Available at http://rbi.org.in/scripts/BS_SpeechesView.aspx?Id=417

Mussa, Michael. 2009. "World Recession and Recovery: A V or an L?" paper presented at the fifteenth semiannual meeting on Global Economic Prospects, April 7. Available at www.iie.com/publications/papers/mussa0409.pdf

OECD. 2010. *OECD Economic Outlook No 87*, volume 2010/1, May.

Paul, Ron. 2003. "Fannie and Freddie. Testimony before the Financial Services Committee of the US House of Representatives." Available at http://www.lewrockwell.com/paul/paul128.html

Paulson, Henry M. Jr. 2009. Remarks on: The Role of the GSEs in Supporting the Housing Recovery before the Economic Club of Washington, January 7, 2009. Available at http://www.treas.gov

Rajan, Raghuram. 2005. "Has Financial Development Made the World Riskier?" proceedings of a symposium on the Greenspan Era: Lessons for the Future, Federal Reserve Bank of Kansas City, USA.

———. 2010. *Fault Lines*. Princeton: Princeton University Press.

Ram Mohan, T.T. 2009. "The Impact of the Crisis on the Indian Economy," *Economic and Political Weekly*, 55 (13): 107–14.

Rangarajan, C. 2009a. "International Financial Crises and Its Ramification." Available at hipa.nic.in/crangranjan.pdf

———. 2009b. "The International Financial Crisis and Its Impact on India," August 6, 2009, speech at the Bureau of Parliamentary Studies and Training, Lok Sabha, Parliament House, New Delhi. Available at 164.100.47.132/LssNew/bureau/Dr.C.Rangarajan.pdf

Rant, Vasja. 2008. "Anatomy of the Global Financial Crisis." Available at miha.ef. uni-lj.si/_dokumenti3plus2/191083/Globalfinancialcrisis.ppt

Reddy, Y.V. 2009. *India and the Global Financial Crisis: Managing Money and Finance*, New Delhi: Orient Blackswan.

Reinhart, Carmen M. and Kenneth S. Rogoff. 2009. "The Aftermath of Financial Crises," NBER Working Paper 14656. Available at http://www.nber.org/papers/w14656

Reserve Bank of India (RBI) 2009. *Annual Policy Statement, 2009–10*. Mumbai: Reserve Bank of India. Available at www.rbi.org.in

———. 2010. *Handbook of Statistics on the Indian Economy*. Mumbai: Reserve Bank of India. Available at www.rbi.org.in

Rosen, Richard. 2007. "The Role of Securitization in Mortgage Lending," Chicago Fed Letters, November 2007, Chicago, USA.

Roubini, Nouriel Stephen Mihm. 2010. *A Crash Course in the Future of Finance*. New York: Penguin.

Samuelson, Robert. 2009. "Will U.S. Recovery Go Global?" *Washington Post*, June 29, Washington D.C., USA.

Securities and Exchange Commission. 2008. "Report and Recommendations Pursuant to Section 133 of the Emergency Economic Stabilization Act of 2008: Study on Mark-to-market Accounting," Washington D.C., USA.

Shiller, Robert. 2007. "Understanding Recent Trends in House Prices and Home Ownership," presentation at the 2007 Jackson Hole Symposium, Kansas City Fed on Housing, Housing Finance, and Monetary Policy, Kansas City USA.

Shiller, Robert. 2008. *The Subprime Solution: How Today's Global Financial Crisis Happened, and What to Do about It*. Princeton: Princeton University Press.

Singh, Manmohan. 2010. Remarks by the PM of India at the Toronto G-20 summit, June 27. Available at http://pmindia.nic.in/speeches.htm

Stiglitz, Joseph. 2010a. "What Kind of Theory to Guide Reform and Restructuring of the Financial and Non-Financial Sectors," presentation at the INET Inaugural Conference. Available at http://ineteconomics.org

————. 2010b. "Needed: A New Economic Paradigm," *Financial Times*, August 20.

Subbarao, D. 2008. "Lessons from the Global Financial Crisis with Special Reference to Emerging Market Economies and India," RBI Bulletin, November, Reserve Bank of India, Mumbai.

————. 2009a. "Impact of the Global Financial Crisis on India: Collateral Damage and Response," speech delivered in Tokyo, RBI Bulletin., Reserve Bank of India, Mumbai.

————. 2009b. "Risk Management in the Midst of the Global Financial Crisis," RBI Bulletin, June, Reserve Bank of India, Mumbai.

————. 2009c. "Global Financial Crisis: Questioning the Questions." RBI Bulletin, August, Reserve Bank of India, Mumbai.

Taylor, John B. 2007. "Housing and Monetary Policy," NBER Working Paper, National Bureau of Economic Research, Cambridge, Massachusetts, USA.

US Treasury. 2008a. "Blueprint for a Modernized Financial Regulatory Structure." Available at www.ustreas.gov/press/releases/reports/Blueprint.pdf

————. 2008b. "Policy Statement on Financial Market Developments: The President's Working Group on Financial Markets." Available at http://www.treas.gov/press/releases/reports

Verschoor, Curtis C. 2009. "Did Repeal of Glass–Steagall for Citigroup Exacerbate the Crisis?" *Strategic Finance*, February 2009.

Virmani, Arvind. 2009. *The Sudoku of India's Growth*. New Delhi: Academic Foundation.

White, William. 2006. "Is Price Stability Enough," BIS Working Paper No. 205, Bank for International Settlements, Basel, Switzerland.

Wilmers, Robert G. 2009. "Where the Crisis Came From," *Washington Post*, July 27.

Wolf, Martin. 2009. "Fixing Global Finance," presentation at the Global Interdependence Center, Philadelphia on March 9, 2009, Philadelphia, USA.

Zingales, Luigi. 2008. "Causes and Effects of the Lehman Brothers Bankruptcy," testimony before the Committee on Oversight and Government Reform United States House of Representatives on October 6, 2008, Washington D.C., USA.

Index

About the Authors

Adarsh Kishore is Chairman of Axis Bank Ltd. He has held several important positions, such as Principal Finance Secretary to the State Government of Rajasthan, Principal Secretary to the Chief Minister of Rajasthan, and Union Finance Secretary of Government of India. He has also served as Executive Director for Bangladesh, Bhutan, India, and Sri Lanka at the IMF, Washington D.C., USA. He has published several papers in academic journals and books such as *Economic Reforms: State–Market Synergy* (1996).

Michael Debabrata Patra is Senior Adviser to Executive Director for Bangladesh, Bhutan, India, and Sri Lanka at the IMF. He is a career central banker with 25 years of experience in the Reserve Bank of India (RBI) in key policy positions and had held the position of Adviser-in-Charge in the Monetary Policy Department before joining the IMF. He has published in national and international journals.

Partha Ray is Director, Department of Economic and Policy Research, RBI. He is a career central banker with 20 years of experience in the RBI. During August 2007–April 2011, he was Adviser to Executive Director for Bangladesh, Bhutan, India, and Sri Lanka at the IMF. He has published in national and international journals.